D0230422

Quality Costing

Quality Costing

Second edition

B.G. Dale

Reader in Quality Management and
Director of the Quality Management Centre,
UMIST, UK

and

J.J. Plunkett

formerly Total Quality Management Project Officer,
UMIST, UK

CHAPMAN & HALL

London · Glasgow · Weinheim · New York · Tokyo · Melbourne · Madras

Published by Chapman & Hall, 2–6 Boundary Row, London SE1 8HN, UK

Chapman & Hall, 2–6 Boundary Row, London SE1 8HN, UK

Blackie Academic & Professional, Wester Cleddens Road, Bishopbriggs, Glasgow G64 2NZ, UK

Chapman & Hall GmbH, Pappelallee 3, 69469 Weinheim, Germany

Chapman & Hall USA, One Penn Plaza, 41st Floor, New York NY 10119, USA

Chapman & Hall Japan, ITP-Japan, Kyowa Building, 3F, 2-2-1 Hirakawacho, Chiyoda-ku, Tokyo 102, Japan

Chapman & Hall Australia, Thomas Nelson Australia, 102 Dodds Street, South Melbourne, Victoria 3205, Australia

Chapman & Hall India, R. Seshadri, 32 Second Main Road, CIT East, Madras 600 035, India

First edition 1991
Reprinted 1992 (twice), 1993
Second edition 1995

© 1991, 1995 B.G. Dale and J.J. Plunkett

Typeset in 10/12 Times by Mews Photosetting, Beckenham, Kent
Printed in Great Britain by T.J. Press, Padstow, Cornwall

ISBN 0 412 60590 2

A catalogue record for this book is available from the British Library

Library of Congress Catalog Card Number: 94-72022

∞ Printed on permanent acid-free text paper, manufactured in accordance with the proposed ANSI/NISO Z39.48-1992 and ANSI/NISO Z39.48-1984 (Permanence of Paper).

Contents

Preface

This book is one of the few English language texts devoted to the subject of quality costing. The material is based on research work carried out at the Quality Management Centre, Manchester School of Management, UMIST, over the last 13 or so years. It will provide managers with sound practical advice on how to define, identify, collect, measure, analyse, report and use quality costs. The text covers all the main aspects of quality costing and an attempt has been made to structure the first half of the book in the sequence by which organizations should set about a quality costing exercise – definitions, collection, reporting and use.

The first chapter is a new one. It examines the concept of TQM and the role of quality costing within a TQM approach. This is followed by an introductory chapter on quality costing which covers background material and traces the historical development of the concept. There are separate chapters on quality cost definitions, collection of quality costs, analysis and reporting of quality costs, and the uses of quality costs. Examples from manufacturing organizations and non-manufacturing situations are used throughout the first six chapters to illustrate key points. This second edition, in addition to bringing the text up to date, provides more data and examples on the 'how to' of quality costing.

The next four chapters are case studies which provide considerable detail on quality costing in companies from the mechanical and electronics industries. The data on the case studies have been gathered as part of a research project and to preserve anonymity the companies are not referred to by name. The case studies illustrate how four different companies have set about analysing their main areas of operation to highlight where quality costs were incurred and how they were collected and reported. A deliberate attempt is made to present the situation as it was. In this way, potential cost collectors can gain some insight into the type of situations and difficulties they may encounter and the issues which need to be resolved in undertaking a quality costing exercise. The case studies also include guidance on potential sources of cost information and the typical questions which occur in a quality cost collection exercise.

This second edition of the book contains two new case studies. The first is Girobank PLC. This shows how they have applied quality costing to financial services. The second is International Computers Ltd. This examines how they have used the concept of quality costing to develop a total cost of ownership model. These two case studies are written in a different way to the earlier cases. They are briefer, tend to focus on specific issues and benefits achieved, and because they are named companies the information provided is more conservative.

The final chapter is a summary and provides key point guidance on how companies can go about setting up a quality costing system.

During the last decade or so there has been considerable interest from Western manufacturing industry, public sector organizations, commerce, and the service sector on the subject of TQM and the process of quality improvement. However, the majority of organizations, certainly in the first few years of their TQM journey usually need to justify the cost effectiveness of the investment in a process of continuous quality improvement to their main board, in particular, when it is located in an off-shore country, and to shareholders. Consequently, an increasing number of organizations are actively engaged in the collection and reporting of quality costs and others are looking for sound practical advice on how to go about it. It is also not uncommon to find organizations who, after collecting and using the results of quality costing for some years, wish to assess how they might make more use of the data.

This book provides useful advice to organizations setting out on a quality costing exercise and to those in the early stages of designing a quality cost collection and reporting system. It will help to prevent cost collectors going up blind alleys. It will also assist those organizations already collecting cost by giving pointers on how to develop and refine their current methods.

The book will prove useful to practitioners and academics, and undergraduate and postgraduate students from a variety of disciplines, in particular, those taking courses leading to BSc and Masters qualifications in quality management. People studying for professional examinations which involve aspects of TQM will also find the book to be of benefit. Quality managers, technical managers, technical specialists, and accountants should find the book of particular interest as they are usually the personnel involved in co-ordinating a quality costing exercise, setting up systems and providing the data. The Chief Executive Officer and board members will also benefit from reading the book. They will see in the text hard evidence of the financial benefits accruing to an organization from pursuing a process of continuous quality improvement.

In revising the book, account has been taken of the comments of practitioners using the first edition and from my academic colleagues and peers. I sincerely hope the new edition reflects continuous improvement in the spirit of TQM.

The book is dedicated to the memory of my friend and colleague Dr Jim Plunkett and provides some recognition of his first class research into the subject of quality costing.

B.G. Dale
Quality Management Centre,
Manchester School of Management, UMIST

Glossary of terms

ABC	activity based costing
ASQC	American Society for Quality Control
BS	British Standard
BSI	British Standards Institution
CEO	Chief Executive Officer
CIMA	Chartered Institute of Management Accountants
COC	costs of conformance
CONC	costs of non-conformance
DAN	defect advice note
DPA	departmental purpose analysis
DTI	Department of Trade and Industry
EDI	electronic data interchange
ESH	effective standard hour
FMEA	failure mode and effects analysis
ICOM	input controls output and mechanism
IDEF	computer aided manufacturing integrated program definition
JIT	just in time
LQS	local quality system
MRP	materials requirements planning
NEDC	National Economic Development Council
NMUK	Nissan Motor Manufacturing (UK) Ltd
NSB	net sales billed
PAF	prevention appraisal and failure
PAT	project action teams
PCB	printed circuit boards
POC	price of conformance
PONC	price of non-conformance
QCD	quality cost delivery
QFD	quality function deployment
Q-MAP	quality management activity planning

QUIPS	quality improvement planning sheets
RFI	radio frequency interference
SPC	statistical process control
TCO	total cost of ownership
TPM	total productive maintenance
TQM	total quality management
UK	United Kingdom
UMIST	University of Manchester Institute of Science and Technology
US	United States of America
VAT	value added tax
ZD	zero defects

Structure of the book

The first six chapters of the book provide a thorough explanation of the concept of quality costing. They are:

- Chapter 1 – The role of quality costing in total quality management,
- Chapter 2 – An introduction to quality costs,
- Chapter 3 – Definitions of qualty costs,
- Chapter 4 – Collection of quality costs,
- Chapter 5 – Reporting of quality costs,
- Chapter 6 – Uses of quality costs.

These chapters explore the background and historical development of quality costing within the context of total quality management (TQM) and examine the practicalities of defining, collecting, reporting and using quality costs. Named and unnamed examples from both manufacturing and service environments are used to illustrate some of the key points in the text.

There is a considerable amount of published literature on quality costing and this is drawn upon to explain specific issues and reflect different points of view on the subject. In addition the most authoritative pieces of reading are pointed out to the reader. The American Society for Quality Control (ASQC) and the British Standards Institution (BSI) have made key contributions to the literature and assisted in developing the knowledge base of the subject; reference is made throughout these six chapters to their respective publications.

The following six chapters are actual case studies. They are:

- Chapter 7 – Case Study, Company 1,
- Chapter 8 – Case Study, Company 2,
- Chapter 9 – Case Study, Company 3,
- Chapter 10 – Case Study, Company 4,
- Chapter 11 – Girobank PLC,
- Chapter 12 – International Computers Ltd (ICL).

Chapters 7 through to 10 provide considerable detail on the state-of-the-art of quality costing in four companies drawn from the mechanical and electronics industries. The material was collected as part of a Science and Engineering Research Council (SERC) research project. These case studies illustrate how four different companies have set about analysing their main areas of operation to highlight where quality costs were incurred, how they were collected and reported and how the data were used to facilitate continuous improvement. A deliberate attempt is made to present the situation as encountered in the research, warts and all. In this way, potential cost collectors can gain some insight into the type of situations and difficulties they may encounter and the issues which need to be resolved in undertaking a quality costing exercise. The case studies also provide guidance on the potential sources of cost information which are available within organizations, cost collection methods, reporting formats and the typical questions which arise in quality costing. These four case studies were undertaken in the mid-1980s. The data were collected through the research process and because of the detail provided the companies are not referred to by name in order to preserve anonymity.

The final two case studies are based on Girobank PLC an International Computers Ltd (ICL), Ashton-under-Lyne manufacturing facility. There are few published examples of quality costing in a non-manufacturing setting and the Girobank case shows how the concept can be applied in a financial institution. The International Computers Ltd case is interesting as it shows how the quality costing concept was used as the basis for developing a total cost of ownership model for dealing with supplier selection and development and other internal and external decisions. The model addresses the way in which ICL is progressing towards the lowest cost of owning a part. Organizations are always on the lookout for new angles on quality costing and this case provides such an example.

The final chapter (Chapter 13 – Setting up a Quality Costing System) draws upon the main issues in the preceding chapters and provides key pointers on how organisations should set about quality costing. The chapter also provides a list of dos and don'ts which acts as a quality costing *aide-mémoire*.

The role of quality costing in total quality management | 1

1.1 INTRODUCTION

Quality costing is just one of a number of quality management tools and techniques which an organization can use in the introduction and development of total quality management (TQM). Organizations considering the use of quality costing must appreciate what quality costing can and cannot do and its potential in TQM. Like any other tool and technique, management has got to decide if it needs to use quality costing and, if so, when and in what form. It should always be kept in perspective. Management also needs to consider what commitment, resources and expertise are required to make the best use of quality costing. These issues along with the method of approach to the identification and collection of costs are some of the crucial factors in making the best use of the technique.

The purpose of this chapter is to introduce the reader to the concept and key elements of TQM and to examine the role of quality costing in TQM. It opens by examining TQM and its main elements and tracing the evolution of quality management. The importance of quality in a business context is discussed and the case made for quality costing.

1.2 WHAT IS TOTAL QUALITY MANAGEMENT?

There are perhaps as many definitions of TQM as there are writers on the subject. The definition used by the Quality Management Centre at UMIST is:

> TQM is the mutual co-operation of everyone in an organisation and associated business processes to produce products and services which meet the needs and expectations of customers.

Recently two definitions of TQM have been published in different British Standards:

> A management philosophy embracing all activities through which the needs and expectations of the customer and the community, and the objectives of the organisation are satisfied in the most efficient and cost effective way by maximising the potential of all employees in a continuing drive for improvement (BS4778: Part 2 [1]).

> Management philosophy and company practices that aim to harness the human and material resources of an organisation in the most effective way to achieve the objectives of the organisation (BS7850: Part 1 [2]).

Whilst there are a number of common threads running through these two definitions it is surprising that such an eminent body as the British Standards Institution could not agree upon a standard definition for the term.

TQM means that a disciplined approach to business must be adopted, based upon a fundamental belief in the need for continuous and company-wide improvement. The process of quality improvement is the means of making progress towards TQM.

In today's markets, customer requirements are becoming increasingly more rigorous and their expectations of the product/service in terms of its conformance, reliability, durability, interchangeability, performance, features, appearance, serviceabilty, environment and user-friendliness and safety are also increasing. At the same time, it is likely that the existing competition will be improving and new and lower cost competitors may emerge in the market place. The organization which claims that it has achieved TQM will be overtaken by the competition. Once the process of quality improvement has been halted, under the mistaken belief that TQM has been achieved and the ideal state reached, it is much harder to restart the process, differentiate the organization's products and service, and gain the initiative on the competition. This is why TQM should always be referred to as a process and not a programme.

Starting a process of quality imrpovement and then developing and fostering its advancement should be a long-term organizational objective; it often takes at least 10 years to put the basics into place. There are: no quick fixes; no one quality management technique and/or tool which is a panacea for all quality ills and is more important than another; no short-cuts; and no ready-made packages which can be plugged into guarantee success. Continuous quality improvement requires patience, tenacity and considerable commitment from people at every level in the organization, in particular the board of directors and senior management team.

Despite the divergence of views on what constitutes TQM, there are a number of common elements running through the various definitions. These elements are now discussed. The material is taken from Dale *et al.* [3] and is based on the practical and research experience of the UMIST Quality Management Centre.

1.2.1 Commitment and leadership of the Chief Executive Officer

Without the total commitment of the Chief Executive Officer (CEO) and his/her immediate executives and other senior managers, nothing much will happen on TQM and anything that does will not be permanent. They have to take charge personally, provide direction and exercise forceful and visible leadership.

1.2.2 Planning and organization

This features in a number of facets of the quality improvement process, including:

- developing a clear long-term strategy for TQM which is integrated with other business strategies and plans;
- building quality into designs and processes;
- developing prevention-based activities (e.g. mistake proofing devices);
- putting quality assurance procedures into place which facilitate closed-loop corrective action;
- planning the approach to be taken to the effective use of quality systems, procedures and quality management tools and techniques, in the context of the overall strategy;
- developing the organization and infrastructure to support the improvement activities;
- pursuing standardization, systemization and simplification of work instructions, procedures and systems.

1.2.3 Using tools and techniques

To support and develop a process of continuous and company-wide quality improvement an organization will need to use a selection of quality management tools and techniques. Without the effective employment of tools and techniques it will be difficult to solve problems. The tools and techniques should be used to facilitate improvement and be integrated into the routine operation of the business. The organization should develop a route map for the tools and techniques which it intends to apply. The use of tools and techniques helps to get the process of improvement started, employees using them feel involved and that they are making a contribution, quality awareness is enhanced and behaviour and attitude changes start to happen.

1.2.4 Education and training

Employees should be provided with the right level of education and training to ensure that their general awareness of quality management concepts, skills and attitudes are appropriate and suited to the continuous improvement philosophy. TQM also provides a common language throughout the business. A formal programme of education and training needs to be planned and provided on a timely and regular basis to enable people to cope with increasing complex problems. This programme should be viewed as an investment in developing the ability and knowledge of people and helping them realise their potential. Without training it is difficult to solve problems and without education, behaviour and attitude changes will not take place. The training programme must also focus on helping managers to think through what improvements are achievable in their areas of responsibility.

It also has to be recognized that not all employees will have received and acquired adequate levels of education. The structure of the training programme may incorporate some updating of basic educational skills in numeracy and literacy, but it must promote continuing education and self development. In this way, the latent potential of many employees will be released.

1.2.5 Involvement

There must be a commitment to the development of employees, with recognition that they are an asset which appreciates over time. All available means from suggestion schemes to various forms of teamwork must be considered for achieving broad employee interest, participation and contribution in the process of quality improvement. Management must be prepared to share some of their powers and responsibilities. This also involves seeking and listening carefully to the views of employees and acting upon their suggestions. Part of the approach to TQM is to ensure that everyone has a clear understanding of what is required of them and how their processes relate to the business as a whole. The more people who understand the business and what is going on around them, the greater the role they can play in quality improvement. People have got to be encouraged to control, manage and improve the processes which are within their sphere of responsibility.

1.2.6 Teamwork

Teamwork needs to be practised in a number of forms. Consideration needs to be given to the operating characteristics of the teams employed, how they fit into the organizational structure and the roles of team sponsor, leader, member and facilitator. Teamwork is one of the key features of involvement and without it, difficulty will be experienced in gaining the commitment and participation of people throughout the organization.

There is also a need to recognize positive performance and achievement and celebrate and reward success. People must see the results of their activities and that the improvements made really do count. This needs to be constantly encouraged through active communication. If TQM is to be successful it is essential that communication must be effective and widespread.

1.2.7 Measurement and feedback

Measurement needs to be made continually against a series of key results indicators – internal and external. The latter are the most important as they relate to customer perceptions of product and/or service improvement. The indicators should be developed from external and internal benchmarking, as well as customer surveys and other means of external input. This enables progress and feedback to be assessed against a roadmap or checkpoints. From these measurements, action plans must be developed to meet objectives and bridge gaps.

1.2.8 Culture changes

It is necessary to create an organizational culture which is conducive to continuous quality improvement and in which everyone can participate. Quality assurance practices also need to be integrated into all of an organization's processes and functions. This requires changing peoples' behaviour, attitudes and working practices in a number of ways.

- Everyone in the organization must be involved in 'improving' the process under their control on a continuous basis and take personal responsibility for their own quality assurance.
- Employees must be inspecting their own work.
- Defects must not be passed, in whatever form, to the next process. The internal customer–supplier relationship (everyone for whom you perform a task, service or provide information is a customer) must be recognized.
- Each person must be committed to satisfying their customers, both internal and external.
- External suppliers and customers must be integrated into the improvement process.
- Mistakes must be viewed as an improvement opportunity.
- Honesty, sincerity and care must be an integral part of daily business life.

Changing people's behaviour and attitudes is one of the most difficult tasks facing management, requiring considerable powers and skills of motivation and persuasion; considerable thought needs to be given to facilitating and managing culture change.

1.3 THE EVOLUTION OF QUALITY MANAGEMENT

The evolution of quality management can be traced through four main stages – inspection, quality control, quality assurance and total quality management (see Dale *et al.* [3] for details).

- *Inspection*. 'Activities such as measuring, examining, testing, gauging one or more characteristics of a product or service and comparing these with specified requirements to determine conformity'. (BS4778: Part 1; ISO 8402 [1]).
- *Quality control*. 'The operational techniques and activities that are used to fulfil requirements for quality'. (BS4778: Part 1; ISO 8402 [1]).

- *Quality assurance.* 'All those planned and systematic actions necessary to provide adequate confidence that a product or service will satisfy given requirements for quality'. (BS4778: Part 1; ISO 8402 [1]).
- *Total quality management.* This requires that the principles of quality management are applied in every branch and at every level in the organization. It is both a philosophy and a set of guiding principles for managing an organization.

The first two stages of inspection and quality control are based on a detection approach to the management of quality. With this approach the emphasis is on the product, procedures, service deliverables and the downstream producing and delivery processes. Consequently, considerable effort is expended on after-the-event inspection, checking and testing of the product and/or service and providing reactive 'quick fixes' in a bid to ensure that only conforming products and services are provided and delivered to the customer.

Quality assurance and total quality management are based on prevention, which concentrates on product, service and process design. There is a clear emphasis on planning quality into the upstream processes.

This evolution is shown in diagrammatic form in Fig. 1.1, taken from Dale *et al.* [3]. This figure also shows some of the typical characteristics of each stage of evolution. These four stages are progressive and embracing. That is quality control embraces inspection, quality assurance embraces quality control and TQM embraces quality assurance.

It is when an organization starts to change its approach from detection to prevention that quality costing is considered by the senior management team. This awareness of quality costing starts to surface when management becomes aware that its current approach to quality management is deficient. Prior to this only a few pieces of quality cost data in the form of scrap, rework, repair, testing, product replacement, service compensation and warranty are collected.

1.4 THE IMPORTANCE OF QUALITY IN A BUSINESS CONTEXT

In the last decade many organizations have come to appreciate the strategic importance of TQM to their corporate health. They have realized that TQM will enable them to become and remain competitive in both home and international markets. TQM not only leads to improved productivity, higher standards, improved systems and procedures, improved motivation, and increased customer satisfaction, but also lower costs and bottom line savings. It means quality at the most effective costs. Consequently, a process of continuous and company-wide quality improvement has been started.

Quality is regarded by most producers, customers and consumers as more important than ever in their manufacturing, operations, service and purchasing strategies (Ryan [4], Hutchens [5], McKinsey [6], Lascelles and Dale [7] and Buzzell and Gale [8]. To understand why, we need only recall the unsatisfactory

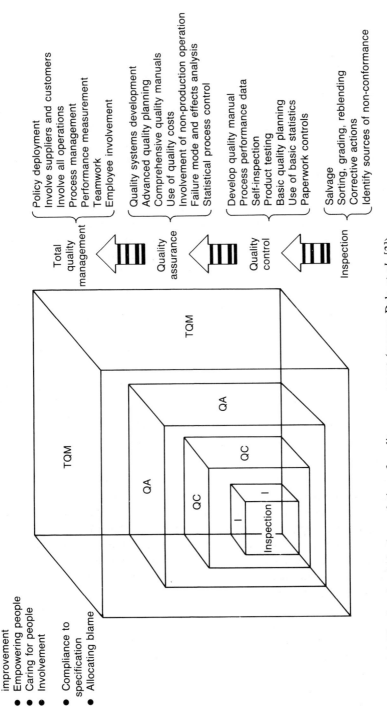

- Continuous improvement
- Empowering people
- Caring for people
- Involvement
- Compliance to specification
- Allocating blame

Policy deployment
Involve suppliers and customers
Involve all operations
Process management
Performance measurement
Teamwork
Employee involvement

Total quality management

Quality systems development
Advanced quality planning
Comprehensive quality manuals
Use of quality costs
Involvement of non-production operation
Failure mode and effects analysis
Statistical process control

Quality assurance

Develop quality manual
Process performance data
Self-inspection
Product testing
Basic quality planning
Use of basic statistics
Paperwork controls

Quality control

Salvage
Sorting, grading, reblending
Corrective actions
Identify sources of non-conformance

Inspection

TQM

QA

QC

Inspection

Figure 1.1 The four levels in the evolution of quality management (source: Dale *et al.* [3]).

examples of product/quality service we have experienced, how we felt about them, the actions we took, and the people we told about the experience and the outcome. Waiting for a customer complaint is too late. Quality concerns and near misses need to be monitored to provide a mechanism for turning concerns into improvement opportunities and retaining customers. An organization should always be aware that niggling incidents can cause aggravation to the customer. Whenever a customer becomes dissatisfied it results in loss of goodwill. It leads to extra effort being expended by personnel within the organization, first investigating what has gone wrong and then trying to put right what went wrong. These unsatisfactory experiences result in actual costs above budget, which directly impact on bottom-line performance and result in erosion of market share.

An order, contract or customer which is lost on the grounds of nonconforming product and/or service quality is much harder to regain than one lost on price or even delivery grounds. The customer could be lost for ever – in simple terms the organization has been outsold. If we doubt the truth of this statement we need only to consider the number of organizations which have gone out of business or lost a significant share of a market and consult the reported reasons for this. Quality is one of the factors which is not negotiable. In today's business world, the penalties for unsatisfactory product quality and poor service are likely to be punitive. When the management of an organization compares its profit-to-sales ratio to its quality-costs to salesturnover ratio it will be found that the costs of quality is of the same order as profitability. This provides an immediate indication of the importance of quality to its survival. Goodman and Adamson (*Anon.* [9] estimate that:

> . . . the cost of not meeting customer expectations to a British company manufacturing products which people buy several times a year, with each purchase producing a $25 profit, would be $1.5 million lost profit annually.

It requires some considerable effort to sustain a process of continuous and company-wide quality improvement. More often than not, the management of an organization, in particular one based in the West, will need to justify to its parent company, board and shareholders that the investment in the improvement process is cost effective. Some people may argue that there should be no need to justify investment in quality-improvement activities, taking the line that the benefits will always outweigh the costs. The environment in the West is such that organizations and their managements are judged over relatively short time periods. Indeed, this is one of the criticisms made of executives, that they place too much emphasis on short-term objectives. This short-termism is often engendered by the financial institutions. Committing huge expenditure in quality improvement activities as a blanket approach without some measure of their cost effectiveness and whether or not the money spent is concentrated on the right activities can be considered a blind act of faith and is contrary to the way in which the majority of Western businesses operate. Executives, after 12 months of TQM activities in terms of training, teams and projects tend to become nervous if tangible benefits are not starting to surface, 'What are the benefits and payoff from all this investment and effort expended on initiatives to improve the quality of output?' A number of writers (e.g. Schaffer and Thomson [10] have criticized some of those TQM approaches heavily orientated to cascade training and action-centred activities and which fail to produce early results and savings. The ultimate measure of the effectiveness of improvement has got to be economic.

In Japanese organizations the situation is quite different. Investment in improvement initiatives over a long period of time without thought of immediate benefits, appears to be accepted without question by senior managers, shareholders and financial institutions. There are a number of well publicized examples where Japanese companies have established a manufacturing plant outside of Japan and planned for it not to break even for at least five years from start-up. The Japanese have considerable tangible evidence over the last 30 years or so of the wisdom of pursuing this long-range view.

In addition to quality, organizations need to be competitive on cost and delivery (QCD). In today's climate a considerable number of organizations need to achieve substantial cost reductions if they are to survive. Consequently, intense effort is being expended by management in deciding what their core businesses are, and identifying waste and non-value adding activity. In the automotive industry, suppliers are often assisted by their customers in this activity by a joint analysis of all costs using an 'open book' and target cost approach. Many organizations, particularly in complex and high-technology industries are vulnerable to any breakthrough in rival organizations in relation to quality improvement and technology. In many instances quality-related costs are a major potential source of the necessary savings. Quality costing is one of several tools and techniques which can assist companies with improving quality, and identifying and eliminating excessive cost, waste and non-value adding activity.

1.5 THE CASE FOR QUALITY COSTING

Whilst there is clearly a good case for quality costing, it is not a panacea for quality problems and must not be treated as an end in itself. The bottom line objective, as with any other quality management tool and technique, is to improve performance. It is also important that reducing the level of quality costs should not be the main reason for an organization starting a process of quality improvement; satisfying customer needs and expectations is much more important.

Quality costing may be considered by some to be more useful for organizations taking the first steps along the TQM journey than it is for those who have considerably more operating experience of TQM. However, a number of world-class organizations do employ quality costing measures as an indication of internal quality performance. Quality costing is about knowing what non-quality is costing the organization, tracking the causes and effects of the problem, working out solutions using quality improvement teams and monitoring progress.

A knowledge of quality costs helps managers justify the investment in quality improvement, assists them in monitoring the effectiveness of the efforts made and to assess the impact of various improvement activities. It is used to reduce the number of errors and mistakes along with the associated costs. In this way it will free-up employees' time and help to use them in a more effective way. Quality costing expresses an organization's quality performance in the language of the board, the senior management team, shareholders and financial institutions – money. It is often found that boards and senior management teams are unmoved by quality assurance data but are spurred into action when the same data are expressed and presented in monetary terms. The majority of management consultants when contacted to assist an organization with its introduction of TQM will carry out an assessment of quality costs. This analysis, no matter how broad brush, is used to indicate the potential for TQM. It is not unusual to find that the representations of financial institutions and venture capitalists on company boards start to take a particular interest in quality when they come to realize the potential loss of profit caused by waste and failure to meet requirements. Operators and line supervision are also found to react positively when failure data, in addition to the normally expressed measure of numbers and percentages, are presented in monetary terms. This reaction happens when they have the opportunity to compare the costs of non-conformance to their salaries.

Sullivan [11], [12], in an issue of *Quality Progress* (the Journal of the American Society for Quality Control (ASQC) devoted to quality costs, quotes half a dozen 'top quality professionals' in support of quality costing and also from the accounting fraternity. Claret [13], Cox [14] and Morse *et al.* [15] also acknowledge the need for quality costing.

The following are comments made by Chief Executive Officers in the Department of Trade and Industry booklet *The Case For Costing Quality* (Dale and Plunkett [16]).

> Quality costs allow us to identify the soft targets to which we can apply our improvement efforts. (John Asher, Managing Director, Crown Industrial Products)

> Four years ago we could still use quality as a selling feature for our product, now that's all changed. If you are still a supplier to the automotive industry today, you will have achieved a high level of quality that is the accepted norm in the industry. Those companies who have failed to improve their quality are no longer suppliers. Customers expect to share in the benefits of our continuous quality improvement efforts through agreed cost reduction programmes and extended warranty agreements. Without tracking quality costs we could seriously impair

our bottom line profitability and not know the reason why. (Tony Harman, Managing Director, Garrett Automotive)

With the prospect of increased competition as a result of activities surrounding 1992, it is important for us to continually improve our operational methods. The formal measurement of quality costs is central to that process, and has the added benefit of showing us how we can tackle certain areas of costs. (John Barbour, Managing Director, John Russell (Grangemouth) Ltd)

Quality must be one of the cornerstones for a growing company, otherwise spectacular growth can be followed by an equally rapid descent and quality costs are one of the measures by which this can be monitored. (Ian Elliot, Managing Director, Pirelli Focom)

From the foregoing comments one might imagine that no company could afford to be without a quality cost collection system. Not so, many organizations have no form of quality costing and many managers do not understand the concept; measurement of costs is not possible without a base level of understanding. Some of those who say they understand it have commented that they find the concept complicated, long-winded and cumbersome and requires considerable extra work. They go on to say that the exercise is unnecessary as the major problem areas should be known. For example, a major supplier of clothing to a retailing company with a first-class reputation for the quality of its goods, does not measure quality costs. Discussions revealed that its senior management appeared to think that the company's ability to satisfy such a quality-conscious customer at competitive prices shows that they are running a tight ship. This is in spite of it having a large 'seconds' shop at the factory site and it considering opening three high street outlets for the sale of 'seconds'. In some industries there is a ready market for off-specification and downgraded products. One company manufacturing microcassettes and floppy discs claimed to have zero defects. When challenged about this, they pointed out that they had customers for all downgraded products. In later discussions about the loss of profit resulting from downgraded product the point was made that if through improvements they managed to produce more of their product to specification it would result in a set of dissatisfied customers for the downgraded product!

In 1971 the Department of Trade and Industry (Mensforth [17]) recorded disappointment at how few firms collect and analyse quality costs. More recent surveys by Roche [18] and Duncalf and Dale [19] showed that only about one third of the companies they studied collected quality costs. The research work carried out at the UMIST Quality Management Centre on the subject of quality costing over the last 12 or so years confirms these findings. It is believed that less than 40% of companies collect and measure their quality costs in a systematic manner. The two main reasons given for the lack of a formal system of quality cost collection are 1. the lack of resources and 2. that the current data and reports are not in a form which allows the extraction of cost information.

Inevitably there are those who question or oppose the consensus view in relation to quality costing. Sitting [20] maintains that there are no such things as quality costs, but he concedes that it is important to analyse the relationship between total production cost (including quality costs) and quality. Tsiakals [21] warns that quality cost reporting alone does not improve quality and reduce cost (neither does quality cost analysis). Morse [22], writing from an accountant's viewpoint, also warns that organizations should not expect too much from the quality costing activity. Some managements hold the view that the measurement of quality costs can actually deflect attention from their reduction and be detrimental to quality improvement. At UMIST we have no evidence to support or refute this point of view. Other managements say they have no need to undertake a quality costing exercise in their organization to know they are at least 10% of annual sales turnover.

On a more positive note, all the signs are that the interest from organizations in the concept of quality costing is growing. A number of organizations are now seeking and getting practical evidence on quality-related costs and others are developing formalized quality costing systems. They are keen to develop their knowledge of the concept to help them better understand the effectiveness of their decisions on wastage and to save money. This is particularly the case in the automotive industry where companies such as the Rover Group and Nissan Motor Manufacturing (UK) Ltd (NMUK) are looking closely at the cost base of their suppliers and for evidence of quality cost collection and use. The NMUK Quality Management System Requirements [23] for suppliers has been structured using the 20 clauses of ISO 9001/BS5750: Part 1 [24]. There are five extra requirements in addition to these 20, one of which is quality costs:

The supplier shall establish systems and procedures for the analysis of quality costs. This shall be made available to Nissan on request.

In the project management section of the Rover Group Supplier Business Specification [25], one of the requirements is:

Quality Cost Analysis and Review.
Including:

- internal and external quality costs
- improvement programmes, where *continuous improvement* can be formally demonstrated by means of for example: Cmk, Cpk, productivity and total cost.

1.6 SUMMARY

In this chapter the concept and elements of Total Quality Management have been explored in brief. The purpose was to set quality costing in the context of its use in TQM. An examination of the evolution of quality management was presented through the stages of inspection, quality control, quality assurance and to TQM. It is argued that organizations only start to recognize the use of quality costing when they start to recognize the limitations of a detection approach and switch their resources into more prevention based activities.

There is no ideal way of starting, developing and fostering TQM. Each organization is different in terms of processes, products, history, culture and people and what works well in one situation may not necessarily be as effective in another. It is not simply a matter of applying a package. Senior management need to devote time to think through the issues and develop the TQM approach to suit the needs of the organization. The same can be said to be true of quality costing and management must make up their own minds on the value of the quality costing concept and assess whether or not it is worth the effort. The point is made that whilst there is clearly a good case for quality costing it is like any other quality management tool and technique, and organizations need to decide when, how and whether to use it.

REFERENCES

1. BS4778: *Quality Vocabulary: Part 1 (1987): International Terms* (ISO 8402: 1986) and Part 2 (1991): *Quality Concepts and Related Definitions*, British Standards Institution, London.
2. BS7850: Part 1 (1992) *Total Quality Management: Guide to Management Principles*, British Standards Institution, London.
3. Dale, B.G., Boaden, R.J. and Lascelles, D.M. (1994) Total quality management: An overview, in *Managing Quality* (ed. B.G. Dale), 2nd edn, Prentice Hall.
4. Ryan, J. (1988) Consumers see little change in product quality. *Quality Progress*, December, 16–20.
5. Hutchens, S. (1989) What customers want: results of ASQC/Gallup survey, February, 33–6.
6. McKinsey and Company (1989) Management of quality: the single most important challenger for Europe, European Quality Management Forum, 19 October, Montreux, Switzerland.
7. Lascelles, D.M. and Dale, B.G. (1990) Quality management: the Chief Executive's perception and role. *European Management Journal*, **8** (1), 67–75.
8. Buzzell, R.D. and Gale, B.T. (1987) *The Profit Impact of Marketing Strategy Principles: Linking Strategy to Performance*, Free Press, New York.
9. *Anon.* (1993) Customer service can reap rich rewards. *Strategic Insights into Quality*, **1** (1), 13–15.

10. Schaffer, R.H. and Thomson, H.A. (1992) Successful change programs begin with results. *Harvard Business Review*, January/February, 80–9.
11. Sullivan, E. (1993) Quality costs: current ideas. *Quality Progress*, **16** (4), 24–5.
12. Sullivan, E. (1983) Quality costs: current applications. *Quality Progress*, **16** (4), 34–7.
13. Claret, J. (1981) Never mind the quality. *Management Accounting*, May, 24–6.
14. Cox, B. (1982) The role of the Management Accountant in quality costing. *Quality Assurance*, **8** (3), 82–4.
15. Morse, W.J., Roth, H.P. and Poston, K.M. (1987) *Measuring Planning and Controlling Quality Costs*, Institute of Management Accountants/ASQC Quality Press, Milwaukee.
16. Dale, B.G. and Plunkett, J.J. (1990) *The Case for Quality Costing*, Department of Trade and Industry, London.
17. Mensforth, E. (1971) *Report of a Committee on the Means of Authenticating the Quality of Engineering Products and Material*.
18. Roche, J.G. (1981) *National Survey of Quality Control in Manufacturing Industries*, National Board of Science and Technology, Dublin.
19. Duncalf, A.J. and Dale, B.G. (1985) How British industry is making decisions on product quality. *Long Range Planning*, **18** (5), 81–8.
20. Sitting, J. (1963) Defining quality costs. *Proceedings of the 7th EOQC Conference*, Copenhagen, 9–17.
21. Tsiakals, J.J. (1983) Management team seeks quality improvement from quality costs. *Quality Progress*, **16** (4), 26–7.
22. Morse, W.J. (1983) Measuring quality costs. *Cost and Management*, July/August, 16–20.
23. Nissan Motor Manufacturing (UK) Ltd (1992) *Nissan Quality Standard for Suppliers – Quality Management System Requirement (QA 001 Section 4.0)*, Nissan Motor Manufacturing (UK) Ltd, Washington and Nissan Motor Iberica SA.
24. BS5750: Part 1 (1987) (ISO 9001: 1987) *Quality Systems: Specification for design/development, production, installation and servicing*, British Standards Institution, London.
25. Rover Group (1992), Supplier Business Specification RG.2000 – A Suppliers Guide to Total Customer Satisfaction, Rover Group, Birmingham.

An introduction to quality costing

2

2.1 INTRODUCTION

This chapter draws upon the published literature on quality costs. It provides guidance on some of the most authoritative reading on the subject, including an outline of the historical development of quality costing as a subject. The chapter opens by discussing, in brief, what is meant by quality costs. The point is made that the ideas of what constitutes quality costs have been changing rapidly in recent years. This changing view is also mirrored in organizations as the operating experience of TQM grows. The problem of in-built inefficiencies such as excess material allowances, excess paper and forms, deliberate over-makes and production over-runs and their impact on the level of quality costs is explored. The scale of quality costs is discussed and the point made that they are likely to range from 5 to 25% of an organization's annual sales turnover. The chapter closes by reviewing the role of accountants in quality costing.

2.2 WHAT ARE QUALITY COSTS?

There is by no means a uniform view of what is meant by a quality cost and what should be included under the quality cost umbrella. Definitions is a key feature in quality costing and Chapter 3 is devoted to this topic. A quality cost is defined in BS4778: Part 2 [1] as:

> The expenditure incurred by the producer, by the user and by the community, associated with product or service quality.

and a quality-related cost as:

> The expenditure incurred in defect prevention and appraisal activities plus the losses due to internal and external failure.

Ideas of what constitutes quality costs have been changing rapidly in recent years. Whereas in the early 1980s the costs of quality were perceived as the cost of running the quality assurance department, plus scrap, rework, testing and warranty costs, it is now widely accepted that they are the costs incurred in the design, implementation, operation and maintenance of an organization's quality management system, the cost of organizational resources committed to the process of continuous and company-wide quality improvement, the costs of system, product and service failures, and non-value added activity and wastage in all its various forms.

Quality systems may range from simple inspection to systems surpassing the requirements of the BS5750/ISO 9000 quality management system series of standards [2] or any other recognized Quality System Standard e.g. The Ford Motor Company Q-101 Quality System Standard [3]. System failures can result in obsolescent stocks, lost items, production or operation delays, missed meetings, additional work, scrap, rectification work, late deliveries, additional transportation costs, poor service and non-conforming products and services. Product and/or service failures result in warranty, guarantee and product liability claims, complaint administration and investigation, product recall, additional customer service costs and loss of customer goodwill.

At one time, there was little awareness by both company staff and the general public of the cost of service failure. Today this is changing. For example, the author was travelling from Manchester International Airport to London Heathrow on an internal flight used by many passengers to connect with world-wide flights. After the vast majority of people had boarded the aircraft the pilot announced that due to computer failure/too few staff at the checking-in desks, he was delaying take-off by a few minutes to allow the remaining passengers to come on board. This was followed by a later announcement that there were 25 breakfast trays too few, this led to a further delay. The plane took off approximately 30 minutes late. The cumulative effect of the late take-off and traffic congestion was a one hour delay in arriving at London Heathrow. This resulted in short-term stress and had the potential to cause passengers to miss connecting flights and to separate baggage from passengers. The terms 'service failure', 'poor quality', 'cost and expenses arising from the problem' were commonly used by passengers to sound off about the problem.

So quality-related costs are not, as is sometimes thought, just the cost of quality assurance, inspection, monitoring, testing, and scrap materials, components and products. Quality-related costs arise from a range of activities and involve a number of departments in an organization, all of which impinge on the quality of the product and service. For example:

- sales and marketing,
- design, research and development,
- purchasing, storage, handling,
- production or operations planning and control,

- manufacturing/operations,
- delivery, construction, installation,
- service.

Nor are they wholly determined or controlled from within an organization. Suppliers, subcontractors, stockists, agents, dealers and customers can all influence the incidence and level of quality-related costs. In non-manufacturing organizations which tend to have more operations which need to be integrated and co-ordinated to produce a seamless service, the incidence of failure is likely to be higher and consequently so are the costs of quality. A good example of this is air travel – passenger checking-in and boarding with the flightcrew, catering with the flightcrew, flightcrew with the terminal building, terminal building with ground services and passengers with baggage handling.

2.3 QUALITY COSTS AND IN-BUILT INEFFICIENCIES

When considering the nitty-gritty of quality costs there is considerable controversy about which activities and costs are quality related. Many quality-related costs are excess production/operation costs arising from the inability to 'get things right first time'. Considerable potential savings can be identified by examining closely the costs of quality-related operations themselves, e.g. inspection, appraisal, auditing, guarantee and warranty undertakings.

There are in-built inefficiencies such as excess material allowances, excess paper and forms, excess production/operations starts, deliberate overmakes (i.e. the customer wants 100 of a particular product type but because of the risk of failure 110 have to be put into the system to guarantee the 100) and production overruns (i.e. the customer wants 100 of a particular product type but because of poor process control the company cannot make just 100; the customer is expected to accept and pay for the excess quantity). These, though, are not regarded specifically as production and operating costs, and may in fact have their origins in engineering, technical, manufacturing and operating inefficiency. The same may also be true of the provision of standby machines, equipment and personnel, additional supervision, some safety stocks and items, and other contingency arrangements. Similarly, in an engineering situation, excess and selective fitting owing to variability of machined parts is often an accepted practice. This can be considerably reduced or even eliminated by the use of statistical process control (SPC).

Snagging facilities to avoid stopping production in line manufacturing are another form of in-built inefficiency. An example met with was in the manufacture of engines. In the company in question, it is sometimes not possible to complete assemblies because the requisite components are not available at the assembly line. Hence incomplete engines are diverted to a snagging area where finishing is carried out, e.g. fitting fuel pumps and starter motors. The quality assurance manager at the site maintained that the cost of the facility was a quality cost, and specifically, a failure cost. His reasoning was that the snagging operation is necessary because there has been a failure somewhere in the system and that the cost of compensating for the failure is a quality cost. Many people would reason that because systems are imperfect it is necessary to provide contingency facilities, such as snagging areas, and that their operating costs are just another built-in burden. However, there is no reason why the principle of accountability should not apply and the function responsible for the failure (purchasing, stores, logistics, planning and materials management) be made accountable for the cost.

Lack of attention to maintenance of process and equipment performance may result in built-in costs by the acceptance of inadequate levels of capability and more non-conformances than are necessary. Maintenance budgets are frequently decided on an arbitrary or general experience basis without taking due regard of the particular process needs. Maintenance should be preventative in the sense of prevention of non-conformances rather than preventing breakdown. Failure to do this is tantamount to building in unnecessarily high levels of non-conformance with consequential in-built costs. Japanese companies and an increasing number of European organizations are now actively pursuing total productive maintenance (TPM). This philosophy recognizes that machines and equipment are a key determinant of production and operation quality and it is people who maintain machines and improve their efficiency and effectiveness. Consequently, TPM encourages the involvement of everyone in this activity. For further details of TPM see Nakajima [4].

In engineering type situations, excess use of materials for starts, ends and off-cuts are built-in manufacturing costs which arise from inattention to details of the process. Wastage of materials on starts can be reduced by using scrap or cheaper materials, and end-wastage can be minimized by accurately counting the output and stopping (as opposed to running down) the producing machinery. Non-conformances may be minimized by careful attention to the available standard dimensions of raw materials and to techniques such as computer-aided nesting to utilize fully the available material.

The junk mail advertising of a myriad of services from insurance policies, and financial deals and arrangements to double glazing and offers on food stuff, whilst loosely classed as marketing, is considered by the author to be another example of in-built inefficiency and waste.

The principal problem arising from built-in inefficiencies, apart from their direct costs, is that they distort the base values against which important judgements are made and, ironically, the more the base values are used the more firmly entrenched and accepted the built-in efficiencies become.

2.4 QUALITY COSTS AND DELIVERY PERFORMANCE

A cause of poor quality which is not usually specified, but which is widely acknowledged, arises from the quality-delivery dilemma. Sometimes quality is only achieved at the expense of a default on delivery, or vice versa. There are two areas of cost which are commonly encountered: 1. the batch of product is delivered by courier service to meet the schedule and satisfy the customer, and 2. the batch is split to ensure that the customer's production line is not brought to a standstill. Manufacturers of large heavy goods, in particular for overseas customers, can face very severe cost penalties if agreed shipping dates are not met; the same is true in the construction, leisure and entertainment industries if completion dates are not met. Having to compromise leads to taking short cuts and also tends to increase the amount of product passed on concession, and tends to increase inventory levels.

In the context of accounting, contract work, and other matters with terminal dates or deadlines, there is often an implicit acceptance of a lower standard of quality provided that the deadline is met. Thus, for example, accountants furnish estimates if exact data is not available, and there are a greater number of errors in latest news articles than in feature articles in newspapers. Perhaps it is similar evidence of the effects on quality of tipping the balance in favour of delivery, which makes organizations try hard to maintain a more balanced situation.

The quality–delivery dilemma is probably an important factor in the poor delivery performance of some organizations, even though, according to the quality fraternity, goods often progress through to delivery with indecent haste. On the other hand, production and operations people complain constantly that quality considerations impede output and the meeting of production and service schedules.

There is probably some truth in the assertion that production and operations people use quality as an excuse for poor delivery. This might be credible if deliveries were a matter of hours, or even days, late. But when deliveries are weeks, or even months, behind schedule for supposedly quality-related reasons the implications are that the company must have serious quality problems and one wonders what the cost consequences might have been if the quality procedures had been by-passed in order to deliver on time.

2.5 A SHORT HISTORY OF QUALITY COSTING

It was the American who first identified and defined quality costs. However, definitions of quality-related costs have changed just as perceptions of TQM and quality improvement have changed and it is difficult to determine when quality-related costs were first so called. Almost all the early papers on quality costing mention only inspection, rework, repair and warranty costs (i.e. elements of what are now called appraisal and failure categories of quality-related costs). The term 'quality costs' was certainly in use in Western Europe in the late 1950s and early 1960s and may have originated with the categorization of costs into prevention–appraisal–failure, which is attributed to the seminal paper of Feigenbaum [5] in the mid 1950s. Quality costs featured in a 1957 British Productivity Council film *Right First Time*. In the discussion notes accompanying the film the costs of quality were broken down into: costs of failure, costs of appraisal and costs of prevention. The notes state:

> These costs build up roughly as follows:
>
> – Failure 70 per cent
> – Appraisal 25 per cent
> – Prevention 5 per cent
> – and the total may well amount to between 4 and 14 per cent of the turnover of the company.

The notes go on to say:

> The company then starts to put its own house in order, first by determining its quality costs. The shock of realising that these amount to between 15 and 20 per cent of factory costs inspires immediate action.

In 1967 the American Society for Quality Control (ASQC) published *Quality Costs – What and How* [6] in which quality costs are defined only by category and by reference to Feigenbaum. This booklet which was revised in 1970 and 1974 has now been withdrawn. It is now entitled *Principles of Quality Costs* (Campanella [7]). It is a definitive short work on the subject, even though it did not include all the cost elements which might be identified as being quality-related in a TQM approach. It takes the 'What' concept and quality cost definitions from Feigenbaum's book *Total Quality Control* [8], but adds sources for finding cost data and gives a lot of good advice on what to include, what to leave out, and specific warnings to be cautious in interpreting and using cost data. However, only about one-third of the book is taken up with quality cost definitions. The rest is about getting management attention and approval, cost collection and tabulation, quality cost trend analysis and corrective analysis, business reports to management, and audit and follow-up. In short, the emphasis is on the use of cost information.

The style of presentation is such that the booklet is helpful and encouraging rather than authoritative and dictatorial in getting its message across. The booklet's messages are spelled out simply and clearly (though perhaps too wordily for some), supplemented with plenty of illustrative charts and exhibits with explanatory notes. The reader is led gently but firmly along the path of getting approximate costs to attract management attention and approval of a quality cost programme, involving other departments, selection of an initial project, definition of cost elements, collection, analysis, presentation, reporting to management, audit and follow-up, with lots of good advice along the way. The fact that the emphasis is on measuring and reducing (or optimizing) the major quality cost categories and elements rather than on the currently more popular quality cost improvement projects approach, does not invalidate or detract from the value of the strategy or advice in any way.

Other ASQC publications which deal best with practical aspects of how to do quality costing are: *Guide for Reducing Quality Costs* [9] and *Guide for Managing Supplier Quality Costs* [10]. The former publication has now been withdrawn. However, material from both these guides has been incorporated into the second edition of *Principles of Quality Costs* (Campanella [7]).

The *Guide for Reducing Quality Costs* (the first edition was published seven years later than *Quality Costs – What and How*) develops the uses of quality costing by directing attention to quality improvement projects and to the involvement and responsibilities of technical, marketing and purchasing functions in quality matters. It deals with identifying problem areas and the analysis of quality costs. It makes specific recommendations on reducing failure and appraisal costs, prevention of quality costs and measuring improvement, as well as providing case study examples. The idea of projecting failure and appraisal costs as desirable targets for cost reduction but regarding prevention as a cost-saving activity is a commendable one. Under the heading 'prevention of quality costs' ways are listed in which marketing, design, quality assurance, and indeed management in general, can help to prevent appraisal and failure costs from arising.

The *Guide for Managing Supplier Quality Costs* (the first edition was published three years later than the *Guide for Reducing Quality Costs*) is an acknowledgement of the fact that companies purchase some of their quality problems. Today, many major Western organizations are now devoting considerable resources to developing partnership sourcing relationships with their supplier communities and working more closely with them on quality improvement initiatives; details are given, for example, by Galt and Dale [11] and Lloyd *et al.* [12]. The guide wastes no time before getting down to methods of vendor control, the visible and hidden quality costs related to vendor control, and methods of applications of quality cost to vendor control. The instruction and advice is detailed, specific and clear, as in the other two ASQC publications. Two themes are pursued, identifying and attacking vendor-related problems through joint projects with the vendor and motivating the vendor to adopt his own quality cost programme.

The only major criticism to be made of the three publications is that the whole emphasis is on reducing costs. Nowhere is mooted the alternative approach of improving quality without increasing costs. Many companies regard quality as being of such prime importance that they are unwilling to put it at risk for the purpose of cost reductions. Indeed, some companies are looking to quality expenditures as areas for profitable investment.

In more recent times the American Society for Quality Control Quality Costs Committee have produced three books. Grimm [13] and Campanella [14] are the editors for two books of papers from ASQC's Annual Technical Conference/Quality Congress. It is claimed that these source books 'contain the best of today's thinking about quality costs'. The first volume covers information from the period 1970–82 and the second volume from 1983–7. Campanella [7] is the editor of a book which is a product of the Quality Costs Committee of ASQC's Quality Management Division. It includes material from other committee publications such as *Guide for Reducing Quality Costs* and *Guide for Managing Supplier Quality Costs*. As mentioned earlier, this book replaces *Quality Costs – What and How*. With coverage of quality costs in service industries this is a much more rounded book than its predecessor. It is an excellent publication and should be compulsory reading for anyone undertaking work on the collection and use of quality-related costs.

The British Standards Institution's publication BS6143 *Guide to the Determination and Use of Quality Related Costs* [15], which was published in 1981, is, in many respects an abridged version of *Quality Costs – What and How*, but it is a poor imitation. The standard has now been revised. The stated primary intention is to provide guidance on the operation of a quality costs system within a manufacturing organization. As judged by the list of contents, the guide promises much but fails to deliver on these promises. The presentation of the Standard does not engender a flexible approach to collecting costs, even though it may have been intended. It does not reflect accurately the incidence and distribution of costs in manufacturing and non-manufacturing situations as encountered in the UMIST research. The emphasis in the Standard tends to reflect the magnitude of quality activities rather than quality-related costs.

The flaws in the Standard are discussed in some detail by Plunkett and Dale [16]; these include, in addition to the ones mentioned above, the following.

- 'Some cost elements in BS6143 are inappropriate to manufacturing industry and are more suited to the heavy fabrication industry.'
- 'It is difficult to find generic terms to describe specific tasks or activities having the same broad objective in different industries or types of manufacture. This makes collation and comparisons of data from different sources very difficult.'
- 'The Standard permits reporting net costs by deduction of income from sales of scrap from quality costs. This is not good practice because it subsidizes poor quality. Also, the type and quantity of scrap sold at a particular time may bear no relation to current output.'

- 'The cost element checklists in the Standard can be useful thought starters when collecting quality costs, but they can also act as blinkers.'
- 'The Standard should make specific recommendations on the quality-relatedness of testing and running-in operations, and on the accounting of overheads and scrap'.

Whilst there is little doubt that many of the faults of the Standard derive from the abridging process and editing down, it also bears one of the hallmarks of committee work. How else would prevention activities which account for say 2% of quality costs (BS6143 'typical data') be broken down into eight minutely detailed elements whilst internal failure costs (63% of quality costs – same data source), though having seven elements, is not analysed in nearly so much detail. In another instance, an example cites 14 prevention elements, six appraisal, seven internal failure, and five external failure elements. All in all, users would have been better served if the committee had adopted ASQC's *Quality Costs – What and How* and incorporated material from the other two publications, though it has to be admitted that the style and content of such a document would be unusual for a British Standard.

Many of these criticisms have been taken into account in an extensive revision of the Standard. The Standard which is now titled *Guide to the Economics of Quality* [17, 18] is published in two parts. Part 1 of the guide 'Process cost model' outlines a model for applying quality costing to any process or service-manufacturing or non-manufacturing. The method is based on process modelling and emphasizes the importance of process measurement and process ownership. The Philip Crosby method of categorizing costs – price (cost) of conformance (POC) and price (cost) of non-conformance (PONC) – has been used in the model to simplify cost classification. Part 2 of the guide 'Prevention, appraisal and failure model' is a revised version of the classical model of quality costing used in manufacturing industry. Rather perversely, Part 2 of the Standard appeared in print in 1990 and Part 1 in 1992. Part 2 contains more general information on quality costing and it would have been better if this had been classed as Part 1.

Prior to the publication of BS6143 in 1981 considerations of quality costing were mentioned in BS4891 [19] in 1972 under the heading 'Economics of quality assurance' – the notion that in each manufacturing situation there should be an optimum quality level corresponding to a minimum manufacturing operation or quality cost. This notion of an economic level of quality was sustained in PD6470 [20] (published in 1973 with revisions in 1975 and 1981). This concept is questioned by many writers, including Plunkett and Dale [21] and Fox [22].

Quality costing has been used primarily by manufacturing industry, but today there is growing interest from commerce, the public sector and service organizations. There is now clear evidence of quality costing being used in a variety of non-manufacturing situations including financial institutions, transport and distribution, health care, and the travel and holiday industry. For example, Dale and Plunkett [23] describe the use made of quality costing by British Airways Technical Workshops (the workshops are responsible for the overhaul and repair of items removed from aircraft), John Russell (Grangemouth) (a transportation and warehousing company), National Westminster Bank (see Chapters 3 and 4 – the Bank refers to quality costing as the cost of making mistakes) and Girobank (see Chapter 11).

A draft international standard (ISO 10014 *Guide to the Economics of Total Quality Management*) has been prepared and is available for comment; this standard reflects a number of developments which have taken place in the subject during the last few years.

2.6 WHY ARE QUALITY COSTS IMPORTANT?

Quality costs are important, first, because they are large: very large. In 1978 they were estimated by the UK Government to be £10 000 million, equal to 10% of the UK's Gross National Product. There is no reason to suppose that they are any less now. The findings of an NEDC task force on Quality and Standards published in 1985 [24], claims that some 10 to 20% of an organization's total sales value is accounted for by quality-related costs. Using the figure of 10%, it is estimated in the report that UK manufacturing industry could save up to £6Bn each year by reducing such costs. Various studies carried out by UMIST and information volunteered by a variety of organizations have shown that quality-related costs commonly range from 5 to 25% of company annual sales turnover. The costs depend on the type of industry, business situation or service, the view taken by the organization of what is or is not a quality-related cost, the approach to TQM, and the extent to which continuous quality improvement is practised in the organization. Crosby [25] claims that manufacturing companies incur costs amounting to 25–30% of their sales by doing things over again, while in service companies he estimates that 40–50% of operating costs are wasted. Blades [26], transposing the type of quality costs experienced in manufacturing and the private sector to the UK National Health Service, claims this could result in a loss of between £6Bn and £11Bn per year. From the UMIST experience it is estimated that an organization who is not progressive in its approach to quality improvement should consider their quality costs to be around 10–14% of annual sales turnover.

Second, 95% of the quality cost is usually expended on appraisal and failure. These expenditures add little to the value of the product or service, and the failure costs, at least, may be regarded as avoidable. Reducing failure cost by eliminating causes of non-conformance can also lead to substantial reductions in appraisal costs. The UMIST research evidence on quality costing suggests that quality-related costs may be reduced to one-third of their present level, within a period of three years, by the commitment of the organization to a process of continuous and company-wide quality improvement.

Third, unnecessary and avoidable costs make goods and services more expensive. This in turn affects competitiveness and, ultimately, wages, salaries and standards of living.

Fourth, despite the fact that the costs are large, and that a substantial proportion of them are avoidable, it is apparent that the costs and economics of many quality-related activities, including investment in prevention and appraisal activities, are not known by many companies. Such a state of affairs is surely indefensible in any well-run business.

2.7 PUBLISHED QUALITY COST DATA

In this context data means real numbers. The literature is strewn with numbers, many of them fictitious. It is not always easy to tell the difference. Some examples may use real figures under fictitious company names. It should be noted that much of what has been written on quality costs is of a qualitative nature and that, with few exceptions, the quantitative data are broad and unqualified. However, so far as is able to be judged, what now follows relates to real numbers.

The literature which contains numerical quality cost data falls conveniently into three groups:

1. figures of costs for quality to nations and multi-national corporations;
2. comparisons between industries and industry groups;
3. individual company experience.

2.7.1 Costs of quality relating to nations and multi-national corporations

From the first group, MacGregor [27] puts the ubiquitous UK quality cost of £10 000M per year (1978 prices) into perspective when he equates it to the income from Value Added Tax (VAT) plus the income from tourism and North Sea oil. He also quotes an unnamed major international industrial company achieving annual savings of $22M rising to $42M over five years by eliminating quality problems. Wheelwright and Hayes [28] reveal that IBM's quality costs in the early 1980s were 30% of their manufacturing costs. Rohan [29], from the aircraft industry, where costs are huge anyway, discloses that despite an annual expenditure of $30M on quality assurance, defects and other quality problems were costing the Fairchild Republic Co. a further $20M each year. After getting to grips with the problems they reduced quality-related losses by more than 80%. Mayben [30], from military aircraft manufacture, is less forthcoming about expenditure and losses, but returns on investment of quality improvements ranging from 2:1 to 20:1, and on one project an estimated saving of $11M over 10 years, make impressive reading. For sheer scale of quality costs and savings ITT are well to the front and even Jones' [31] $30M of quality cost improvements planned for 1977 seems small when compared to Groocock's [32] reported $460M and $550M quality costs in 1978 and 1979, respectively, for the European operation alone.

2.7.2 Costs of quality comparisons between industries and industry groups

Information showing quality cost levels and distributions of expenditure are useful if only to reinforce the warnings about comparisons of data. The periodical *Quality* [33], reporting data across 11 industry groups, at two levels of sophistication of cost collection and expressed against two bases (net sales billed and direct labour), shows clearly the folly of attempting to make comparisons across industry boundaries. The only cross-industry research known to the authors is by Gilmore [34–6] in which he investigates 10 industry groups, different company sizes, and production-to-quality-personnel ratios, looking for differences in total quality costs and in prevention-appraisal-failure distributions.

Robertson [37] draws on data from the National Council for Quality and Reliability saying that for the average UK organization quality-related costs are divided in the proportions: 5% prevention costs, 30% appraisal costs and 65% failure costs. He goes on to say that they may be 4–20% of sales turnover, and that concentrating on prevention may alter the failure-appraisal-prevention ratio to 35:20:10 whilst achieving savings of 1.5 to 6.5% of turnover.

Abed and Dale [38] from an analysis of the quantitative data contained in the quality costing literature found that the quality cost categories expressed as a percentage of total quality costs are: prevention (5%), appraisal (28%) and failure (67%). Total quality costs as a percentage of annual sales turnover averaged 9.2% with a range from 2 to 25%.

2.7.3 Cost of quality from individual companies

Contributions from individual companies are valuable because many reveal how they measured quality costs and how they achieved their cost reductions. Revealing actual data gives their contributions an authenticity lacking in papers without data.

Richardson's [39] paper from the engineering industry is an excellent example. Starting with one in six of the total complement of personnel on the quality budget and a reject rate of 6% giving quality costs of 13.2% of sales turnover, the company reduced the personnel in its quality assurance function from 125 to 35 whilst defect rates fell from 6% to 4% through a series of quality-improvement activities, giving around 10% of annual sales turnover (worth £1M) as real savings. Add in enhancement of the company's price competitiveness owing to the savings, and its improved ability to respond to order requirements because of the obvious reduction in lead time, and one is left with a story which spells success by any standards. Paradoxically, this success was achieved by applying the quality assurance manager's joke, 'We can reduce our quality costs tomorrow – just sack the inspectors and checkers'.

Garvin [40], using the example of air-conditioning equipment, notes that Japanese manufacturers' warranty costs are about 0.6% of sales. At the best US companies it was 1.8% and at the worst 5.2%. Further, the total costs of quality incurred by Japanese producers were less than one-half of the failure costs incurred by the best US companies.

From a survey and study in the machine-tool industry, Burns [41] reports quality costs as 5% of estimated sales turnover, of which approximately 60% were failure costs. The proportions of measured quality costs falling into the main categories of quality costs were: prevention 3.3%, appraisal 40.3% and failure 56.3%. This level of prevention investment was compared to a level of 13% claimed from a similar survey carried out in West Germany. From the company in which Burns carried out a detailed case study he reports a reduction in quality costs of 1.6% of sales turnover between the year of measurement (1970) and a post-study audit of 1973 costs.

Webb [42] compares meat processing industry costs with general industry costs as in Table 2.1. This example serves to reiterate the dangers of generating expectations from comparisons. The inclusion of machinery maintenance as a prominent quality cost also illustrates how major quality parameters differ from one industry to another.

Moyer and Gilmore [43] in a study of a steel foundry jobbing-shop making castings for the valve industry include 'quality image loss' of 5% of sales turnover, thereby boosting external quality costs alone to 15.5% of sales. Debiting returned castings at sales value, despite noting that it should be at manufacturing cost plus profit margin, also helps to keep the costs well inflated. By the time all the other quality-related costs are gathered in they arrive at a staggering 38% of sales, apportioned as 6% prevention, 14% appraisal and 80% failure.

Table 2.1 Comparison of the costs in the meat processing industry with those in industry in general (Webb [42])

	General industry (%)	Meat industry (%)
Failures	65	79
Appraisals	25	8
Prevention (machinery maintenance, etc.)	8	10
Prevention (technologies, etc.)	2	3
Percentage of sales	10	6

The following are examples of quality costs taken from the Department of Trade and Industry publication *The Case for Quality Costing* (Dale and Plunkett [23]). (Unless stated all current quality costs are based on 1988 figures.)

- In 1980 the quality costs of Bridgeport Machines were 4% of sales turnover (£1M); by 1988 they had fallen to 2% of sales turnover.
- British Aerospace Dynamics quality costs are 11% of the total cost of production.
- In British Airways Technical Workshops, staff time on quality-related matters is spent in the ratio: prevention (19.4%), appraisal (6.8%) and failure (22.9%).
- The costs of quality in Courtaulds Jersey have been reduced from 12.1% to 7.6% of sales turnover over a period of four years.
- The cost of quality in Standfast Dyers and Printers (another Courtaulds company) have been reduced from 20% to 7% of sales value over a period of four years.
- In 1986, the quality costs at Crown Industrial Products were 13% of raw material usage costs; by late 1988 they were down to 8%.
- In 1986 the quality costs of Garrett Automotive (Turbocharger Division) were 6.5% of sales turnover; by 1988 they had fallen to 4% of sales turnover.
- At Grace Dearborn the cost of quality is 20% of sales turnover.
- In 1987 the cost of quality at ICL (Manufacturing and Logistics) was £60M.
- In 1988 the costs of quality at John McGavigan were 22% of sales turnover.
- At National Westminster Bank, 25% of operating costs is absorbed in the difference between the cost actually incurred in accomplishing a task and the cost of a 'right first time' approach.
- Philips Components Blackburn have reduced their plant-wide quality costs by 60% over a period of six years.

The following three contributions by Huckett [44], Krzikowski [45] and Kohl [46] are special because they give quality costs and changing distributions between categories of cost over periods of six to eight years.

Huckett [44] recounts the achievements of the 1984 British Quality Award winners, Rank Xerox Ltd at their Mitcheldean site. Reduction in the cost of quality is one of their key measurements of results and their data shows a steady reduction from 6% of manufacturing cost in 1979 to a little over 1% in 1984.

Krzikowski [45] presents an excellently detailed paper on quality in the cash register manufacturing business. He indicates total quality costs as a percentage, probably of manufacturing cost, though it is not specifically stated. However, he shows the changes in distribution of prevention-appraisal-failure costs as the total costs fall from 6.4% to 4.4% over a period of six years. The data is unusual in that prevention costs were increased to a point where they caused the total costs to rise, but it is clear from the text that this is entirely owing to a one-off training exercise for inspectors.

Kohl [46], from the Allis-Chalmers Corporation, claims a 35% reduction in 1970 of 1969 quality costs of \$1.6M, in addition to conserving interest costs by 6.3% by improving cash flow. Over 18 months 'the portion of the specification cost dollar spent on internal failures was also reduced by 2 cents to $\frac{7}{10}$ cent', giving a saving of \$405 000. At one factory the inspection force was reduced by 43% whilst at another the total costs of quality were reduced by 70%, equivalent to 3% of sales turnover (i.e. from 4.5 to 1.5% of sales turnover). However, by far the most interesting data is the 'allocation of the quality dollar' to prevention-appraisal-failure and the total quality costs for the years 1967 to 1974. These indicate the substantial reduction in total failure costs noted above and an even more dramatic change in the relative expenditures (e.g. external failure costs falling from 46% to 6% of the total, whilst prevention expenditure was increased two-fold).

The following three contributions from Payne [47], Knock [48] and Hesford and Dale [49] are more recent but show similar trends to the earlier publications.

Payne [47] (formerly quality improvement manager of the 1987 British Quality Award winner, Philips Blackburn) reports cost of quality savings of £1.6 million per annum over a five-year period as a result of the company's quality improvement initiative. He goes on to give details of a quality cost analysis at the Philips sister plant at Hazel Grove. For the power bipolar device cost of quality (non-conformance, appraisal and failure) reduced from a 1988 figure of 35.8% of factory turnover to 18.1% in 1991 and for Power MOS devices from 29.7% in 1989 to 15.7% in 1991.

Knock [48] from York International (designer and manufacturer of air-conditioning and industrial refrigeration systems) outlines how a quality assurance programme reduced the cost of quality. This, measured as a cost of sales, has been reduced from 13.5% in 1985 to 3.7% in 1991. The cost of on-site failures has been reduced by more than 80% and the cost of factory failures by 96% during the same period.

Hesford and Dale [49] report on a quality costing exercise carried out across the five principal sites of the British Aerospace Dynamics Division. The Division manufactures guided weapons, equipment and underwater systems. The results show that the total quality costs were some 11% of the total cost of production. Twenty-two per cent of these total costs fell into the prevention category, 30% into appraisal and 48% into failure costs. Prevention costs comprise some 13 individual elements with the largest single cost being that of calibration and maintenance of inspection and test equipment at 3.5% of total quality cost. In the appraisal category, which includes 11 individual elements, the major cost activities were inspection at 8% and test at 7%. The failure costs include 11 individual elements, with engineering changes being the largest single element at 23% of the total quality cost and 2.5% of the cost of production.

2.8 WHY MEASURE QUALITY COSTS?

The measurement of costs allows quality-related activities to be expressed in the language of management. This, in turn, allows quality to be treated as a business parameter along with, for example, marketing, research and development, and production/operations. Drawing quality costs into the business arena helps to emphasize the importance of quality to corporate health and will help to influence employee behaviour and attitudes at all levels in the organization towards TQM and continuous quality improvement. The emphasis should be on identifying improvement opportunities and not just costing areas of failure nor should it be considered as just another financial measure.

Quality cost measurement focuses attention on areas of high expenditure and wastage and identifies potential problem areas and cost-reduction and improvement opportunities. It allows measurement of performance and provides a basis for internal comparison between products, services, processes and departments. Measurement of quality-related costs also reveals quirks and anomalies in cost allocation, standards and procedures for disposal of products which may remain undetected by the more commonly used production/operation and labour-based analyses. It can uncover non-conformances that conventional accounting procedures do not pick up. The questioning of the norm helps to identify situations which have been overlooked or ignored by traditional practices. Measurement can also obviate the dumping of embarrassing after-sales costs under quality-related headings.

Finally, and perhaps most importantly, measurement is the first step towards control and improvement.

2.9 ACCOUNTING, ACCOUNTANTS AND QUALITY COSTING

The initiative to collect and analyse quality costs comes, in general, from the quality assurance department; sometimes it is driven by the board of directors and senior management team but rarely does the initiative come from the accounting and financial department. Initiatives emanating from accountants seem to be prompted only by the high costs of inspection and checking activities or scrap appearing in labour or material cost analyses, respectively. The collection of quality costs should be a joint exercise between quality assurance, technical specialists and accountants. Accountants should be involved from the outset of the exercise. The costs should be produced or endorsed by the accounts department who should also be specifically charged with responsibility for avoiding double-counting. Quality assurance and technical specialists frequently complain about the lack of initiative taken by accountants in the quality costing exercise and their unwillingness to co-operate. There is a view that accountants tend to raise barricades in anticipation of an onslaught from quality assurance managers in search of accurate quality costs.

The collection of quality costs and their analysis, and reporting of quality costs is dealt with in Chapters 4 and 5, respectively, in this chapter, however, it is important to review the contribution, or lack of it, by accountants to the subject of quality costing. In the last two years the author has had a number of interesting discussions on the concept of quality costing with accountants who have had some positive comments to make on the topic.

The accountancy literature does not contain a lot of articles on quality costs. A few contributions worth noting have been found and are reported here together with some views of accountants and accountancy from the quality assurance and management literature.

Jorgensen [50] was clearly unhappy with his local accountancy department, and its staff when he wrote that:

The accounting systems in most factories are built upon rather conservative principles, which rarely provide for the instant and relevant information necessary to run a quality control department.

A great amount of energy and tact is necessary on the part of the Quality Control Department in order to overcome this difficulty ... quality control must make a habit of using the data from traditional accountancy with a great amount of suspicion and must try to convince the accountants of the justice of this suspicion.

Krzikowski [45] was equally gloomy when he noted that:

An exact calculation of the quality costs would demand a radical change in the Accounts Department – as radical as the introduction of the accounting systems in German companies about 30 years ago.

Jorgensen and Krzikowski were writing 30 years ago. But 10 years later Brown [51] still felt constrained in his ability to give guidance on establishing and controlling quality costs, thus:

Unfortunately, due to the differences in accounting procedures within industry, it is not possible to lay down hard and fast rules for establishing and controlling quality costs. This paper sets down the basic principles behind any quality cost investigation, bearing in mind that the procedures and make-up of costs will vary as the accounting procedures vary.

This does suggest that the gap between engineer and accountant was getting narrower.

At about the same time Mandel [52] was offering a statistician's alternative to cost accountancy – random time sampling. Referring to the inability of conventional cost-accounting systems to provide the special type of cost information required for quality costing, especially with respect to personnel and machine costs, he suggests 'an effective and efficient method of costing, called random time sampling which meets the costing requirements of relevance, accuracy, simplicity, and economy' and has been found to be 'a highly acceptable alternative to the conventional cost accounting system'. It is also less subjective, and cheaper, but it does not appear to have caught on so far as can be gauged from published information on quality costing systems.

Olson [53] found that the company's accounting department benefitted from his improvement to a discrepant materials reporting and action system by generating information it could not get previously. He cites an example that on one single day there was a total of $160 000 worth of rejected materials and parts. Apparently that information could not have been available before, and must be of considerable value to company management. A very important point emerging from this is that cost data cannot be any better than the underlying time or materials or labour data. If these are uncontrolled there is no way they can be costed properly.

Hallum and Casperson [54] appear to have a good working relationship with accountants in their organization. They open their paper with a description of their accounting system. Costs carry three labels: the kind of costs (e.g. wages, salaries, materials), the place of the cost or the department debited, and the purpose of the cost (e.g. production, sales, product development, and quality control). This makes life much easier when collecting quality costs, though no doubt there are some misallocations through wrong labelling and differences of opinion about the purposes of expenditures. Ironically, Hallum and Casperson work for the same company whose accountants were so distrusted by Jorgensen 12 years before.

An indication of the receptiveness of management accountants to quality costing initiatives is provided in a more recent case at the British Aerospace Dynamics Division. Hesford and Dale [49], writing about the reaction of the finance people, say:

The site finance managers were very receptive and impressed at the level of documentation behind quality cost recording. They were anxious to ensure that all costs were auditable or at least traceable to original source data or criteria. If percentage allocations or apportionment routines were to be used, this was of little concern to the accountants, provided source data were traceable to accounts and that the methodologies were consistent. Finance management's main concern was to avoid double counting in the cost elements within the failure category. With reference to this they provided useful advice for areas to be checked out in detail.

In the special quality costs edition of *Quality Progress*, Sullivan [55] reports a member of ASQC's Quality Costs Technical Committee as saying:

The emphasis in quality costs is to get the accounting people involved . . .

and that the committee

. . . has been in contact with representatives of professional associations of accountants to develop better ways of capturing quality costs.

If the system is properly explained, finance and accounting departments are generally glad to help set up a cost system, according to Feigenbaum 'This gives them the opportunity to measure major costs that just haven't been measured'.

There is little doubt that during the last 20 years or so there has been a considerable change in attitude towards accountants and what may be expected of them.

In the opposite corner, whilst not writing a great deal about quality costs, the accountants have some worthy champions of their cause. Morse [56] shows a sensitivity to the problems of gaining the co-operation of quality assurance personnel when he writes of the inappropriateness of the expression 'cost of quality' (as opposed to quality costs) in that it implies a trade-off between cost and quality, and of the effects its use is likely to have. Nonetheless he is firm in the accountants' assertion that the ultimate purpose of a quality cost system is to give management a means of planning and controlling costs.

Cox [57] looks at quality from the point of view of the community at large, from the users' standpoint and from the manufactuers' and/or providers' angle. For the user he identifies aspects of product failure which cannot be quantified in money terms but which result in a loss to the manufacturer in terms of negative goodwill. For the manufacturer and provider he points out that whilst anything spent on achieving conformance to specification represents a charge against profits (and hence the manufacturers'/providers' objective must be to minimize quality costs for the particular specification), sometimes he has no choice as to how much he must spend. For example, products which are likely to cause severe loss of life or ecological disaster require that the original specification must be right and the quality effort must be absolute. The possibility of death or injury to individuals imposes moral and legal constraints which will require close attention to quality assurance, with relatively high quality-related costs. In cases where the only consequence of failure is loss of profit the manufacturer is in a position to trade quality costs against profit. An examination of where a manufacturer's products stand in this quality–cost spectrum is an advisable precursor to an organization undertaking a quality costing exercise.

In a second contribution Cox [58] does his profession an excellent service by setting down what a management accountant does. He briefly discusses long-term planning, budgeting and quality costing, and closes on a practical note that the management accounting function has just as many constraints on its resources as any other function and will need to be persuaded that the results obtained from a cost-collection exercise are likely to be worth the time and effort. Sensibly too, he warns against expecting accountants to be arbiters in disputes between departments over allocations of costs.

Claret [59], whilst recognizing that:

> ... accountants are frequently seen as responsible for many of the ills of society ...,

is at pains to point out that the accountant does not make the decisions which result in the ills. He discusses the limitations of the accountant's contribution to quality-related matters and makes some suggestions for improvement. In particular he points out that accountants usually get involved in capital investment but, in many businesses, do not get involved in revenue investment decision (e.g. in production engineering and new designs). He appeals to accountants to get themselves involved in all kinds of investment decisions and suggests some self help by urging them to develop models

> ... which allow them to test the relationships between costs, quality, investment, and improved turnover through improved quality.

The quality assurance profession must look forward with interest to the publication of such a model.

Sandretto [60] in a paper which goes much further than Cox's explanation of what management accounting is about, stresses that although conceptually simple, cost accounting is not an all-purpose management tool. It is very much a matter of horses for courses. Uses of costs information, inputs, outputs and operation constraints, various manufacturing situations (e.g. job order production, discrete part products, few material inputs) and service companies, together with influences of various factors on cost control and analysis and the conflicting needs for control and analysis, are all discussed in a paper which, although not specifically about quality costs, is excellent background material for any cost-collection exercise.

Morse et al. [61] report on the results of a study undertaken by the three authors (all accountants) for the National Association of Accountants (now the Institute of Management Accountants). The book is split into three sections: 'Framework for a quality cost reporting system', 'Case studies' and 'Analysis and summary'. It is aimed at management accountants as an introduction to quality costs and provides excellent advice on the type of tasks which need to be undertaken in designing and implementing a quality cost reporting system.

Dobbins and Brown [62] argue for a spirit of partnership between the quality assurance and accounting functions instead of them adopting an adversarial position. The paper describes typical cost accounting statements and shows their relationship to quality cost analysis data elements. Much useful guidance is provided on methods for collecting and reporting quality costs and helping to develop a co-operative relationship between the accounting and quality assurance functions.

2.10 SUMMARY

The evidence suggests that the cost of non-quality, waste, non-value-added activity and a range of in-built inefficiencies can be some 5 to 25% of an organization's annual sales turnover. It is estimated from the UMIST research experience that, on average, these costs in an organization whose approach to quality management is rooted in detection-based activities is around 10–14% of annual sales turnover. However, much of the published data on quality costs is broad and unqualified. Some effort has been made in this chapter to highlight the key pieces of published numerical data.

The Americans have had a considerable impact on quality costing. The American Society for Quality Control has been particularly influential and has produced much useful advice on the subject.

Sometimes accountants and quality managers end up taking an adversarial position in a quality costing, rather than working in partnership to collect the data. The key role of accountants has been reviewed. The point is made that management accountants during the last two years have adopted a more positive stance towards quality costing.

REFERENCES

1. BS4778: Part 2 (1991) *Quality Vocabulary: Quality Concepts and Related Definitions*, British Standards Institution, London.
2. BS5750/ISO 9000 (1987) *Quality Systems*, British Standards Institution, London.
3. Ford Motor Company (1990) *World-Wide Quality System Q-101*, Ford Motor Company, Plymouth, MI, USA.
4. Nakajima, S. (1988) *Introduction to Total Productive Maintenance*, Productivity Press, Cambridge, MA.
5. Feigenbaum, A.V. (1956) Total Quality Control. *Harvard Business Review*, **34**(6), 93–101.
6. ASQC Quality Costs Committee (1974) *Quality Costs – What and How*, American Society for Quality Control, Milwaukee.
7. Campanella, J. (ed.) (1990) *Principles of Quality Costs: Principles, Implementation and Use*, ASQC, Quality Press, Milwaukee.
8. Feigenbaum A.V., 1961, Total Quality Control, McGraw Hill.
9. ASQC Quality Costs Committee (1977) *Guide for Reducing Quality Costs*, American Society for Quality Control, Milwaukee.

10. ASQC Quality Costs Committee (1987) *Guide for Managing Supplier Quality Costs*, American Society for Quality Control, Milwaukee.
11. Galt, J. and Dale, B.G. (1990) Customer supplier relationships in the motor industry: a vehicle manufacturer's perspective. *Proceedings of the Institution of Mechanical Engineers*, **204** (D4), 179–86.
12. Lloyd, A., Dale, B.G. and Burnes, B. (1994) Supplier development: a study of Nissan Motor Manufacturing (UK) and her suppliers. *Proceedings of the Institution of Mechanical Engineers*, **208**(D1), 63–68.
13. Grimm, A.F. (ed.) (1987) *Quality Costs: Ideas and Applications*, Vol. 1, ASQC Quality Press, Milwaukee.
14. Campanella, J. (ed.) (1989) *Quality Costs: Ideas and Applications*, Vol. 2, ASQC Quality Press, Milwaukee.
15. BS6143 (1981) *Guide to the Determination and Use of Quality Related Costs*, British Standards Institution, London.
16. Dale, B.G. and Plunkett, J.J. (1988) Quality-related costing: findings from an industry-based research study, *Engineering Management International*, **4** (4), 247–57.
17. BS6143 Part 1 (1992) *Guide to the Economics of Quality: Process cost model*. British Standards Institution, London.
18. BS6143 Part 2 (1990) *Guide to the Economics of Quality: Prevention, appraisal and failure model*. British Standards Institution, London.
19. BS4891 (1972) *A Guide to Quality Assurance*, British Standards Institution, London.
20. PD6470 (1981) *Management of Design for Economic Production*, British Standards Institution, London.
21. Plunkett, J.J. and Dale, B.G. (1988) Quality costs: a critique of some 'economic cost of quality' models. *International Journal of Production Research*, **28** (11), 1713–26.
22. Fox, M.J. (1989) The great 'economic quality hoax'. *Quality Assurance*, **15** (2), 72–4.
23. Dale, B.G. and Plunkett, J.J. (1990) *The Case for Costing Quality*, Department of Trade and Industry, London.
24. *Anon*. (1985) *Quality and Value for Money*, National Economic Development Council, London.
25. Crosby, P.B. (1985) *The Quality Man*, BBC Education and Training.
26. Blades, M. (1992) Healthy Competition. *TQM Magazine*, **4** (2), 111–13.
27. MacGregor, A. (1983) Making profit for quality. *Quality Today*, June, 2–3.
28. Wheelwright, S.C. and Hayes, R.H. (1985) Competing through manufacturing, *Harvard Business Review*, January/February, 99–109.
29. Rohan, T.M. (1987) Quality or junk? Facing up to the problem. *Industry Week*, December 12, 72–4 and 78–9.
30. Mayben, J.E. (1983) Quality percepts – new profits from the modern QA program. *Quality Progress*, **16** (1), 24–9.
31. Jones, J.S. (1978) Quality costs and quality improvement. *Chartered Mechanical Engineer*, February, 76–7.
32. Groocock, J.M. (1980) Quality-cost control in ITT Europe. *Quality Assurance*, **6** (3), 37–44.
33. *Anon*. (1977) Quality cost survey. *Quality*, June, 20–2.

34. Gilmore, H.L. (1974) Product conformance cost. *Quality Progress*, June, 16–19.
35. Gilmore, H.L. (1983) Consumer product quality control cost revisited. *Quality Progress*, **16** (4), 28–32.
36. Gilmore, H.L. (1984) Consumer product quality costs. *Proceedings of the World Quality Congress*, Brighton, 587–95.
37. Robertson, A.G. (1971) *Quality Control and Reliability*, Pitman, London.
38. Abed, M.H. and Dale, B.G. (1987) An attempt to identify quality-related costs in textile manufacturing. *Quality Assurance*, **13** (2), 41–5.
39. Richardson, D.W. (1983) Cost benefits of quality control: a practical example from industry. *BSI News*, October.
40. Garvin, D.A. (1983) Quality on the line. *Harvard Business Review*, September/October, (65–75.
41. Burns, C.R. (1976) Quality costing used as a tool for cost reduction in the machine tool industry. *Quality Assurance*, **2** (1), 25–32.
42. Webb,N.B. (1972) Auditing meat processor quality control costs. *Quality Progress*, February, 13–15.
43. Moyers, D.R. and Gilmore, H.L. (1979) Product conformance in the steel foundry jobbing shop. *Quality Progress*, May, 17–19.
44. Huckett, J.D. (1985) An outline of the quality improvement process at Rank Xerox. *International Journal of Quality and Reliability Management*, **2** (2), 5–14.
45. Krzikowski, K. (1963) Quality control and quality costs within the mechanical industry. *Proceedings of the 7th EOQC Conference*, Copenhagen, September, 42–8.
46. Kohl, W.F. (1976) Hitting quality costs where they live. *Quality Assurance*, **2**(2), 59–64.
47. Payne, B. (1992) Accounting for improvement. *TQM Magazine*, **4** (2), 95–98.
48. Knock, A. (1992) Information holds the key. *TQM Magazine*, **4** (2), 99–102.
49. Hesford, M.G. and Dale, B.G. (1991) Quality costing at British Aerospace Dynamics: a case study. *Proceedings of the Institution of Mechanical Engineers*, **205** (G5), 53–7.
50. Jorgensen, J. (1963) Utilising quality cost information. *Proceedings of the 7th EOQC Conference*, Copenhagen, September 49–59.
51. Brown, A.C. (1973) Budgeting for the determined standard. *The Quality Engineer*, **37**(3), 73–5.
52. Mandel, B.J. (1972) Quality costing systems. *Quality Progress*, December, 11–13.
53. Olson, R. (1982) Putting QC into good form. *Quality Progress*, January, 35–7.
54. Hallum, S. and Casperson, R. (1975) Economy and quality control. *Proceedings of the 19th EOQC Conference*, Venice, 11–22.
55. Sullivan, E. (1983) Quality costs: current ideas. *Quality Progress*, **16** (4), 24–5.
56. Morse, W.J. (1983) Measuring quality costs. *Cost and Management*, July/August, 16–20.
57. Cox, B. (1979) Interface of quality costing and terotechnology. *The Accountant*, June 21, 800–1.
58. Cox, B. (1982) The role of the management accountant in quality costing. *Quality Assurance*, **8** (3), 82–4.
59. Claret, J. (1981) Never mind the quality. *Management Accounting*, May, 24–6.

60. Sandretto, M.J. (1985) What kind of a cost system do you need? *Harvard Business Review*, January/February, 110–18.
61. Morse, W.J., Roth, H.P. and Poston, K.M. (1987) *Measuring Planning and Controlling Quality Costs*, Institute of Management Accountants/ASQC Quality Press, Milwaukee.
62. Dobbins, R.K. and Brown, F.X. (1991) Quality cost analysis: QA versus accounting. *Quality Forum*, **17** (1), 20–8.

Definitions of quality costs

3.1 INTRODUCTION

The focus of this chapter is quality cost definitions. The chapter opens by examining the importance of definitions to the understanding, collection and use of quality costs. The various ways of classifying and categorizing costs are examined from the traditional prevention-appraisal-failure (PAF) categorization to other more innovative and alternative methods. The different types of cost elements associated with each cost category are reviewed and the more difficult elements to identify and collect are highlighted. The potential difficulties associated with quality cost definitions are discussed with some suggestions for overcoming them. The chapter closes by arguing the case for identifying in more detail costs associated with concessions, modifications and engineering changes.

3.2 THE IMPORTANCE OF DEFINITIONS

By their very nature costing exercises require rigorous definitions and those concerned with quality costing are no exception and in any cost-collection exercise the costs must be relevant to the topic. Therefore the importance of definitions to the collection analysis and use of quality costs cannot be overstressed. Without clear definitions there can be no common understanding or meaningful communication on the topic. The definition of what constitutes quality costs is by no means straightforward and there are many grey areas where good production/operations practices overlap with quality-related activities. Unfortunately there is no general agreement on a single broad definition of quality costs.

Quality costs may be regarded as one criterion of an organization's quality performance – but only if valid comparisons can be made between different sets of cost data. Clearly the comparability of sets of data is dependent on the definitions of the cost categories and elements used in compiling them. If definitions are not established and accepted, the only alternative would be to qualify every item of data so that it might at least be understood, even though it may not be comparable with other data. Admittedly there are difficulties in finding generic terms to describe specific tasks or activities having the same broad objectives in different industries, organizations or types of manufacture and service – private or public. This makes the collation and comparison of data from different sources very difficult. Consequently, the value of much of the published quantitative data on quality-related costs, may be questionable because of the absence of precise definitions and lack of qualification.

In view of this it is surprising that many bodies, practitioners, management consultants and writers on quality costs appear to be reluctant to get to grips with the problem of definitions *per se*. A number of definitions of quality-related costs are in fairly specious terms. Many writers avoid the issue altogether, though some have at least faced up to it before neatly sidestepping it. Some cost collectors and writers state or imply their definitions of quality-related costs. In other cases it is evident from the test, tables and figures, and/or discussions that the cost collector's view of what constitutes a quality-related cost is at odds with commonly accepted views. But despite obvious differences in interpretation, definitions of what constitutes quality costs are not discussed. Accountants are similarly not very forthcoming with definitions of costs which make clear how, for example, overheads should be dealt with or how scrap should be costed and this adds to the problem. Admittedly there are difficulties in preparing unambiguous acceptable definitions and it is understandable that most people writing on the subject avoid the issues.

A variety of definitions associated with quality costing are given in BS4778: Part 2 [1] and BS6143: Parts 1 and 2 [2,3].

Quality cost is defined in BS4778: Part 2 as:

> The expenditure incurred by the producer, by the user and by the community, associated with product or service.

Quality-related cost is defined in BS4778: Part 2 as:

> The expenditure incurred in defect prevention and appraisal activities plus the losses due to internal and external failure.

Quality-related cost is defined in BS6143: Part 1 as:

> Cost in such categories as prevention cost; appraisal cost; internal failure cost; and external failure cost.

In BS6143: Part 2 it is defined as:

> Cost in ensuring and assuring quality as well as loss incurred when quality is not achieved.

Whilst the meaning of these three different definitions of quality-related cost are the same, the lack of standardization may be seen as somewhat puzzling to the would-be cost collector. The same is true of small differences in definitions of prevention cost, appraisal cost, internal failure cost and external failure cost, given in BS4778: Part 2 and BS6143: Part 2. Having said this these standards do provide useful definitions of a range of quality costing and accounting terms.

It is interesting to report that over-ambition or overzealousness may prompt quality assurance specialists and management consultants to try to maximize the impact of quality costs on the Chief Executive Officer (CEO) and members of the senior management team; consequently they tend to stretch their definitions to include those costs which have only the most tenuous relationship with the quality of the product and service. This is not necessarily for self-aggrandizement, but to try to create a financial impact. The problem with this attempt to amplify quality-related costs is that it can backfire. Once costs have been accepted as being quality related, there may be some difficulty in exerting an influence over the reduction of costs which are independent of quality considerations. It is not always easy to disown costs after one has claimed them, especially if ownership is in a 'grey area' and no one else wants them. Without exaggerating them the figure will almost certainly be big enough to provoke positive action.

In relation to this point of over-ambition the following questions are posed.

- Is the typically quoted figure of quality costs as 25% or so of annual sales turnover realistic?
- What is the basis for figures which are frequently quoted in excess of this 25%?
- What are the likely reactions of senior management when the quality costs which have been calculated turn out to be less than this figure?
- What can be said to executives whose response to this claim of 25% is along the lines, "If the organization is incurring costs of this magnitude how are we managing to survive?"

The point being made here is that the question of definitions which is fundamental to the whole exercise of gathering and using quality-related costs is in general not given sufficient thought. The fact that there are not yet agreed definitions of some of the fundamental terms of quality costing should warn cost collectors of the uncertainties and difficulties which may be met when attempting to measure and report quality costs. Attention to definitions may obviate many of the obstacles to establishing quality costing as a management tool, for as the eminent philosophers Aristotle and Socrates respectively have observed:

How many a dispute could have been deflated into a single paragraph
if the disputants had dared define their terms.

and

The beginning of wisdom is the definition of terms.

3.3 QUALITY COST CATEGORIES

A most striking feature of the quality costing literature is a preoccupation with the prevention-appraisal-failure (PAF) categorization model. This is also the case when organizations categorize their quality costs.

The prevention-appraisal-failure cost elements are defined in BS6143: Part 2 [3] as:

Prevention cost. The cost of any action taken to investigate, prevent or reduce the risk of non-conformity or defect.

Appraisal cost. The cost of evaluating the achievement of quality requirements including e.g. cost of verification and control performed at any stage of the quality loop.

Internal failure cost. The costs arising within an organisation due to non-conformities or defects at any stage of the quality loop such as costs of scrap, rework, retest, reinspection and redesign.

External failure costs. The costs arising after delivery to a customer/user due to non-conformities or defects which may include the cost of claims against warranty, replacement and consequential losses and evaluation of penalties incurred.

The external failure costs are more serious, in that they are experienced by the customer with all the potential damaging implications. They are the most costly to direct and correct. The cost of finding a faulty part once installed in a system is likely to far outweigh the cost of the part itself.

There can be little doubt that the prime reason for this is the adoption categorization of the PAF by the American Society for Quality Control (ASQC) Quality Costs Committee and subsequent incorporation into its various quality costing publications [4]. Subsequent adoption of this approach by various writers and the British Standards Institution (BSI) BS4891 [5] and BS6143 [6] has resulted in it becoming very firmly entrenched in the current wisdom on quality costing, so much so that although it was devised to deal with manufacturing industries, attempts have been made to apply its principles directly to other quite different industries. Aubrey and Zimbler [7], for example, claim to have successfully applied the approach in banking; Webb [8] has applied it to meat processing; and Ball [9] may be only a step away from using it when he looks at how the basic tenets of industrial quality assurance can be applied to hospital quality assurance. The PAF method has also been used in more recent times by British Airways Technical Workshops

(Dale and Plunkett [10]), National Westminster Bank (Ibbotson [11] and Hilti (Great Britain) Ltd, (a sales and marketing organization selling a range of fastening systems into the construction industry) (Wilshaw [12]).

It should be noted that the arrangement of cost elements into the categories of prevention, appraisal and failure tends to be a post-collection exercise carried out to accord with convention. Categorization of costs in this way seems to be of greater interest to quality assurance managers than to anyone else in the business. A corollary of this approach is the preoccupation with in-house quality-related costs, with little specific attention being paid to supplier or sub-contractor generated quality costs or to customer-related costs.

The widespread use and deep entrenchment of the prevention-appraisal-failure categorization of quality costs invites analysis of the reasons for it. After all, arrangement of data into these categories is usually done for reporting purposes, after the collection exercise. It adds nothing to the data's potential for provoking action. It may facilitate comparison with earlier data from the same source, but even this may not be valid because of the irrelevance of current warranty and guarantee costs, where these are applicable and/or included, to other current costs.

There are some general and specific advantages to be gained from this type of categorization. Among the general advantages are that it is easy to understand and may prompt a rational approach to collecting costs, and it can add orderliness and uniformity to the ensuing reports. Among the specific advantages of this particular categorization are, first, its universal acceptance, second, its conference of relative desirability of different kinds of expenditure, and third, and most important, it provides keyword criteria to help to decide whether costs are, in fact, quality related. The last-mentioned point may explain why neither Feigenbaum, the originator of the categorization, nor the ASQC Quality Costs Committee, defines the term 'quality costs'. Matters are judged to be quality related if they satisfy the criteria set by their definitions of prevention, appraisal and failure.

With the development of total quality management, the need to identify and measure quality costs across a wide spectrum of company activities and functions has arisen and the traditional prevention-appraisal-failure approach is in some respects unsuited to this new requirement. Among its limitations are:

- The quality activity elements as defined do not match well with the cost information most commonly available from accounting systems.
- To the unwary, because of the distribution of cost elements, it can lead to more focus on the prevention and appraisal components than on failure costs.
- It is not broad enough to account for many of the activities of non-manufacturing areas.
- There are many quality-related activities in grey areas where it is unclear to which category they belong.

- In practice, the categorization is often a post-collection exercise done in deference to the received wisdom on the topic.
- The categorization seems to be of interest only to quality assurance personnel. The cost categories do not always align with the business activities of the organization, which makes the link between quality improvement and quality costs difficult to identify.
- It is not an appropriate categorization for the most common uses of quality-related cost information.

There are alternatives to the prevention-appraisal-failure approach which are different but do not necessarily conflict with it because they use the same costs collected under different headings. Chief among these alternatives (or supplementary) categorizations is division of costs into direct and indirect, theoretical and actual, controllable and uncontrollable, discretionary and consequential costs, value adding and non-value adding and price of conformance (POC) and price of non-conformance (PONC).

The principal argument for Crosby's [13] broader categorization which measures only the POC and the PONC is that it can be applied company-wide and that it focuses attention on the cost of doing things right as well as the costs of getting them wrong. This is considered to be a more positive all-round approach which will yield improvements in efficiency as well as in quality. In theory all costs to the company should be accounted for under such a system. In practice, departments identify key-result processes against which to measure their performance and costs. Details of one such process cost model are given in BS6143: Part 1 [2].

Moyes and Rogerson [14] have devised classifications such that, in an industry where quality-related costs may account for up to one-third of the project cost, the main items of cost were found to arise from only four topics: validation inspection, special procedures, repair and rectification, and quality engineering.

Based on work carried out at ICL, Nix has devised a total cost of ownership model (see Nix *et al.* [15] and Chapter 12). The model was developed for use in ICL as a data extraction system. It is used to focus on externally sourced product cost elements to assist the collaborative efforts of ICL and its suppliers to optimize cost and improve quality. The following definitions are used.

- Total cost of ownership – those costs associated with acquiring, possessing and sustaining a conforming product as it exists throughout its life cycle.
- Costs of acquiring a product – those costs that are concerned with ensuring a conforming product is available for manufacture.
- Costs of possessing – those reactive costs that ensure the conformance of a product.

Table 3.1 Quality cost matrix

	Supplier/subcontractor	In-house	Customer
Prevention	SOA, feedback, advice, training Vendor assessment and rating Certification and accreditation Develop existing and alternative sourcing Audits and site inspection Joint quality planning	Training Statistical process control Quality circles Quality engineering Quality planning Design of experiments	Joint quality planning Field trials Evaluation customers packing, handling and storage arrangements Market research Customer audits and inspections
Appraisal	Incoming inspection Sorting Organizing returns and replacements Inspections at suppliers site Material certification/traceability	Inspection and tax Product testing Calibration Checking procedures	Product sign-off/certification Liaise with customer inspection
Internal Failure	Work costs to point of scrapping Rework costs Negotiate rework/sort prices Machining defective materials Lost production and disruption owing to defective material Negotiate reimbursements	Isolation of causes of failures Reinspection Modifications and concessions Scrap and associated costs Rework and associated costs Downgrading	Discount on goods accepted on concession Downgraded goods sold cheaply
External failure	Costs attributable to but not recoverable from supplier Complaint handling Receipt and disposal of defective goods	Analysis and correlation of feedback data	Complaint handling Customer returns Free of charge replacements Field repairs
Warranty	Costs attributable to suppliers but not recoverable	Analysis and correlation of feedback data	Warranty payments Warranty claim checking and negotiation
Other	Excess stocks to buffer delivery failures Preparation of specifications	Records of quality-related activities Quality performance reporting Quality costing Interdisciplinary quality task groups	Product liability provision/insurance

- costs of sustaining – those proactive costs that ensure conformance will be maintained in the future.

Another approach is to consider the activities relating to supplier, company and customer. This idea came from observing quality assurance departments at work and the realization that the PAF concept of quality activities, for all its virtues, relates more to historical reporting of costs than to the activities of the company. It is suggested that costs categorized under 'supplier', 'company', and 'customer' headings would relate more closely to the way companies work. Quality costs categorized in this way would relate better to other business costs and would be easier for people to identify with. Clearly the prospects for success of a costing system will depend on how well the system matches with other systems in the company and the way the company operates. This form of categorization must have distinct operating advantages and it can be applied to both manufacturing and service situations.

The business and the quality concepts of costing could be met by the simple expedient of a supplier-company-customer v. prevention-appraisal-failure matrix, as illustrated in Table 3.1. (The Table also indicates some of the major cost elements which might be included in the matrix.) This proposal has the merit of having new categories which closely match the business activity whilst retaining the advantages of the established (PAF) categorization. Further reference to alternative approaches are made in Chapters 4 and 6 on the collection and use of quality costs respectively. However, in the absence of a suitable broad definition of quality-related costs, definitions of prevention, appraisal and failure costs are good criteria for deciding whether or not particular costs are quality related, despite their limitations as cost categories.

3.4 QUALITY COST ELEMENTS

Definitions of the categories and their constituent elements are to be found in most standard texts. Detailed guidance is give in BS6143: Part 2 [3], AS2561 [16] and Campanella [17]. Inevitably there are examples of disagreement to be found as to what is included under the cost categories of prevention, appraisal and failure. However, there is general acceptance and common understanding of the nature of costs in these categories, despite some ambiguities and differences in wording which occur. This is not detrimental to the process of cost collection provided there is consistency in the decision making and treatment of the costs.

Within each of the four main cost categories there are many cost elements from which the total quality cost may be synthesized. BS6143: Part 2 [3], AS2561 [16] and Campanella [17] identify a list of cost elements under the cost categories of prevention, appraisal, internal failure and external failure. Such lists act as a guideline for the purpose of quality cost collection. Some of the elements listed are not relevant to particular industries, and service-related organizations. On the other hand, many elements identified by practitioners are peculiar to an industry (e.g. service and manufacturing) or even a manufacturing unit sector or situation. Such elements, by their definition, are not identified in either of these publications.

Some writers (e.g. Oseberg [18]) point out that individual cost definitions relevant to the company organization, types of products, number of products and the degree of controlled processes, or automation, need to be established. Papers by Burns [19] (from the machine tool industry), Garvin [20] (writing about air conditioning equipment manufacture), Grant and Rogerson [21] (from the process plant industry), Schmidt and Jackson [22] (on diesel engine manufacture), Brown [23] and Abed and Dale [24] (on the manufacture of textiles), and Blank and Solorzano [25], Groocock [26] and Brennan et al. [27] (on electrical electronic manufacture) all make it clear that each case is different. With the developing interest by commerce, the public sector and service organizations in the concept of quality costing this is likely, in the near future, to identify a number of 'new' cost elements. A good example of this is the failure/complaints list of elements used by National Westminster Bank in *The Cost of Making Mistakes* exercise, an example of which is provided in Fig. 3.1. The list is used by the personnel of each section of a branch, in conjunction with the administration manager, to help decide which activities to focus on.

Business situations may also play a part in what might be included in quality cost elements. Burns [19] for example, lists intangibles which include loss of reputation and goodwill, whilst for others additional capital requirements imposed by the pursuit of quality improvement may be of prime importance, as reported by Besterfield [28] and Kirkpatrick [29]. Brewer [30] includes pilferage losses, sales and marketing operations ('costs attributable to over-staffing and related expenses resulting from inflated sales projection; sales and marketing costs associated with defect complaints, investigations and soothing irate customers; excessive promotional or advertising expenses to market low quality products'), expenses attributable to financial management, industrial relations and materials procurement causes. Mertz [31], too, points the finger at sales staff dealing with problems instead of selling, and at financing additional inventory to cover for scrapped work. Witts [32] gives a comprehensive picture from the car industry of the inputs to product quality (and hence cost) from design through to warranty control – and identifies areas for improvement in all of them. Garvin [20] also provides food for thought on sources of quality costs when he discusses them under: 'programs, policies and attitudes, information systems, product design', production and work force policies, and vendor management. In one case encountered in the course of the UMIST research, the quality assurance manager included stock losses

Failures/complaints list

This list of activities was compiled from research in 100 branches. **It is not** exhaustive and Assistant Managers – Section Heads are asked to make additions appropriate to your branch.

securities
☐ Chase customers for information
not taken or requested at outset
Formalities correction
security prepared but not used

unpaids
☐ Unpaids balancing difficulties/tracing payee/errors
Stops investigation

counter
☐ Access differences
Cash/till errors
    Correct discrepancies
    Credits – incorrect additions
    Customer queries
    Customers unprepared at tills

foreign
☐ Chase customers and other banks/
branches for instructions
Customer queries not related to Foreign
Investigating errors

machine room
☐ Clearing Department queries
Credits – incorrect additions
Credit Clearing errors
☐ Giro/Rem errors
Keying error investigation
Mis-sorted work
Stops investigation (when things go wrong)
VDT failure
☐ Vouchers mis-sorted/wrong account number

Key
☐ Most often selected Improvement
Areas – by branches in pilot study.

Figure 3.1 Failure/complaint list (source: Ibbotson and Goodstadt [11])

in his quality costing reports. He contended that much of the material which gets lost is non-conforming work which is deliberately obscured by operators.

A cost element which many contributors to the literature list without comment is 'lost opportunity costs'. These are market related costs which have a direct impact on business performance. They are considered by some to be a special category of external failure costs. Indeed, some of the failure costs given in BS6143: Part 2 [3] can be identified as lost opportunity. This element is mentioned so frequently that one might expect to find it and its constituent elements defined and discussed at some length. This is not so. Most people have ideas about how they may be incurred, and in broad terms, what they are, but there is great reticence about quantifying them, though the general inference is that they must be huge. The following are some typical examples of lost opportunity costs which have been encountered:

- *Losses caused by substandard product.* The revenue difference between downgraded and top grade product.
- *Unplanned substitution of material.* Substitution of higher cost material, component or product because of problems with the original. This also includes sourcing from a higher cost supplier because the lower cost supplier is experiencing problems.
- *Lost capacity.* The capacity taken up by the production of defective material, components and products.
- *Loss of custom, goodwill, sales opportunities, revenue and profit.*
- *Cost effective maintenance of processing equipment.* The difference between the cost of effective equipment maintenance and that of repeated repairs, in breakdown mode, of processing equipment, with subsequent product contamination and lost sales opportunity.
- *Utilization of sales personnel.* Sales personnel delivering product to the customer when they should be out selling.

The Chartered Institute of Management Accountants (CIMA) [33] define opportunity cost as, 'The value of a benefit sacrificed in favour of an alternative course of action'.

However, rarely do business and management dictionaries define lost opportunity cost. It can be considered to be the sum total of an organization's 'lost opportunity cost' and can only amount to the difference in profit accruing from their current output and the output they might reasonably aspire to. Given the swings and roundabouts of trade, the lost opportunity cost of a single failure is probably relatively small.

3.5 DIFFICULTIES ASSOCIATED WITH QUALITY COST DEFINITIONS

It must be appreciated that problems of rigorous definitions arise only because of the desire to carry out a quality costing exercise. Consideration of quality in other contexts (e.g. education and training, supply, design, document and engineeering changes, and statistical process control) does not require such sharp distinction to be made between what is quality related and what is not. But there is ample evidence to show that, even when collecting costs, collectors do not feel constrained to stick to rigorously defined elements. By and large collectors devise their own elements to suit their own industry, commercial or service situation, within the framework of the widely accepted prevention-appraisal-failure categorization. The result is a proliferation of uniquely defined cost elements which preclude comparison of data from different sources. Fortunately there have been few attempts and no success in proliferating categories of costs. There is little doubt that, in general, proliferation of categories and elements adds to the difficulties of cost definitions and limits the broad uses of quality costs. As well as being undesirable this may also be unnecessary.

Two of the salient points which are important to any discussion of quality costing are that accounting systems do not readily yield the information needed, as it is presently defined, and that rigorous definitions of quality activity elements are necessary only for costing purposes. Thus there is an apparently absurd situation of defining elements in a way which makes them difficult to cost. Elements are usually identified from specific activities or expenditures arising from product and/or service non-conformance (in the broadest sense) without much consideration of the ease of measurement and costing. Given that accounting systems are unlikely to change radically to accommodate quality costing difficulties, there should be greater consideration of the accounting aspects when defining quality cost elements. The hope is that activity based costing and throughput accounting will start to change accounting systems. The objective must be to re-define cost quality elements to align with the business activities of the company and fit in with the costing structure. Warranty cost is an example of such an element. It is clearly quality related, it is part of the business agreement between a company and its customers, and the company must make financial provisions to meet its liabilities. Another example is the quality costing situation encountered in some companies in which most of the data comes directly from cost centres or labour-booking accounts.

When considering definitions of quality and their susceptibility to costing, the accountant's preference for definitions which are constrained to meeting specification has much to commend it. Open ended definitions such as the definition of quality as 'fitness for purpose', whilst commendable, admit too many intangibles and makes quality costing more difficult. If, say 'fitness for purpose' is the quality objective it must be met through suitable specifications and measures of customer needs, expectations and delight. The cost collectors must not be left in the difficult situation of trying to decide what features and parameters affect the product's and/or service's suitability for its purpose.

There are differing views between the quality fraternity and the accounting fraternity of what quality is about and hence the cost of quality. Accountants appear to be uncompromising in their insistence that, for the purposes of quality costing, the definition of quality needs to be constrained or qualified by bringing 'meeting specification' into their definitions. Whilst the correctness of this may be debatable, it is understandable that accountants (who, after all, are likely to be charged with the responsibility of putting costs on the identified cost elements) do not want open-ended definitions adding to their problems. The difficulties which accountants face in gathering quality costs stem not only from a lack of agreement on definitions of quality and related activities but also because considerations of quality bring in parameters not usually noted or measured in management accounting reporting. Furthermore, there is lack of definitions of quality-related costs in purely accounting terms. There are a small number of quality definitions (e.g. quality-related costs, prevention cost, appraisal cost, internal failure cost, external failure cost, quality cost variance, cost of conformance, cost of non-conformance) in the CIMA's official terminology [33]. The profession could do the quality fraternity and themselves a service if it pronounced judgements on a few of the major issues such as allocation of overheads, valuation of scrapped goods and materials, and double counting. To its credit the CIMA have published a guide/workbook by Rooney and Rogerson [34] to assist organizations in assessing their quality costs. A number of worked examples are given in the guide, including one to assess the costs of implementing a quality system which meets the requirements of BS5750: Part 2.

The problem of whether or not testing and running-in activities involving some adjustment of the product are a quality cost arises at most companies. Carson [35] is positive that testing is about detecting defects, that it is an appraisal cost, and that there is an onus on the manufacturing/operations department to 'get it right first time'. Testing is effectively proving the fitness-for-purpose of the product and/or service in one or more respects. There may well be cases where such testing ought not to be necessary, but is, and hence incurs a quality cost. However, in many cases the state of the technology may be such that testing is unavoidable. An organization may be unable to give guarantees to its customers without testing the product. The customer may specify that every product is tested and that a test certificate be attached to the product. An organization may be unable to get insurance cover without testing. In the end, the decision whether or not to test may be taken out of the organization's hands, irrespective of whatever they think can be achieved without testing. In such circumstances should testing be regarded as a quality cost or a purely production activity? And if it is treated as a quality cost, is it an appraisal or a prevention cost?

Executives appear to hold diverse views of whether or not testing should be considered as a quality cost. The first is that it should not if testing is unavoidable and/or it is a contractual requirement of the customer. The second is that in all cases it should. The argument for this latter view is it is only by measuring and reporting testing activities on a regular basis and keeping the costs under top management's attention will actions be taken by them to reduce the costs. A case in point is that of an organization manufacturing a safety critical product and where all the testing has to be viewed by either second or third party inspectors. In addition to the actual testing activities themselves the cost of travel and hotel accommodation of these inspectors is treated as a quality cost. The objective was that by increasing the confidence of the customer(s) in the organization's control over its process and commitment to continuous improvement they would be prepared to reduce the degree to which the testing was required to be witnessed. The monthly reporting of this large cost would focus senior management's attention on giving some time to this line of persuasion.

Because each case is different it is not possible to offer a general solution to this problem of what is a quality cost and what is considered as the basic work of a department (i.e. the essential activities which are involved in supplying products and/or services) other than to suggest that if there is serious doubt, the cost should not be defined as being quality related where it is unlikely to be amenable to change by quality management influences. It is always better to underestimate rather than overestimate the costs of quality. Other suggested criteria are that an item is quality related when 1. if less is spent on it, failure costs increase and 2. if more is spent on it, failure costs decrease.

Similar problems of categorization arise for costs generated by functions other than quality assurance and production/operations. Notable examples are the contributions of the purchasing function to supplier quality assurance and assistance to suppliers in ensuring the fitness for purpose of purchased goods, and the activities of engineering and design departments involved with concessions and design modifications prompted by product quality considerations. Quantifying, classifying and costing such inputs are very difficult and are seldom done, but they can amount to significant proportions of the prevention and internal failure expenditure categories respectively.

There are those factors which serve to ensure the basic utility of the product, guard against errors, and protect and preserve product and service quality. Examples are the use of design codes, preparation of engineering and adminstrative systems and procedures, capital premiums on machinery, document and drawing controls, handling and storage practices, provision of 'clean areas', and protection for parts and assemblies. Whether such factors give rise to costs which may be regarded as being quality related is a matter for judgement in individual cases.

There is also the question of whether quality-related costs should include a portion of the costs of site services such as catering and security. The consensus opinion that they should not, but some practitioners feel that the full costs of quality are not being measured if some such allocation for this activity is not made.

Obviously such problems need to be discussed with purchasing, engineering, production/operations and accountancy personnel, as appropriate, in order to resolve them. It is unlikely, however, that there will be a uniform view, and it is improbable that the prevailing accounting practices will yield ready-made or satisfactory solutions.

An aspect of definitions which is worth discussing briefly is the sensitivity of costs to changes in quality. It was noted at one company studied that despite dramatic improvements in quality there was little evidence of corresponding changes in quality costs. The matter arose again in a different format at another company where they were looking for a cost reporting system which reflected quality performance. Unfortunately there are many costs which do not change in line with quality improvement. These costs are often large and obscure those costs which do change with quality. The answer to the problem seems to be to identify and isolate those parts of the cost which change (or will ultimately change) in relation to quality improvement and to report them separately, perhaps as projected savings, if necessary. This will be discussed in more detail in Chapters 4 and 5.

An interesting point of definition arises from inclusion of the phrase 'before (or after) transfer of ownership' in defining internal and external failure costs. It appears that the point of transfer of ownership is not unequivocally defined. Whereas many organizations consider delivery to the customer to be the point of change of ownership, others maintain that it is only when the goods have been paid for that they change ownership.

3.6 CONCESSIONS, MODIFICATIONS AND ENGINEERING CHANGES

To anyone investigating costs in manufacturing industry, striking features are 1. the large amount of time and money spent on modifications and engineering changes, and 2. an apparent acceptance, in particular amongst design, engineering and technical pesonnel, that they are facts of organizational life that one must learn to live with. The feeling is given that this is the way organizations go about their respective businesses. It is important to reflect that the main reason there are so many difficult engineering changes is that there was often a problem with the design to begin with. If products were designed right first time using design for manufacture concepts, design reviews, quality function deployment (QFD) and failure mode and effects analysis (FMEA), these types of changes would be kept to a minimum. Thus they might justifiably be categorized as in-built costs. The costs, though hidden, can be substantial and, quite apart from the costs of personnel directly involved, there can be serious implications for inventory levels and even impediments to output if modifications and changes are not kept to a minimum. It is also important to ensure that the processing of the modifications and changes does not become protracted.

There is a need for a new set of definitions to help determine the cost associated with concessions and engineering changes. These are major quality activities but little is known about the cost. It is necessary also to focus attention on these activities to make people more aware of them, and to make accountable those people who are responsible for the costs. It is not good enough just to budget monies to cater for concessions and engineering changes.

It is suspected that in many companies concessions are an expedient way of maintaining schedules and that little account is taken of the disadvantages incurred in deciding to overlook non-conformances. Not least among these are the proliferation of paperwork and engendering lax attitudes towards quality improvement among managers, supervisors, clerical staff and shopfloor workers. In fact, frequent concessions on non-conforming goods are a positive disincentive to people to get operations right the first time.

In many companies goods passed on concession do not feature in quality reporting systems because they have escaped the company's non-conformance reporting system. In some companies goods are supposed only to be passed on concession if they cannot be rectified. It is often easier to find reasons why goods cannot be rectified than it is to rework them. Hence concession systems may become an engineering expediency, or, equally, they may become a production/operations expediency to avoid impediments to output or delays in delivery. All in all it is felt that the quality cost implications of concessions granted on non-conforming goods are probably far greater than can be inferred from the literature on quality costs and discussions on the subject with practitioners. The general feeling is that many of the associated costs may never be picked up using conventional quality costs checklists and guidelines.

There can be no doubt that between concessions, modifications and engineering changes there is a sizeable quality-related activity escaping the quality cost net in most organizations. The prime reason why these costs may not be identified and picked up is because they do not feature in quality non-conformance reports. There is a clear need for additional cost elements to be defined identifying the kinds of quality-related costs which arise from concessions, modifications and engineering changes.

3.7 SUMMARY

The question of definitions is central to the subject of quality costs. Without clear definitions there will be considerable confusion and misunderstanding of what is considered to be a quality cost and what is normal business practice.

Many writers on the subject of quality costing state or imply their definitions of quality costs. In other cases it is evident that the writers' view of what constitutes a quality cost is at odds with commonly accepted views. However, despite obvious differences in interpretation, definitions of what constitutes quality costs are not fully discussed, and accountants are similarly not very forthcoming with definitions of costs which make clear how, for example, overheads should be dealt with or how scrap should be costed.

A most striking feature of quality costing is the preoccupation with the prevention-appraisal-failure categorization, even though arrangement into these categories tends to be a post-collection exercise carried out to accord with convention. Categorization of costs in this way seems to be of greater interest to quality managers than to anyone else. There is a need for organizations to consider other forms of categorization to better suit their business practices.

REFERENCES

1. BS4778: Part 2 (1991) *Quality Vocabulary – Quality Concepts and Related Definitions*, British Standards Institution, London.
2. BS6143: Part 1 (1992) *Guide to the Economics of Quality: Process cost model.* British Standards Institution, London.
3. BS6143: Part 2 (1990) *Guide to the Economics of Quality: Prevention, appraisal and failure model.* British Standards Institution, London.
4. ASQC Quality Costs Committee (1970) *Quality Costs – What and How*, American Society for Quality Control, Milwaukee.
5. BS4891 (1972) *A Guide to Quality Assurance*, British Standards Institution, London.
6. BS6143 (1981) *Determination and Use of Quality-Related Costs*, British Standards Institution, London.
7. Aubrey, C.A., II, and Zimbler, D.A. (1983) Quality costs and improvements. *Quality Progress*, December, 16–20.
8. Webb, N.B. (1972) Auditing meat processing quality control costs. *Quality Progress*, February, 13–15.
9. Ball, L.W. (1984) The relevance of industrial quality assurance to hospital quality assurance. *Quality Assurance*, **10** (3), 84–7.
10. Dale, B.G. and Plunkett, J.J. (1990) *The Case for Costing Quality*, Department of Trade and Industry, London.
11. Ibbotson, I.C. and Goodstadt, P. (1990) Cost of quality: findings from pilot test in *Cost of Making Mistakes*, Quality Service Department, National Westminster Bank, London.
12. Wilshaw, G. (1992) Competitive advantage through total quality management. MSc Dissertation, School of Management, UMIST.
13. Crosby, P. B. (1979) *Quality is Free*, McGraw Hill, New York.
14. Moyes, E.M. and Rogerson, J.H. (1983) *The Reduction of Quality-Related Costs in the Process Plant Industry*, Process Plant EDC.
15. Nix, A., McCarthy, P. and Dale, B.G. (1993) The key issues in the development and use of total cost of ownership model. *Proceedings of the Second International Conference of the Purchasing and Supply Education Group*, University of Bath, April, 247–54.
16. AS2561 (1982) *Guide to the Determination and Use of Quality Costs*, Standards Association of Australia.
17. Campanella, J. (ed.) (1990) *Principles of Quality Costs: Principles, Implementation and Use*, ASQC Quality Press, Milwaukee.
18. Oseberg, M. (1963) Acquiring quality cost information. *Proceedings of the 7th EOQC Conference*, Copenhagen, September, 25–30.
19. Burns, C.R. (1976) Quality costing used as a tool for cost reduction in the machine tool industry. *Quality Assurance*, **2** (1), 25–32.

20. Garvin, D.A. (1983) Quality on the line. *Harvard Business Review*, September/October, 65–75.
21. Grant, I.M. and Robertson, J.H. (1981) The importance of contractual requirements in determining quality costs in the fabrication industry. *Proceedings of the Welding Institute Conference*, November, London.
22. Schmidt, J.W. and Jackson, J.F. (1982) Measuring the cost of product quality. *Automotive Engineering* (Warrendale P.A.), **90** (6), 42–8.
23. Brown, A.C. (1973) Budgeting for the determined standard. *The Quality Engineer*, **37** (3), 73–5.
24. Abed, A.H. and Dale, B.G. (1987) An attempt to identify quality-related costs in textile manufacturing. *Quality assurance*, **13** (2), 41–5.
25. Blank, L. and Solorzano, J. (1978) Using quality cost analysis for management improvements. *Industrial Engineering*, **10** (2), 46–51.
26. Groocock, J.M. (1975) ITT Europe's quality cost improvement programme. *Quality Assurance*, **2** (2), 35–40.
27. Brennan, L., Cullinane, H., O'Connor, C., Punch, D. and Sheil, J. (1990) Quality costs determination on a production line, *International Journal of Quality and Reliability Management* **7** (3) 43–58.
28. Besterfield, B.M. (1979) *Quality Control*, Prentice Hall Inc.
29. Kirkpatrick, E.G. (1970) *Quality Control for Managers and Engineers*, John Wiley and Sons.
30. Brewer, C.W. (1978) Zero based profit assurance. *Quality Progress*, January, 15–27.
31. Mertz, O.R. (1977) Quality role in ROI. *Quality Progress*, October, 14–18.
32. Witts, M.T. (1976) Participation in industry. *The Quality Engineer*, **33** (3), 3–7.
33. The Chartered Institute of Management Accountants (1991) *Management Accounting – Official Terminology*, CIMA, London.
34. Rooney, E.M. and Rogerson, J.H. (1992) *Measuring Quality Related Costs*, The Chartered Institute of Management Accountants, London.
35. Carson, J.K. (1986) Quality costing – a practical approach. *International Journal of Quality and Reliability Management*, **3** (1), 54–63.

Collection of quality costs | 4

4.1 INTRODUCTION

Quality costs are incurred by any organization, whether or not they are collected, measured and reported on a formal basis. The objective of a quality cost collection exercise is to identify these 'hidden costs', 'indirect costs' or 'unbudgeted costs' from various departmental budgets and overheads. Once identified the costs should be allocated to a specific activity. However, some costs – even those directly associated with failure (i.e. scrap, rework and rectification) – are not easy to measure and collect. It therefore should be realized from the outset that quality costing can never be precise.

This chapter explores the whole issue of quality cost collection. It opens by examining a number of possible quality costing objectives and strategies. Various approaches to quality cost collection are discussed and their merits and range of application explored. Some of the practicalities of cost collection are touched upon, including ease of cost element collection, sources of cost data, detail and accuracy. The need for a joint approach between the quality and accountant's functions is emphasized.

4.2 ESTABLISHING THE OBJECTIVES FOR QUALITY COST COLLECTION

There is little point in collecting quality costs just out of curiosity to see what they may reveal. Also, it must not be seen as just another cost monitoring exercise. Many managers have successfully resisted pressure to co-operate in the collection of costs on the grounds that they would not reveal any problems of which they were not already aware from the organization's existing quality management information system. Thus, the effect of the quality costing strategy on the measurement and collection of quality costs is a key issue.

Whilst Leibert [1] and Jenney [2] stress the importance of clear and concise objectives, there has been little comment in the literature on the significance of this. There is little doubt that getting the purposes of the exercise clear at the outset can have a considerable influence on the strategy. It is also of significant importance to the success of the project, avoiding pitfalls and unnecessary work. For example, if the main purpose of the exercise is to identify high-cost problems, coarse scale costs in known problem areas will suffice. If the Chief Executive Officer and members of the senior management team accept that the organization's quality costs are within the normally quoted range and are prepared to commit resources to improvement activities without the detail there is perhaps no point in attempting to refine the data further. If, on the other hand, the purpose is to set a percentage cost reduction target on the company's total quality-related costs, it will be necessary to identify and measure all the contributing cost elements in order to be sure that costs are reduced and not simply transferred elsewhere. If a quality costing exercise is to be repeated there is a need for discipline to ensure that the data collected is comparable with previous reporting. Thus, the matter is important, not only from a philosophical point of view, but from purely practical considerations as well.

The reason for failure to discuss in the literature the implications of differing objectives may be that almost all contributors favour the approach which identifies specific quality improvement projects. This approach initially requires only approximate costs (with which to identify and rank projects and, later, more precise costs, but in a narrow field of activity and cost) to be measured. The universality of this approach is matched only by the prevention-appraisal-failure (PAF) categorization of cost and is largely due to Juran's influence.

Instances of quality management practitioners favouring the Juran and Gryna [3] and Juran [4] approach are too numerous to mention. Juran's advocacy of 'quick and dirty' estimates to identify quality improvement projects which are worth tackling has an immense attraction for the busy manager, though one wonders how quick and dirty an estimate of ± 15% which he uses by way of example may really be. But when faced with his alternative of restructuring the accounting system in order to evaluate accurately total quality costs, the project approach becomes doubly attractive.

It is worth noting that those contributors who give an overview of measurement and collection of quality costs take a circumspect view of the topic. For example, Jenney [2] stresses that minimizing quality costs is not the only criterion. Many writers make the point that accuracy is not a premium and warn not to expect too much from the first attempt at quality cost; the first attempts may well underestimate the costs. The costs collected will tend to increase with operating experience of the system, as more people get involved and as more non-conformances are identifed and quantified. Indeed, it is suggested by Crosby [5] that only one-third of a company's total quality costs are uncovered at the first attempt; this applies to a company which is at the first stage of Crosby's quality management maturity grid – uncertainty. Eldridge and Dale [6] make the point that a cost collector who is inexperienced in the company's operations may unwittingly overlook some of the quality costs. This underestimation is also a result of focusing only on some areas of the business. A non-conformity audit is a good way of checking to see if the internal failure costs have been underestimated.

The true quality costs of an organization can often be swelled by one-off incidents which by their nature are very difficult to cost but which serve to emphasize the importance of quality. The following example illustrates this point. A corrugated cardboard manufacturer was shredding some non-conforming heavy duty cases which included metal staples. The material became stuck in the machine and the staples generated friction which caused a fire. Luckily the fire was put out before it spread through the ventilation system and destroyed the factory.

Therefore, possible quality costing strategies range from measuring and monitoring all quality costs to costing only specific quality improvement projects and activities. An organization's total quality costs inevitably include large immutable costs (e.g. the cost of running a laboratory or test house) and the powerful arguments which are put forward for measuring and presenting on a routine basis only costs which change tend to erode the case for collecting on a regular basis total quality costs. Consequently, before setting up a quality cost collection sytem, it is advisable to examine the potential for change of a cost element in both absolute and relative terms. The inclusion of fixed or immutable costs also has the effect of reducing the sensitivity of costs to performance improving changes. On the other hand, if costs are not being monitored, how does one know that they are not going to change? It is argued by some executives that they need to be presented on a regular basis with these large fixed costs. This keeps costs in the spotlight and will encourage them to pursue some form of action to reduce them. It is also important to know the total quality-related costs, including those which do not change, so that the effects of changes in elemental costs on total costs may be seen. The classic and often-quoted example of failure to do this is that of reducing inspection costs only to increase failure costs by a far greater amount. An acceptable compromise is to carry out occasional total cost exercises, (perhaps every six months) but to monitor regularly (monthly) and emphasize only those costs which are likely to change with improvement activities. The basis of the argument supporting this view is that it is unnecessary to know all the costs to be sure, for example, that quality costs are decreasing.

Another argument, leading to a similar conclusion, is that if a company is looking to reduce costs while improving quality (or vice versa), it needs some measures of quality and cost performance, and of their relationship to each other. Further, this needs only quality maintenance costs and those costs which can or do change with quality improvement. Whilst such arguments are plausible and superficially attractive, they imply that some key costs are sensitive to quality changes and that the relationship is known and understood. In reality, this is far from being the case.

One of the important decisions on quality costing strategy, to be taken at the outset, concerns the assignment of accountability. Deciding in advance who should be accountable for what may produce a very different cost report to one based on the usual quality-based criteria. Also, on the subject of accountability, the production function is the most closely measured and accountable group in manufacturing organizations. Hence, it is usual for cost collection to start there. It is important to make sure it does not end there, for although the manufacturing function has a prime responsibility for quality, all departments in a company contribute to quality, to failure and to costs. The internal customer–supplier concept and the technique of departmental purpose analysis (DPA) is a useful means of getting quality performance measurements and quality improvement activities accepted in non-manufacturing departments and areas.

When actually collecting quality costs it is sometimes easy to lose sight of the fact that the task is primarily a cost collection exercise and that cost collection exercises have other, different, criteria which are sensibly independent of the cost topic. Suitable criteria include purpose, relevance, ease of collection, size, accuracy, completeness, potential for change, recording and presentation, and uses. A set of back-up criteria like these, which are independent of the cost topic, can often provide useful ways out of the dilemma about whether or not particular activities and costs should be included in a costing exercise. They will ensure that the data which are collected are understood and can be qualified. The collection and synthesis of quality costs are very much a matter of searching and sifting through data which has been gathered for other purposes.

4.3 AVAILABLE ADVICE ON QUALITY COST COLLECTION

The aspect of measuring and collecting quality cost, though obviously central to a quality cost reduction exercise is poorly covered by most contributors to the literature. The cost collecting exercise can, of itself, and irrespective of the topic, present all sorts of difficulties. Perhaps this is why even the most eminent writers appear to skip over the subject.

Many papers and books touch on quality cost collection but give little help and guidance to the practitioner setting out to gather quality costs. There is a lack of detailed guidance from accountants and some leading management consultants appear to have sidestepped the problem in their general advocacy of the establishment and use of quality costing. In the case of the latter, they often oversimplify the difficulties encountered in quality cost collection. They typically argue that much of the cost data is readily available and that data can be collected in a few days. Many writers on the subject confine themselves to why and what to collect and some skip lightly onto presentation and use. It should be noted that the often optimistic expectations of the quality fraternity are counterbalanced by the more cautious outlook of the accountants who are expected to do the work.

A brief survey of the accounting literature uncovered little guidance on cost collection exercises in general. It might be imagined that such a common exercise would have generated a considerable body of literature setting down criteria and advising on allocation of overheads and avoiding double counting; not so. Perhaps accountants feel that such matters are too elementary to be worth writing down or that it is unnecessary to give guidance to non-accountants, presumably in the belief that collecting costs is really an accountant's job and that their professional training equips them to deal with the problems which arise. Nevertheless, non-accountants frequently become involved in cost collecting exercises and some informal guidance would surely be welcomed by would-be collectors.

However, a select band of contributors do give guidance on how to do it and show some appreciation of the practicalities likely to be encountered in the exercise. Any project which crosses departmental boundaries and functions and other cost boundaries is almost bound to run into more difficulties than projects contained within a single department. A quality costing exercise is a good example of such a cross-functional project. Accounting systems are not usually set up in such a way that cost collection exercises which cross conventional boundaries can easily be made.

The merits and demerits of the American Society for Quality Control (ASQC) and the British Standards Institution publications have already been discussed at some length in the earlier chapters of this book. However, they both recommend a pilot study approach, principally, perhaps out of recognition of the fact that no two cases are the same and that each organization and/or department needs to develop its own detailed procedures and systems within the framework outlined in these publications.

Some writers advocate starting the cost collection exercise by looking at internal failure costs. Hallum and Casperson [7] show how straightforward cost collection can be, given a cost accounting system which appears to be purpose designed for cost collection exercises. Blank and Solozarno [8], Booth [9], Hagan [10] and Alford [11–13] all clearly have first-hand experience of collecting quality costs and it shows in their thoroughly practical papers on the subject.

4.4 VARIOUS APPROACHES TO QUALITY COST COLLECTION

There are a wide variety of ways in which organizations can set about collecting and measuring quality costs. The approach taken is dependent upon the objectives of the exercise and the audience for the resulting data. It should always be tailored to the needs of the organization. If the aim is to obtain an indication of the company's total quality costs, the PAF approach could be used. In some cases, analysis at company level is inadequate as the problems would be in terms too global to generate ownership at departmental or process level. On the other hand analysis at too detailed a level might lead to a trivialization of problems.

If it is considered important to determine the costs being incurred on a departmental basis, PAF may prove inadequate. A more broadly based method may need to be used to uncover issues not addressed by the traditional PAF approach. The PAF approach is more suited to gathering costs which are related to the manufacturing function. An activity based approach may need to be used for the non-manufacturing functions. It has been observed on more than one occasion that, when the PAF methodology has been applied to non-manufacturing areas, there has been considerable disagreement on what activities are classified as prevention and appraisal. It has also been found that discussions with departmental managers and staff are easier to hold in terms of their actual daily activities than in the usual quality costing terms of prevention, appraisal and failure.

In deciding the approach there are a number of issues to be considered, including:

- Are quality costs to be collected across the whole organization or on a project/department/business unit basis?
- Should the method of collection be applicable at different levels of the business?
- Is a pilot study to be used? If so, should this be based on business unit, product, department, function or process?
- Are failure costs to be collected as a first step in quality cost reporting and use, before progressing to the measurement of appraisal and then prevention costs?
- In a manufacturing situation should the emphasis first be on the manufacturing function followed by the non-manufacturing areas? Is a different method required for these two areas of activity?

It is important that the first approach is soundly based. The majority of management consultants when contracted by an organization to assist with the introduction of total quality management will carry out a quality cost survey. This is done as part of the condition setting as a prerequisite to the development and execution of a TQM policy and strategy. The purpose of the quality cost survey is to bring to senior management's attention the potential savings which are achievable through quality improvement. The approach to the collection of costs adopted by the consultants contracted by a major chemical manufacturer to assist with the introduction of TQM was to make each departmental manager responsible for obtaining assessments of the time and resources committed by their staff to carrying out quality-related activities in the

Table 4.1 Measuring quality costs, sales operation 1, time spent in prevention activities.

	Prevention activity	Time spent (%)
P1	In-field training	4
P2	Training courses	3
P3	Customer reviews	2
P4	Planning service activity	1
P5	Planning sales activity	4
P6	Consulting service report reviews	6
P7	Customer monitoring procedures	3
P8	Contract review procedures	0.5
P9	Business reviews	0.5
P10		

Table 4.2 Measuring quality costs, sales operation 1, cost of each item.

	Item	Annual cost (£)
PC1	Training costs	10000
PC2	Laboratory costs	18000
PC3	Chemical test kit	20000
PC4	Research development costs	30000
PC5	Equipment/clothing costs	15000
PC6	Telephone procedures	10000
PC7	Paperwork/stationery	4000
PC8		
PC9		
PC10		

Table 4.3 Measuring quality costs, sales operation 1, total time spent on quality-related activities.

Activity	Time %
Total prevention % time spent (P1 + ... +	24
Total appraisal % time spent (A1 + ... + A10)	12
Total failure % time spent (F1 + ... + F10)	18
Total	54

Table 4.4 Measuring quality costs, sales operation 1, total annual non-pay expenditure on quality-related activities.

Activity	Expenditure (£)
Total prevention direct expenditure (PC1 + ... + PC 10)	107000
Total appraisal direct expenditure (AC1 + ... + AC10)	17000
Total failure direct expenditure (FC1 + ... + FC10)	192000
Total	316000

categories of prevention, appraisal and failure. The data was obtained from a variety of sources. A questionnaire was also used to help obtain estimates from staff of how they spend their time. Each manager was asked to assign these costs to a departmental matrix. Tables 4.1–4 shows an example from the sales operation. Whilst the results of such surveys may fulfil this one-off objective and raise awareness, they do little else. They are, in most cases, based on a large amount of estimated data and, because of the limited time allowed for the exercise, are not soundly based. Organizations wishing to continue with quality costing usually need to start the exercise from scratch.

A summary of the most popular quality cost methods is now examined:

4.4.1 Prevention-appraisal-failure cost element method

Whenever the cost element method is used in whatever form, the first step is to identify the elements of cost, the second is to measure and quantify the elements and the final step is to cost the elements. The usual approach is for a quality assurance and/or technical specialist, in conjunction with other appropriate company personnel, to take responsibility for identifying the elements and provide appropriate quantitative data relating to each element. The accountant will then put costs on the elements which have been identified. It is helpful if the quality assurance and technical personnel work closely with the accountant during this activity.

The list of cost elements identified in publications such as BS6143: Part 2 [14] and Campanella [15] is a useful starting point. They have particular attractions for those with little knowledge of quality cost collection. The list and guidance notes on the cost elements of prevention, appraisal and failure from BS6143: Part 2 follow.

Appendix A. Guidance notes on cost elements of prevention appraisal and failure model

A.1 Prevention costs

These costs are incurred to reduce failure and appraisal costs to a minimum. The usual categories include the following:

(a) *Quality planning.* The activity of planning quality systems and translating product design and customer quality requirements into measures that will ensure the attainment of the requisite product quality. It includes that broad array of activities that collectively create the overall quality plan, the inspection plan, the reliability plan and other specialized plans as appropriate. It also includes the preparation and vetting of manuals and procedures needed to communicate these plans to all concerned. Such quality planning may involve departments other than the quality organization.

(b) *Design and development of quality measurement and test equipment*. Included are the costs of designing, developing and documenting any necessary inspection, testing or proving equipment (but not the capital cost of the equipment in question).

(c) *Quality review and verification of design*. Quality organization monitoring activity during the product's design and development phase to assure the required inherent design quality. Quality organization involvement with design review activities and in verification activity during the various phases of the product development test programme including design approval tests and other tests to demonstrate reliability and maintainability.

This includes quality organization effort associated with that part of process control which is conducted to achieve defined quality goals.

(d) *Calibration and maintenance of quality measurement and test equipment*. The cost of calibration and maintenance of templates, jigs, fixtures and similar items should be included.

(e) *Calibration and maintenance of production equipment used to evaluate quality*. The costs of calibration and maintenance of templates, jigs, fixtures and similar measurement and evaluating devices should be included but not the cost of equipment used to manufacture the product.

(f) *Supplier assurance*. The initial assessment, subsequent audit and surveillance of suppliers to ensure they are able to meet and maintain the requisite product quality. This also includes the quality organization's reviews and control of technical data in relation to purchase orders.

(g) *Quality training*. Includes attending, developing, implementing, operating and maintaining formal quality training programmes.

(h) *Quality auditing*. The activity involving the appraisal of the entire system of quality control or specific elements of the system used by an organization.

(i) *Acquisition analysis and reporting of quality data*. The analysis and processing of data for the purpose of preventing future failure is a prevention cost.

(j) *Quality improvement programmes*. Includes the activity of structuring and carrying out programmes aimed at new levels of performance, e.g. defect prevention programmes, quality motivation programmes.

A.2 Appraisal costs

These costs are incurred in initially ascertaining the conformance of the product to quality requirements; they do not include costs from rework or reinspection following failure. Appraisal costs normally include the following.

(a) *Pre-production verification*. Cost associated with testing and measurement of pre-production for the purpose of verifying the conformance of the design to the quality requirements.

(b) *Receiving inspection*. The inspection and testing of incoming parts, components and materials. Also included is inspection at the supplier's premises by the purchaser's staff.

(c) *Laboratory acceptance testing*. Costs related to tests to evaluate the quality of purchased materials (raw, semi-finished or finished), which become part of the final product or that are consumed during production operations.

(d) *Inspection and testing*. The activity of inspecting and testing first during the process of manufacture, and then as a final check to establish the quality of the finished product and its packaging. Included are product quality audits, checking by production operators and supervision and clerical support for the function. It does not include inspection and testing made necessary by initial rejection because of inadequate quality.

(e) *Inspection and test equipment*. The depreciation costs of equipment and associated facilities; the cost of setting up and providing for maintenance and calibration.

(f) *Materials consumed during inspection and testing*. Materials consumed or destroyed during the course of destructive tests.

(g) *Analysis and reporting of tests and inspection results*. The activity conducted prior to release of the product for transfer of ownership in order to establish whether quality requirements have been met.

(h) *Field performance testing*. Testing is performed in the expected user environment, which may be the purchaser's site, prior to releasing the product for customer acceptance.

(i) *Approvals and endorsements*. Mandatory approvals or endorsements by other authorities.

(j) *Stock evaluation*. Inspecting and testing stocks of products and spares which may have limited shelf life.

(k) *Record storage*. The storage of quality control results, approval and reference standards.

A.3 Failure costs

These are subdivided into internal and external failure costs: internal costs arising from inadequate quality discovered before the transfer of ownership from supplier to purchaser and external costs arising from inadequate quality discovered after transfer of ownership from the supplier to the purchaser.

The internal failure costs include the following.

(a) *Scrap*. Materials, parts, components, assemblies and product end items which fail to conform to quality requirements and which cannot be economically reworked. Included is the labour and labour overhead content of the scrapped items.

(b) *Replacement, rework and repair*. The activity of replacing or correcting defectives to make them fit for use including requisite planning and the cost of the associated activities by material procurement personnel.

(c) *Troubleshooting or defect/failure analysis*. The costs incurred in analysing non-conforming materials, components or products to determine causes and remedial action, whether non-conforming products are usable and to decide on their final disposition.

(d) *Reinspection and retesting*. Applied to previously failing material that has subsequently been reworked.

(e) *Fault of subcontractor*. The losses incurred due to failure of purchased material to meet quality requirements and payroll costs incurred. Credits received from the subcontractor should be deducted, but costs of idle facilities and labour resulting from product defects should not be overlooked.

(f) *Modification permits and concessions*. The costs of the time spent in reviewing products, designs and specifications.

(g) *Downgrading*. Losses resulting from a price differential between normal selling price and reduced price due to non-conformance for quality reasons.

(h) *Downtime*. The cost of personnel and idle facilities resulting from product defects and disrupted production schedules.

The external failure costs include the following.

(1) *Complaints*. The investigation of complaints and provision of compensation where the latter is attributable to defective products or installation.

(2) *Warranty claims.* Work to repair or replace items found to be defective by the purchaser and accepted as the supplier's liability under the terms of the warranty.

(3) *Products rejected and returned.* The cost of dealing with returned defective components. This may involve action to either repair, replace or otherwise account for the items in question. Handling charges should be included.

NOTE. While loss of purchaser goodwill and confidence is normally associated with external failure costs, it is difficult to quantify.

(4) *Concessions.* Cost of concessions, e.g. discounts made to purchasers due to non-conforming products being accepted by the purchaser.

(5) *Loss of sales.* Loss of profit due to cessation of existing markets as a consequence of poor quality.

(6) *Recall costs.* Cost associated with recall of a liability claim and the cost of premiums paid for insurance to minimize liability litigation damages.

To assist with quality cost identification Eldridge and Dale [6] divided cost elements in the BS6143 checklist into three groups:

1. those which it was possible to identify and quantify,
2. activities which were identified but considered to occur too infrequently to be quantified accurately or merit including in the quality costing exercise, and
3. activities which simply did not take place.

A variation on the published checklist method is for the cost collector to analyse the quality costing literature (including these two publications) and identify, from what has been written about the subject, potential elements of cost which are relevant to their organization. These methods are mainly used in cases where the organization is engaged in the manufacture of mechanical and electrical products.

In other manufacturing environments such as paint, chemicals, rubber and textiles, the list of elements which are readily available from the literature (e.g. Juran [4], BS6143: Part 2 [14], Campanella [15] and Feigenbaum [16]) are not necessarily applicable in these cases. It is likely that they will encounter some difficulties in interpreting the terms to suit their environment and some cost elements will simply not apply. Hence cost collectors whilst using such lists as guidance, will be required to develop their own list of cost elements from company specific experience. In preparing the list the cost collector should seek advice from the management accountant who can provide guidance on the flexibility of collecting data on the cost elements under consideration.

The following two examples from the textile and paint industries provide an indication of the type of cost elements considered to be important in these respective cases. Comparison with those given in Table 4.2 will highlight key differences.

Abed and Dale [17] in research carried out in five textile manufacturing organizations identified the following elements.

(a) *Internal failure costs*:
- scrap,*
- rework and repair,*
- trouble shooting,
- re-inspection, retest,
- modification, permits and concessions,
- downgrading.*

(b) *External failure costs*:
- complaints administration,*
- product or customer service, product liability,
- warranty costs and costs associated with replacement.

(c) *Appraisal costs*:
- laboratory acceptance testing,
- inspection and test (including goods inward inspection),*
- in-process inspection,*
- set-up for inspection and test,
- inspection and test material,
- product quality audits,
- review of test and inspection data,
- air conditioning,*
- colour matching,*
- production operatives,*
- machine maintenance,*

(d) *Prevention costs*:
- quality planning and process control,*
- design and development of quality measurement and control equipment,
- calibration and maintenance of production equipment used to evaluate quality,*
- maintenance and calibration of test and inspection equipment.

The elements indicated * are those which, in principle, are more easily identifiable and account for the greatest proportion of measured quality costs.

Pursglove and Dale [18] in discussing the experience of developing and operating a system of quality costing at a paint manufacturer, explain the adaption and additions needed to fit the elements of quality costs identified from the literature to paint manufacture. The following are the elements used.

(a) *Internal failure costs*:
- yield variance,
- mix/usage variance,
- rejected batch raw material,
- unrecorded raw material stock usage,
- stocktake loss,
- rejected batch make cost.

(b) *External failure costs*:
- value write downs,
- external transport,
- administration,
- on-site technical personnel and service,
- settlements,
- technical service investigations,
- dumped products.

(c) *Appraisal and prevention costs*:
- quality control function,
- research laboratory.

The evidence from the field indicates that it is not practical to compile an all-embracing list of quality cost elements to cover all eventualities as attempted in BS6143: Part 2 [14] and Campanella [15], for example. There will always be cost elements which are specific to particular situations and industries. The way forward may be for each industry sector to compile its own list of cost elements. The main purpose of the list of elements given in BS6143: Part 2 [14] and the ASQC Quality Costs Committee publications (e.g. Campanella [15]) is to facilitate quality cost comparison between companies. As already pointed out, such comparisons are both dangerous and fraught with difficulties. Consequently, the main use of the list of elements is to act as a thought promoter and mind opener and to demonstrate to senior managers the type of quality costs their organization is likely to be incurring. However, lists of published cost elements used to identify quality costs can also act as blinkers.

4.4.2 Time-based cost element method

In non-manufacturing situations, the cost elements described in BS6143 Part 2 [14], Campanella [15] and in the popular quality costing literature are often of little use to the cost collector. The same, to some degree, is true in the identification of costs specific to a department or section. As in the case of non-engineering manufacture the cost collector must strive to develop his/her own list of cost elements specific to their situation.

Due to the intangible nature of their jobs the concept of quality costing is often difficult for non-manufacturing personnel to grasp. It is relatively easy to understand the wastage involved in defective material, components and/or product. Not so in the case of: spoilt forms, reprocessed reports, incorrect application of the sales discount policy, incorrect information, unnecessary documentation, excessive adminstration, inefficient procedures, ineffective communications, incorrect data, duplication of paperwork, unnecessary reports, incorrectly directed telephone calls, premium freight charges, abortive sales visits, missed sales opportunities, credit notes and an excessive number of photocopies. The quality costing language is not well understood in non-manufacturing areas. The cost collector needs to have some sympathy with these cultural difficulties and put the concept in the language and environment of the organization or department under study. In a manufacturing organization the non-manufacturing area makes a significant contribution to the total costs of quality of the organization.

National Westminster Bank developed, in the mid 1980s an interesting method of identifying, collecting and measuring elements of quality costs, which they termed *The Cost of Making Mistakes* (National Westminster Bank [19]). The objective of the approach is to focus on areas where mistakes/errors occur and use a planned approach to improvement to put matters right. This approach, which is an example of a time-based cost element method, is now briefly summarized.

1. The administration manager of a branch identifies, with the head of each section and their staff, the areas/activities to be monitored, using a pre-prepared failure/complaints list; the example shown in Table 3.1 is used as a guide. The list of unmeasured or non-routine work was compiled from research in 100 branches and is focused on six basic areas of failure time (e.g. customer complaints, investigation, correction of work, system/equipment failure and checking).
2. Using the statistics monitoring form shown in Fig. 4.1 the staff of a section gather statistics on the areas/activities they have chosen to monitor.
3. The collected statistics are reviewed with the administration manager of the branch and five areas selected for improvement. The objective is to reduce the time spent on each of the five areas by at least 50% using a time-scaled improvement plan.

The point is made that a pilot study of the *Cost of Making Mistakes* exercise has shown that for every hour put into the exercise eight hours have been saved.

4.4.3 Semi-structured cost element identification and measurement methods

The following three semi-structured methods are of use in helping to develop a list of quality cost elements in both manufacturing and non-manufacturing situations. The elements identified can be based on people's activities and physical scrap and waste (i.e. forms, paper, components, material). The

STATISTICS MONITORING FORM

Assistant Manager/Section Head name: _____ Starting Date:_____

ACTIVITY	10 DAY'S STATISTICS (Record time in minutes per day) Day 1 2 3 4 5 6 7 8 9 10		AVERAGE TIME

Figure 4.1 Statistics monitoring form.

former are sometimes termed 'soft' quality costs and the latter 'hard' quality costs. With these methods there will always be a degree of subjectivity with the data and it should be expected that some people will express doubts about the accuracy of the statistics.

These semi-structured methods when focused on the activities of a department and its associated processes have the potential to: develop the internal customer/supplier concept, stimulate change, identify improvement opportunities, empower ownership for quality improvement, and highlight internal management responsibilities through process review. These methods have a wider perspective than a traditional quality costing based exercise and can provide a firm foundation for the application of departmental purpose analysis and activity based costing.

(a) Department based quality cost analysis method

After an introduction by the Chief Executive Officer confirming his commitment to quality costing as an essential aspect of TQM, a quality assurance/technical specialist/management consultant gives a briefing on the concept of quality costing to all department heads and members of the senior management team. Prior to the briefing some organizations use a questionnaire to test the understanding of quality costsing an example from GPT Payphones Systems developed by Frances Machowski is given in Fig. 4.2. The quality costing briefing typically includes what quality costs are; their uses, the concept of cost categories and elements, examples of specific cost elements in the organization, why the organization is setting out to identify quality costs, and the methodology which is to be employed to identify, collect and measure the costs. As part of this briefing, some organizations use a checklist, along the lines of that given in Table 4.5, relating to the various activities of the organization in order to help staff distinguish quality parameters into prevention, appraisal and failure activities. This assists in developing a common understanding within the organization of the three types of cost categories.

The managers are given a briefing pack on quality costs and are requested to make the same presentation to their staff and explain to them the quality costing methodology. As part of the quality costing education process some organizations get staff to take part in a quality costing awareness exercise. This involves them recording on an hourly basis for between one and three days their activities and classifying them as POC or PONC or alternatively prevention, appraisal and failure. Staff at all levels soon start to realize that a considerable amount of their activities is related to failure.

The methodology is for each department (e.g. marketing, personnel, purchasing and finance), using a team approach, to identify elements of quality costs which are appropriate to them and for which they have ownership. Quality management tools and techniques, such as brainstorming, cause and effect

QUALITY COSTS QUESTIONNAIRE

DEPARTMENT :..

JOB TITLE   :..

DATE   :..

PLEASE TICK YOUR ANSWER – CHOOSE ONLY ONE ANSWER UNLESS STATED OTHERWISE

OFFICIAL USE ONLY

1. Do you know what is meant by the term PREVENTION COSTS?

    (a) No

    (b) Yes, please specify......................................

        ....

        ....

1

2. Do you know what is meant by the term APPRAISAL COSTS?

    (a) No

    (b) Yes, please specify......................................

        ....

        ....

2

3. Each of the following statements are possible definitions of quality costs, please enter TRUE/FALSE (T/F) in each of the boxes.

    (a) The cost of having a quality department

    (b) Cost of producing quality products

    (c) Cost of not meeting customer requirements

    (d) Cost of inspection / test

    (e) Cost of introducing BS5750: Part 1

    (f) Costs associated with not getting it right first time

    (g) Cost of making mistakes

3

4. Do you know what is meant by the term INTERNAL FAILURE COSTS?

   (a) No

   (b) Yes, please specify ....

       ....

       ....

4

5. Do you know what is meant by the term EXTERNAL FAILURE COSTS?

   (a) No

   (b) Yes, please specify ....

       ....

       ....

5

6. Which department(s) do you associate with quality costs?

   (a) Quality department

   (b) Production

   (c) Finance

   (d) Marketing

   (e) All departments

   (f) Other, please specify

       ....

       ....

6

7. Do you know what is meant by the term PRICE OF CONFORMANCE?

   (a) No

   (b) Yes, please specify ....

       ....

7

8. Do you know what is meant by the term PRICE OF NON-CONFORMANCE?

   (a) No

   (b) Yes, please specify ....

       ....

8

9. Typically quality costs range between 5% and 25% of annual sales turnover

   What percentage of sales do you think quality costs will be in GPT Payphones?

   (a)   0–5%

   (b)   6–10%

   (c)   11–15%

   (d)   16–20%

   (e)   21–25%

                                                                    9

10. The following is a list of quality cost elements. Please indicate, in the box provided, which department (from the list below) in your opinion, each element is associated with.

    The departments to choose from are :

        Manufacturing (M)

        Engineering   (E)

        Purchasing   (P)

        Quality   (Q)

        Other   (O)

    (a)   Engineering change order

    (b)   Field performance testing

    (c)   Product Inspection

    (d)   Product Test

    (e)   Rework

    (f)   Defective materials

    (g)   Warranty errors

    (h)   Warranty

    (i)   Equipment downtime

                                                                    10

Figure 4.2 Quality costs questionnaire. (Source: GPT Payphones: Francis MacLowski.)

Q11 For each pair of the five statements choose which statement is most important to you and place a tick at the appropriate point

	VERY IMPORTANT	QUITE IMPORTANT	UNIMPORTANT	NEITHER	UNIMPORTANT	QUITE IMPORTANT	VERY IMPORTANT	
ACHIEVE BONUS	—	—	—	—	—	—	—	REDUCE AMOUNT OF REWORK
REDUCE SCRAP	—	—	—	—	—	—	—	IMPROVE QUALITY THROUGH INCREASED INSPECTION
CHOOSE LOWEST PRICE VENDOR	—	—	—	—	—	—	—	PRODUCE QUALITY PRODUCTS
MAKE FEW MISTAKES	—	—	—	—	—	—	—	WORK AT SPEED
ACHIEVE MONTHLY TARGETS	—	—	—	—	—	—	—	WORK EFFECTIVELY

Table 4.5 Categorizing activities

	My view	View of group

1. Dealing with a customer who is querying an invoice.

2. New product training for sales staff.

3. A member of the sales department makes a call on a customer but the person he/she wishes to see is not available.

4. Visual examination of a batch of product to assess the standard of finish.

5. A customer goes bankrupt owing the company £600 000.

6. A person who is responsible for providing material to a production process makes a repeat visit to the stores for extra material in order that a batch of product can be completed.

7. A development engineer carries out trial testing of a new type of product.

8. A quality engineer carries out a process potential study.

9. Audit checking of finished product before passing into the warehouse.

10. Carrying out an appraisal of the accuracy of paperwork/forms.

11. Proofreading a report before distribution.

12. Transporting a batch of product from the manufacturing to the inspection department.

13. Carrying out a survey of customers to obtain their views about the company.

14. Extra costs of working overtime because of a changed schedule.

15. Checking the accuracy of readings of a piece of test equipment.

16. A member of the customer services department calls on a customer at the agreed time and corrects the reported fault(s) to the customer's satisfaction.

17. The Chief Executive Officer chasing the Marketing Department for sales figures.

18. Waiving a customer charge after a disagreement about the work done.

19. Developing standard practices and procedures and instruction manuals.

20. Checking the 'first off' from a production run.

21. Top-up of a plating line with chemicals to bring the process to the required strength.

Table 4.5 (contd)

	My view	View of group
22. Visit customers premises to assess damage caused by one of the company's site services staff.		
23. Sending some urgently needed material by express courier to enable a supplier to commence production of a batch of product.		
24. A visit by one of the company's inspectors to a customer to investigate the reason for repeated rejections of batches of product.		
25. A member of the distribution department phones the sales office to check which type of a particular product the customer wants.		
26. A batch of product is reworked to remove a particular type of defect.		
27. Carrying out market research to determine customer future needs and expectations.		
28. Carrying out a BS5750 Part 1 internal audit.		
29. Offering a customer an alternative choice of product when the first choice is not available from stock.		
30. A member of the maintenance staff returns to a manufacturing department to refix a previous recurring problem with a pump.		
31. A lost time accident.		
32. Equipment start-up and shut-down losses.		
33. The annual cost associated with operating quality improvement teams.		
34. Carrying out gauge and instrument calibration.		
35. Undertaking an assessment of a potential supplier.		
36. Selective fitting due to the variability of manufactured parts.		
37. The disruption caused by outside suppliers to the company's production schedules.		

Code:
B = Basic work
P = Prevention
A = Appraisal
F = Failure

analysis, forcefield analysis and 'why why' diagrams are useful aids to assist staff to identify aspects of their job (i.e. time and materials) which are not always carried out right the first time. This leads to the identification of quality cost elements. The use of time sheets and labour variance reports can help to identify the non-value added time.

Once the elements have been identified, the department heads make a presentation to the technical and/or quality assurance specialists. The presentations made and the relevant synergy which develops during the discussion helps to cut out duplication and refine each department's list of cost elements.

After the elements have been agreed the next step is for each department to determine the amount of time they are spending on each cost element which has been identified. The quality assurance and technical specialists assist the departments in the task. The accountant then works with each department manager and with the technical and quality assurance specialists, as appropriate, in putting a cost on each element identified.

(b) Team based quality cost analysis method

The following are the main steps involved with this approach.

1. A team is formed. The usual members of the team include: quality manager, management accountant, technical manager, production/operations manager and the training manager. Apart from the first two members the remainder of the team membership can be varied to suit the environment of the organization under study.
2. The next step is to hold a one-day workshop on quality costing. As part of the workshop a training session on quality costing is given, covering topics such as: what are quality costs, importance of costs, historical background of quality costing, definitions, collection, reporting, uses, the role of management accountants in quality costing and setting-up a quality cost collection system. The quality costing awareness questionnaire and the quality costing time analysis outlined in the departmental based quality cost analysis method can be employed prior to this training session.

    The senior management team are expected to attend this workshop.
3. The workshop participants clarify the reasons for the need to collect and use quality costs. They also agree the objectives for the exercise. This includes deciding whether to identify quality costs on a department-by-department basis or across the total organization.
4. A quality costing awareness exercise is then carried out. The purpose of the exercise is to:

    (a) help decide what constitutes a quality cost, and

(b) determine the best means of identifying and collecting quality costs.

The workshop participants are asked to consider and debate a number of activities, the details of which are given in Table 4.5. This standard list of questions can be modified to suit the requirements of an organization. Each person, on an individual basis, is asked to state whether each activity is basic work (i.e. the essential activities entailed in supplying the company's products and/or services) or a quality cost. If the activity is considered to be a quality cost they are asked to say whether it is prevention, appraisal or failure. When each participant has completed the exercise, there is a general discussion on the reasoning for each answer and a reconciling of different points of view. The participants soon realize that the activities they have no or least disagreement are the activities related to failure, followed by appraisal. The main areas of contention relate to basic work and prevention activities.

As part of the exercise participants are asked to:

(a) prepare a set of rules for deciding what constitutes a quality cost, and
(b) identify the typical sources of quality cost data which are available in the company

5. The participants then decide the methods which they perceive as the most appropriate and useful to identify elements of quality cost. The usual outcome of this debate is to start to identify the main failure costs across the company or on a departmental basis. A departmental analysis would require the appropriate representatives to be involved in the exercise.

6. The next step is to hold a brainstorming session to identify the major failure costs across the organization. Once a failure cost has been agreed, the management accountant is asked if the data is available from the existing accounting system. If not, the participants discuss how the element should be measured. On a number of occasions this has resulted in the formation of a quality improvement team to address this measurement issue. This activity continues until some 10 major failure costs have been identified and agreed. The idea is to start simple and expand the system in line with operating experience and needs.

7. The team reaches decisions on issues such as the time period over which these agreed elements will be measured, how the data should be reported and the use made of the data in terms of improvement action and projects.

8. The team meets on a regular basis to discuss progress. The team, in conjunction with members of the senior management, as appropriate, reconvenes to identify other activities giving rise to failure cost. This process is continued for appraisal activities and then to prevention, if considered desirable.

(c) Process cost model

The process cost model is outlined in BS6143: Part 1 [20]. The Standard ...

> ... sets out a method for applying quality costing to any process or service. It recognises the importance of process measurement and process ownership. The categories of quality costs have been rationalised to the cost of conformance and the cost of non-conformance. This serves to simplify classification. The method depends on the use of process modelling and the standard gives guidelines on useful techniques ....

Although it does not say so in the Standard the process cost model is based on the computer-aided-manufacturing integrated program definition (IDEF) method (see Ross [21] for details). IDEF is a method for representing complex systems using a standard format in such a way as to allow pictures and words to be coupled together and then presented in the form of an activity diagram (Fig. 4.3). It can be seen that the activity diagram is made up of inputs and outputs which are usually in the form of materials or information. The activity transforms the input into an output. The mechanism is the location where the activity takes place or is the thing which performs the activity. The control is made up of factors or situations

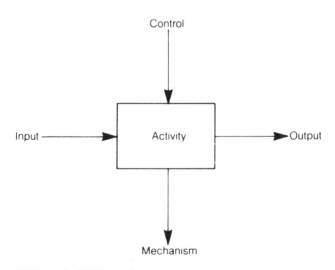

Figure 4.3 IDEF – the ICOM code.

which regulate the activity. A series of activity diagrams form a model of the system, process and procedures being studied. The diagrams are parented down to progressively provide more detail on the activity under study.

This process modelling model was first used for the identification of elements of quality cost by Marsh [22] in work carried out at ICL.

The model employed in BS6143 Part 1 [20] is shown in Fig. 4.4. It is identical to the IDEF-ICOM (input, controls, output and mech-

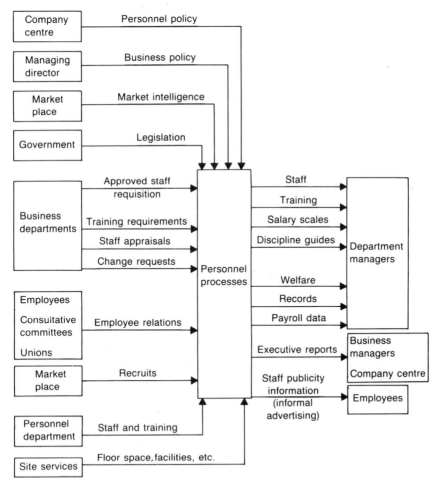

Figure 4.4 Typical process model inputs and outputs for personnel department processes (source: BS6143 Part 1 [20]).

anism) code apart from mechanism being replaced by resources. The methodology focuses on departmental objectives and process ownership, and helps people to identify the costs of conformance (COC) and the costs of non-conformance (CONC) which are associated with the processes for which they have responsibility. This COC and CONC classification has been modified from Crosby's [5] POC and PONC categories. A model of each process is developed, along the lines of Fig. 4.4. The cost elements associated with the process which has been modelled are identified as either a COC or CONC; this is termed a cost model. The Standard contains examples of process models and cost models for a personnel department, manufacturing department, quality assurance department and technical publication unit. The personnel and manufacturing department models reproduced from BS6143 Part 1 [20] are shown in Tables 4.6 and 4.7 respectively.

The IDEF methodology was developed for use by experts for the modelling of manufacturing systems. Substantial research has been conducted by Crossfield [23] in the modelling of quality systems. The opinion was formed that if individuals were to take ownership for modelling their particular aspect of the quality system, a more simpler method was required. This led to the development of quality management activity planning (Q-MAP) for the mapping of quality assurance procedures, information, flows and quality-related responsibilities (Crossfield and Dale [24]) Q-MAP has been used by a wide range of company personnel from shop floor operators to members of the senior management team.

In discussion with managers concerning the collection of quality costs using a process modelling approach there was almost universal agreement that if they and departmental staff were to be responsible for identifying the elements of costs, then the method was too complex. This was the same finding as that reached by Crossfield [23] in relation to quality system mapping. However, if a quality assurance/technical specialist or a management consultant is to take responsibility for the process modelling and identification of costs, then this method is appropriate.

Whilst the process cost model method may facilitate ownership of the costs by each department it sometimes fails to identify those costs which occur between departments. Consequently, some costs are not identified and, even if they are, difficulties are encountered in persuading departmental managers to take responsibility for their ownership and subsequent reduction. This can also lead to departments attempting to minimize their costs at the expense of other departments, and so ultimately the benefits to the organization as a whole are diminished. Cross-function co-operation is necessary if quality costing is to be a success and perhaps the process cost model method is not particularly apt in facilitating co-operation of this type.

Table 4.6 Cost model for a personnel department (source: BS6143 Part 1 [20]).

Key activity	Cost of conformance	Cost of non-conformance
Attitude surveys	Total cost	
Audit of salaries	Total cost	
Appraisals	Cost of appraisals	Cost of progressing non-returns
Industrial action		Total cost
Staff turnover		Total cost
Recruitment costs	Cost of satisfying requirements	Cost of not satisfying requirements i.e. delays, etc.
Sponsored students not joining business		Total cost
Training	Cost of training	Cost of cancellations
Grading panel	Cost of grading	Cost of appeals
Personnel change requests	Cost of those approved	Cost of errors, rejections, referrals, etc.
Preparation of statistics	Routine reports	Cost of special reports, chasing inputs, etc.

Table 4.7 Cost model for a manufacturing department (source: BS6143 Part 1 [20]).

Key activity	Cost of conformance	Cost of non-conformance
Planning, production engineering work study, cost control, materials and process laboratory	Part cost	Part cost (effect of engineering change, planning errors, etc.)
Production inspection and test costs	'Good' hours booked	Re-inspection/retest/fault finding
Test gear depreciation, calibration and preventative maintenance	Total cost	
Breakdowns		Total cost
Production costs	'Good' hours booked	Rework
Material costs	Estimated cost	Scrap cost, overspend
Waiting time		Total cost
Cost of work held due to shortages		Total cost

In summary, the methodology should help to extend the concept of quality costing to all functions of an organization and in this way raise awareness.

4.5 EASE OF COLLECTION AND SOURCES OF COST DATA

Most companies have materials and direct labour costs analysed in considerable detail for the purpose of measuring production efficiencies. However, indirect labour (including staff personnel) costs are seldom analysed in detail even though they may total four or five times the direct labour costs. Thus, prevention is the most difficult of the categories to cost because it depends heavily on estimates of apportionment of time by indirect works and staff who do not usually record how they spend their day. In relation to the prevention cost category, one argument often advanced is, 'If prevention activity is considered desirable, then why bother to cost it?' The case for measuring prevention is to obtain an indication of the scale of an organization's total quality costs.

In those cases where indirect personnel are engaged on single activities or a narrow range of closely related activities (e.g. inspection), the cost is much easier to collect. In practice, however, many personnel are involved in a number of disparate activities, sometimes wholly quality related, sometimes not. For example, personnel from the quality department operate across functional boundaries, in particular between appraisal and prevention activities. This is also the case when departments and activities have been merged.

It is the lack of data about how people spend their time which makes the collection of cost data under the different quality categories and elements difficult. In order to obtain a prevention cost synthesis it is necessary to record or estimate the proportions of time spent by various personnel on each activity. For personnel within the quality assurance department it is presumably with the quality assurance manager's authority to require routine accounting of staff time. Weekly returns on half-day increments would suffice as a time allocation mechanism. The quality-related topics against which to book time, and personnel costs to be used in conjunction with such booking, are discussed later. If this more objective method of analysis is adopted careful consideratoin needs to be given to the period of time over which data collection takes place. Retrospective estimates of the proportions of time spent on various activities tend to be highly subjective (more often than not coloured by recent events) and are 'average' or 'typical' observations. There is also an unwillingness of people to change their initial estimates in the light of changed circumstances. In one organization studied the quality assurance manager's perception of how his three quality engineers spent their time was wildly different from their own analysis. In the same organization a rule used by the quality assurance manager is 'whatever activity accounts for more than 50% of a persons's time, on an on-going basis, shall be identified as the total activity of that person'. In a company manufacturing computers the problem of costing prevention was overcome by considering it to be '20% of the departmental expense of test, plus 30% of the departmental expense of manufacturing engineering, plus 2% of the production direct cost which is estimated to be related to job and quality-related training'.

Some quality-related costs arising within the production function can readily be obtained from routine monthly accounts. Other quality activities such as sorting and inspection work undertaken by production personnel are not so easy to identify and cost. A cost which is not collected and which is very difficult to estimate with acceptable accuracy, is the cost of personnel (other than quality assurance department personnel), part of whose work is generated as a result of failures. Examples are the involvement of purchasing and accounts personnel in dealing with supplier problems and rejected batches, and production control personnel rescheduling rework in terms of components and batches of product. Analysis of failure costs by functional causes (e.g. production, purchasing, marketing) is another type of cost which is not usually readily available. Collecting the costs of the retesting of previously faulty parts, in particular when rework and rectification are an integral part of the process, is also fraught with difficulties. Within manufacturing industry these are regarded as very important costs.

Another consideration in relation to ease of collection is the matter of labelling account codes. It sometimes happens that accounts departments wish to keep separate accounts of some non-routine matter (e.g. a product recall), and give it a title from which it is not immediately obvious that it may be a quality cost. Hence it is prudent to work very closely with the accounts department when investigating quality costs.

The ease of collection of quality cost data is dependent upon identifying cost data sources. BS6143: Part 2 [14] recommends the following as source documents:

(a) payroll analysis
(b) manufacturing expense reports
(c) scrap reports
(d) rework or rectification authorisations/reports
(e) travel expense claims
(f) product cost information
(g) field repair, replacement and warranty cost reports
(h) inspection and test records
(i) non-conformance reports

A number of rich and specific sources of cost data are also identified in each of the case studies (Chapters 7–12). In general, quality costing data is obtained from three main sources:

● normal accounting data (i.e. labour and overhead cost reports) from accounts ledgers,

- company operating systems, procedures, standards and specifications, and

- data specifically calculated or estimated for the quality costing exercise.

As a final point in this section it is most important for an organization to develop quality cost collection guidelines and procedures, for example: apportioning staff time to a quality cost category; how to allocate an activity into different cost categories; what to include in a particular element, and losses caused by sub-standard products. The following are examples of guidelines from Allied Signal Ltd, Turbochargers, Skelmersdale (The company is a manufacturing and assembly facility producing turbochargers for the automotive industry and is the world's largest producer of automotive turbochargers.)

Apportion individuals' time to that quality cost category which represents the individual's primary responsibility. Do not attempt to apportion individuals' time amongst different categories.

The cost of inspection and test incorporated into production operator self-control activities (where inspection or test is not the principal job function of the operator) should be considered as part of the standard cost of product. This cost is desirable. It will normally replace higher independent appraisal cost and need not be estimated or calculated for inclusion in these measurements.

Inspection and test cost normally comprises two elements – initial product inspection and test, and extra inspection test due to product non-conformities. The latter element should really be classified as a failure cost but, since it would be too time consuming to discriminate between the two elements, total inspection and test cost is viewed as a single entity and included in the appraisal category.

4.6 THE LEVEL OF DETAIL IN THE COSTS COLLECTED

An obvious but often overlooked fact is that a costing system only translates other information into costs (i.e. the subject matter needs to be a matter of record before it can be picked up by a costing system). It follows that the potential for costing at a company may be gauged from the sophistication of its management information systems, and also that overambitious pursuit of detailed cost information will, of necessity, proliferate recording and analysis of underlying information. If the management information system and other systems such as ordering, materials management and tracking are unreliable this will complicate the identification and collection of quality costs. On the other hand, a quality cost collection exercise will expose deficiencies in the management information system and uncover anomalies in the reporting and feedback of quality-related data. It may be worth carrying out an audit of the management information and quality reporting systems before embarking on a quality cost collection exercise.

Eldridge and Dale [6] report on two methods they used for improving the accessibility of cost data in a company manufacturing valves.

- Where direct measures were not available or inaccurate then more indirect measures were used. For example, the quantity of castings scrapped during the machining process was not reported accurately but the quantities of castings supplied to the machining process and remaining after machining were reported accurately for material control purposes.
- The Phase 1 exercise highlighted that some quality-related activities were masquerading under manufacturing related titles. For example, 'excess work' was described as non-productive work carried out by direct labour or work not included in the payment-by-results scheme and was closely monitored for management information purposes. In reality, it almost totally comprised rework operations and, because data was available, it was relatively easy to cost these activities.

Difficulties can be encountered even in collecting the most commonly occurring cost element, that of scrap. An organization needs to lay down firm guidelines on what is meant by the term and how it should be collected. For example, in a manufacturing situation the following is typical:

- Non-conforming material scrap costs.
- 100% material cost plus 50% of the finished part total labour/burden cost irrespective of the actual stage of manufacture of the rejected part.
- Scrap costs will include all discarded material regardless of whether accounted for on a scrap note, counted as planned or unplanned yield losses, or otherwise disposed of. They will include such costs as: incorrect design, defective purchased items not charged to supplier and incorrectly performed manufacturing operations.

The characteristics of the industry (i.e. one-off production, timescale for manufacture) are such that there is little opportunity to build up an historical file of meaningful cost data. It is also found that putting costs on scrap and rework in a one-off manufacturing situation is much more difficult than in, say, a high volume low cost production facility.

Care must also be taken not to concentrate only on what is already known with a view to refining it. Size is often regarded as being synonymous with importance, although it is size coupled with relevance and potential for reduction which determines the real importance of costs. Clearly, if refining costs is the object of the exercise, it is probably much more advantageous to refine known large costs than to quantify known sources of small costs. It is also better to pursue a small percentage reduction in a large cost than a large reduction in a small cost, depending on the ease of achievement. What magnitude of cost may be regarded as being insignificant in the cost collection exercise is another problem. Unfortunately, there are no useful guidelines, nor are ratios helpful, although accuracy levels, if known, may give good indications. In the end it becomes a subjective decision about what sum of money is significant in the context of quality costs, or, perhaps, company profit.

It is suggested that all costs which are readily available should be collected, but that cost elements which are likely to be less than £1000 per annum are not worth pursuing. Having decided on a figure, it is important to recognize that it is much more likely that the magnitude of cost may fail to be picked up as part of a large cost element than of a small element. The quality costing strategy must therefore be to concentrate on the large cost items.

It is important also to remember that the size of costs, both absolute and relative, can become grossly distorted under some accounting practices. An example met with is the practice of including full overheads in direct labour charges to quality-related costs; this was done to portray an accurate picture within accounting conventions. The argument for including full overhead allocation to rejected material is that it will not be recovered elsewhere. Eldridge and Dale [6] discuss how they presented to senior management one set of quality cost figures including an overhead allocation and another set which were simply the costs that could be reduced by improvement activities. They report that the figures with no overhead allocation stimulated the most comment from senior management, because they were seen as the avoidable real costs.

Hesford and Dale [25] report that despite the warnings of Dale and Plunkett [26] about dangers of double counting and of gross distortion of quality costs when including a proportion of overheads in labour costs the British Aerospace Dynamics view 'was that the opportunity costs of scrap and rework could be expressed using full overhead rates because a reduction in these costs would facilitate 'good' hours resulting in increased sales potential.'

The result of overhead inclusion means that rework and scrap costs become grossly inflated compared to prevention and appraisal costs which are incurred by salaried and indirect workers. Such a system is, of course, not tenable in that there is some double counting inevitably taking place. Another example of double counting typically encountered was that of the benefit arising from reworking rejected material being subtracted from the quality costs. It was found that this had already been catered for in the cost accounting system. The larger and more complex the cost accounting system the greater the likelihood of double counting. It is recommended that the cost collector stands back from the data which has been collected to check for double counting. A material process flow chart has been found to be useful in identifying potential cases of double counting. Another example of cost distortion is the influence of some countries tax regulations on the valuation of scrap material.

It should also not be forgotten that if the quality costing system demands that information is collected on a regular basis in minute detail, there is a good chance that the system will fall into disuse. Considerable attention needs to be given to the number of cost elements to be collected and the sources of information. Nothing inhibits data gathering so much as having to gather it from a large number of sources. The system should be made as easy and simple and as automatic as possible, with minimum intervention from the cost owners and without significantly increasing paperwork or the burden on accountants. An attempt should be made to ensure that it is an integral part of the job.

4.7 ACCURACY OF DATA

Accuracy is one of the most important criteria in that it has a strong and direct influence on the amount of work involved in the task and on the credibility of the outcome. It is not usually practicable to decide in advance of the task the level of accuracy to which to work, or what is attainable. The precision is usually determined by factors outside the control of the quality cost investigator. However, what must be avoided is the search for unnecessary accuracy delaying the introduction of the cost collection system.

A particularly apt piece of advice on the topic is contained in the following quotation:

It is the mark of an instructed mind to rest content with that degree of precision which the nature of the subject permits and not to seek exactness where only approximation of the truth is possible. (Aristotle)

Because quality cost data are expressed in figures, which are sometimes treated by people as being very precise, there is a danger that a cost report may give an impression of accuracy which is not warranted. The true accuracy of costs is dependent on the underlying data. Knowledge of how these data are obtained and the purposes for which they are used may give good indications of the accuracy which may reasonably be sought or expected. Resorting to underlying data can also have the advantage that corroborative information may be available, though corresponding costs may not be. A case in point is failures under warranty data.

Accuracy of costs is dependent on the quality of underlying data. Knowledge of how those data are obtained, and the purposes for which they are used, may give good indications of the levels of accuracy which might reasonably be sought or expected. For example, in a situation where non-productive hours of direct workers are deducted from total hours before calculating labour and production efficiencies, there may be an incentive to carry out non-productive work (e.g. sorting of conforming from non-conforming product) inefficiently or even to misallocate time at the expense of quality-related costs. Poor control of paperwork may also lead to inaccuracies. In-process rejection notes may provide an example. Each note carries a unique number, but there may be no system for checking that all notes issued are accounted for when it comes to costing the various disposal outlets (scrap and rework). It may be the case that a significant number of rejection notes which ought to go to the quality assurance and accounts departments for costing purposes never get there. In other cases encountered, the incidence of non-conforming components is simply not recorded.

When trying to get a feel for the accuracy of cost information accumulated in accounts departments it is often useful to look for independent measures as corroboration. In one company studied there appeared to be inconsistencies between provision made for warranty claims, actual warranty charges accumulated, product failure rates, and the level of effort devoted to customer rejected products and warranty.

In apportioning personnel time to quality cost elements and categories, the use of actual costs, which may vary from month to month, may not be warranted. Average rates based on annual employment costs will be accurate enough. Nor is it necessary to have an employment cost for every individual. Two or three levels of cost could give sufficient accuracy. These figures may also provide useful checks in making inter-divisional or inter-site cost comparisons. However, if this is considered an objective of the exercise, the difficulties relating to comparisons mentioned earlier in the book should be kept in mind.

Specifying the elements and categories against which to apportion time can lead to inaccuracies if not thought out carefully. If the individual concerned does not think that the elements are appropriate to his/her work he/she will not bother to make accurate entries. It may be as well therefore, in the early stages, to get participants to specify their own element definitions, or to co-operate to provide a comprehensive listing at the outset of the exercise.

In making the above comments it is presupposed that the intention is to build up a reasonably accurate and detailed picture of how and where quality-related costs are incurred. However, as discussed earlier in this chapter, not all quality management practitioners accept that this is necessary. An alternative view is that it is necessary only to identify and analyse the high-cost areas with a view to mounting specific cost-cutting projects. Yet another view is that periodic snapshots of the quality-related cost situation (as opposed to continuous monitoring) are all that is needed. The incidence of such diverse objectives with their differing requirements serves to reinforce the case for a rational approach in which the purposes of the exercise are clearly established at the outset.

Against the background of difficulties with definitions and of knowing what should be included amongst quality-related costs, and the problems of gathering some of the costs, there seems little point in pursuing accuracy even where it is known to be obtainable. On the other hand, costs must be accurate enough and sufficiently robust to be credible even to those whose efficiency or performance is perhaps impugned by the resulting report. Nevertheless, many companies are content with quality costs which are accurate to ± 10% and, seemingly, the greater the cost, the greater the tolerance. A cost report which does not have credibility is a waste of time and, unfortunately, the credibility of a whole report can easily be seriously undermined by a skilled protagonist once a single weakness has been exposed. Staff should feel comfortable with the accuracy of the figures used and generated. It is for this reason that only costs produced or endorsed by accounts departments should be used in the report. Costs produced by accounts departments have greater acceptability and are more likely to be compatible and consistent with other cost efficiency measures.

A final point on the matter of accuracy is that guesses are at best useless. As already mentioned, experience has shown that where people are involved in disparate activities estimates of how and where they spend their time tend to be long-term based and vary widely. The danger of course is that the guesses are either ascribed the same credence as other figures in the report, or they may be identified as a weakness through which the report may be discredited. they will certainly not be kept in their proper perspective. Thus, when data has to be estimated it must be indicated as such.

4.8 THE PEOPLE INVOLVED IN QUALITY COST COLLECTION

In some companies, accountants give the impression that they consider quality assurance and quality improvement as necessary evils, and consequently there are attempts to play down the true costs or savings from improvement activities and projects. On the other hand, engineers, technical and quality assurance specialists are also culpable in making simple operations appear to accountants to be very technical, difficult and complicated. These are important factors which tend to inhibit the collection and use of quality cost data. Everyone who has tried to investigate costs will almost certainly have experienced the frustration caused by the communication barrier which separates the professional management accountant from the non-accountant. An added difficulty is that not all management accountants are aware of the concept of quality costing and the knowledge of those that are is sparse.

An essential precursor to collecting quality-related costs is knowledge of the company in terms of history, culture, people, processes and products. This is not as might at first be imagined an unnecessary consideration for a company carrying out a quality costing exercise. A quality costing exercise requires quality, technical and accounting knowledge, and few people at the right level in the organization are likely to have all the knowledge which is necessary.

Thus costing should be a joint exercise. If accounts people try to do it alone, they are likely to miss a lot of the detail or even be misled by people with axes to grind. The accountants usually seek guidance from quality assurance staff on what to measure. On the other hand, if quality assurance and technical people go it alone they may, for example, fail to discover costs which tidy-minded accountants have tucked away out of sight, and consequently the costs collected and presented will lack credibility. In addition they may not be aware of the true meaning or relative sensitivity of certain cost data. They may also have difficulties in interpreting the cost data which is available from the costing system and what it actually means. It should be remembered, however, that management accountants are always under pressure to produce all sorts of costs and, if quality costing is to get off the ground in a company, they need to be convinced that there is some worth in the exercise. A positive factor in getting accountants departments involved is that any measure put into place by them usually helps to focus management's attention on the metric.

Hesford and Dale [24] reporting on the future quality costing strategy of the British Aerospace Dynamics say:

> In the future, site finance managers will need to become more involved in the collection of quality costs to increase the confidence of senior management in the validity of quality cost data as a measure of operational performance.

4.9 THE VIEWS OF QUALITY MANAGERS AND ACCOUNTANTS

An interesting feature of the treatment of measurement and collection of cost data is the contrast between the apparent optimism of the majority of quality management specialists and management consultants about how easy it should be (at least to get started) and the caution of the accountants and a few quality management specialists. This interdisciplinary difference of outlook is so marked that those from the quality fraternity who advocate caution are made to appear as spiritless pessimists who are more aware of the obstacles than of the opportunities. However, deeper study reveals that despite their apparent optimism about the ease of the measurement of costs, most quality management specialists acknowledge that it may take years to establish a good system of measurement and collection. Reasons for the differences in outlook may arise from fundamentally different perceptions of costing exercises. It is clear that most quality management specialists think in terms of pilot schemes or improvement projects requiring approximate costs to be measured in a small segment of the business. Accountants on the other hand are professionally, if not naturally, concerned with the precision and completeness of costs. They therefore wish to see how the mini-exercise or improvement project stands in relation to the whole business. This of course requires much more information to be got, much of which may appear to the quality assurance professional to be irrelevant.

Management accounting is based on tried and tested rules with well defined practices and procedures. Accountants tend to be precise and pay considerable attention to detail. In general, accountants do not like dealing with grey areas. Quality costing is very much a grey area with few rules, procedures and practices and with a considerable degree of ambiguity. This is perhaps why accountants have difficulty getting to grips with the concept.

The differences have also given rise to (or at least reinforced) prejudices amongst the quality fraternity about accountants and accounting systems. Whilst there are indeed difficulties, it is being less than fair to modern management accountants to suggest that they cannot or will not accommodate the needs of quality management and technical specialists requiring data which is out of the ordinary.

4.10 COMMITMENT OF SENIOR MANAGEMENT

As a final point it is important to remember that in addition to having the necessary mechanism in place for collecting quality-related costs, it is also necessary for the Chief Executive Officer and members of the senior management team to have the will and commitment to support the quality cost collection process and to use the data. They must use judgement to assess the degree of quality cost quantification and cost of quality in relation to targets which it is necessary to meet in order to meet the objectives set for quality cost collection and use. Management must ensure that there is a real incentive to report and reduce costs of quality. The concept of quality costing must have credibility at all levels in the organization, and senior management can play a key role in this.

4.11 SUMMARY

The strategy to be adopted for collecting quality costs will be influenced by the purpose of the exercise. Getting the purpose clear at the outset can go a long way towards avoiding pitfalls and unnecessary work. Senior management must be involved in developing and agreeing the strategy.

The chapter has reviewed a number of strategies together with the type of issues which have a bearing on the collection methods. However, irrespective of the strategy adopted, what will be got from the exercise should be stressed to all concerned. This helps to overcome the resistance of the department managers who may view quality costing as a low priority. There is also a need for developing a company standard and operating procedure on quality cost collection and reporting.

When establishing a qualty cost collection procedure for the first time, five points must be kept in mind.

1. The methodology adopted for the collection of costs must be practical and relevant in that it must contribute to the performance of the basic activities of the organization.
2. There is no substitute for a thorough examination of the operating process in the beginning. Modifications to the procedure may be made later, as necessary, with hindsight and as experience of applying the procedure grows.
3. People will readily adopt ready-made procedures for purposes for which they were not intended if they appear to fit the situation. Hence the 'first-off' should be soundly based.
4. Procedures should be 'user friendly'.
5. The management accountant must be involved from the outset.

REFERENCES

1. Leibert, F.P. (1968) Guidelines on the gathering and implementation of quality costs. *The Quality Engineer*, **32** (2), 39–43.
2. Jenney, B.W. (1974) Motivation for quality. *The Quality Engineer*, **38** (1), 5–7.
3. Juran, J.M. and Gryna, F. (1993) *Quality Planning and Analysis*, McGraw-Hill, New York.
4. Juran, J.M. (ed.) (1988) *Quality Control Handbook*, McGraw-Hill, New York.
5. Crosby, P.B. (1979) *Quality is Free*, McGraw-Hill, New York.
6. Eldridge, S. and Dale, B.G. (1989) Quality costing: the lessons learnt from a study in two parts. *Engineering Costs and Production Economics*, **18** (1), 33–44.
7. Hallum, S. and Casperson, R. (1975) Economy and quality control. *Proceedings of the 19th EOQC Conference*, Venice, 11–22.
8. Blank, L. and Solorzano, J. (1978) Using quality cost analysis for management improvement. *Industrial Engineering*, **10** (2), 46–51.
9. Booth, W.E. (1976) Financial reporting of quality performance. *Quality Progress*, February, 14–15.
10. Hagan, J.T. (1985) Quality costs II: the economics of quality improvement. *Quality Progress*, 18 (10), 48–51.
11. Alford, R.E. (1979) Quality costs – where to start – Part I. *Quality*, August, 36–7.
12. Alford, R.E. (1979) Quality costs – where to start – Part II. *Quality*, September, 70–1.
13. Alford, R.E. (1979) Quality costs – where to start – Part III. *Quality*, October 40–2.
14. BS6143: Part 2 (1990) *Guide to the Economics of Quality – Prevention, Appraisal and Failure Model*, British Standards Institution, London.
15. Campanella, J. (ed.) (1990) *Principles of Quality Costs: Principles, Implementation and USE*, ASQC Quality Press, Milwaukee.
16. Feigenbaum, A.V. (1983) *Total Quality Control*, McGraw-Hill.
17. Abed, M.H. and Dale, B.G. (1987) An attempt to identify quality-related costs in textile manufacturing. *Quality Assurance*, **13** (21), 41–5.

18. Pursglove, A.B. and Dale, B.G. (1990) Developing a quality costing system: key features and outcomes. Unpublished paper, Manchester School of Management, UMIST.
19. National Westminster Bank (1991) *The Cost of Making Mistakes*, Package, Quality and Customer Service Department, National Westminster Bank, London.
20. BS6143: Part 1 (1992) *Guide to the Economics of Quality-Process Cost Model*, British Standards Institution, London.
21. Ross, D.T. (1980) *Architects Manual ICAM Definition Method*, IDEFO, Cam-i Inc., Texas.
22. Marsh, J. (1989) Process modelling for quality improvement. *Proceedings of the Second International Conference on Total Quality Management*, London, IFS Publications, 111–21.
23. Crossfield, R.T. (1989) A study of some key techniques used in planning for total quality management. MSc Thesis, Manchester School of Management, UMIST.
24. Crossfield, R.T. and Dale, B.G. (1990) Mapping quality assurance systems: a methodology. *Quality and Reliability Engineering International*, **6** (3), 167–78.
25. Hesford, M.G. and Dale, B.G. (1991) Quality costing at British Aerospace Dynamics: a case study. *Proceedings of the Institution of Mechanical Engineers*, 205 (G5), 53–7.
26. Plunkett, J.J. and Dale, B.G. (1988) Quality-related costings: Findings from an industry-based study. *Engineering Management International*, **4** (4), 247–57.

Reporting of quality costs | 5

5.1 INTRODUCTION

The growth of interest in quality as a contributor to competitiveness and marketability has stimulated organizational concern for the economic effects of quality. Companies are now beginning to amass and use quality cost data but in a limited way, using mainly scrap and rework analysis and warranty claims. It is encouraging to find such facts being used even if they are not assembled as a formalized quality costing report. Because scrap and rework costs frequently amount to an impressive sum of money, there is often a tendency to assume that they represent the whole cost, or indeed a reluctance to investigate more closely in case they turn out to be even larger. The preparation of quality costs and their presentation and reporting in a formal manner are aspects of quality costing to which organizations have perhaps given insufficient attention. Quality cost reporting is not yet widely accepted as one of the normal activities in reporting of quality performance.

The objectives of quality cost collection and the views on what costs should or should not be collected on a regular basis have been discussed in Chapter 4. This chapter examines the key issues to be considered in the reporting of quality costs. It opens by examining how costs can be extracted from existing systems. This is followed by examining some fundamentals of quality cost reporting and typical reporting formats. The chapter closes by discussing the merits of economic cost of quality models.

5.2 EXTRACTING QUALITY COSTS FROM EXISTING COMPANY SYSTEMS

Quality cost information needs to be produced from a company's existing system. It is easier to develop a quality costing system in a 'greenfields' situation as opposed to attempting to break into an established system. A common fallacy is that larger companies have accounting systems from which it is relatively easy to extract quality-related costs. In general, such companies have large immutable accounting systems and practices which are often imposed by a head office function with little flexibility to provide quality costs. The situation is compounded if the head office is remote and located in another country. On the other hand, smaller companies are less likely to have a full-time professionally qualified person responsible for management accounting.

Some of the difficulties in obtaining quality cost data are related to organizational structures and with the accountancy systems used. it is well known that accounting systems are inflexible. Few companies set up matrix accounting systems which allow costs to be collected by topic (e.g. product and service quality) across the traditional functional groups (e.g. sales, production/operations, research and development) and it is seldom the case that all the costs attributable to a topic such as quality are incurred under a single cost centre. The use of activity based costing (ABC) systems ('Cost attribution to cost units on the basis of benefit received from indirect activities e.g. ordering, setting-up assuring quality (CIMA [1]) should make it easier to gather quality-related costs; details of ABC are provided by Innes and Mitchell [2] and Bailey [3]. These systems are used to enable more accurate calculations of product costs to be made and tend to focus on values at an activity level. This enables the quality cost associated with an activity to be obtained more easily. ABC is of particular benefit in identifying costs in non-manufacturing areas. A process management structure in which a manager is responsible for a complete process regardless of functional structures is also an aid to the identification, collection and reporting of quality cost data.

There is a widely held view that cost information is easily obtainable if a company wishes to obtain it. We do not subscribe to this view. For example, Eldridge and Dale [4] reporting on a quality costing exercise carried out in an organization employing around 300 personnel across two sites and manufacturing industrial valves state:

> Very little information existed in a form that could be directly transferred into a quality cost report. Much of the quality cost information was buried so deep in the accounting system that retrieval was impracticable. On the other hand a considerable amount of information lay dormant.

They also say:

> Quality cost items such as rework were lost in the accounts and whilst the servicing section keep very comprehensive records of all warranty work, the warranty activity was not monitored. The only account that included quality costs was headed – 'castings rejected'.

Companies which collect quality costs have developed their systems as one aspect of gathering quality-related information in attempting to monitor quality peformance. Another factor has been the economic and competitive pressure which has caused companies to look in more detail at appraisal activities and the costs of failure, with a view to facilitating improvements and reducing costs. Such companies have based their systems and methods on what they are doing in terms of the technology, product type, processes and dealings with suppliers and customers, rather than on any published list of cost elements, or categorization into the classical activities of prevention, appraisal and failure.

5.3 SOME FUNDAMENTALS OF QUALITY COST REPORTING

In order for matters to become part of a routine costing system it is first necessary to record the activity or transaction routinely. Once it has been decided which costs are relevant to the organization, and which are insignificant, it is important to collect and display all those costs which have been decided upon, and also to indicate the existence, by a suitable description, of the relevant costs which cannot yet be quantified. Eldridge and Dale [4] suggest that two categories should be used in a separate section of the quality cost report for these unquantifiable costs 'identified but not quantified' and 'not identified but it is thought to comprise a quality cost'. This is important, because, first, reporting only part of the costs, without some form of qualification, can be very misleading, and, second, reporting the existence of unquantified costs keeps them in view of management, helps to ensure they are not forgotten and encourages attempts to find ways of measuring them.

The creation of a quality-related cost file, integrated with the existing costing system but perhaps with some additional expenses codes should not present many problems; collecting the data will be much more difficult. Those quality cost elements which come from within the quality assurance department may be easy to obtain but those from other departments may be more difficult, especially if it is suspected that the data may be used to attack them and their staff in some future improvement activity. Nevertheless, provision should be made in the file for collecting such data, even though it may take a long time to obtain satisfactory returns on a routine basis.

The following two examples from Allied Signal Ltd, Turbochargers, Skelmersdale plant show the detail for two particular cost categories (appraisal equipment costs and rework costs), the activities encompassed within each category and the appropriate departmental account codes from which the data is collected.

Quality cost category – appraisal equipments costs

Cost of inspection, test and laboratory equipment used by personnel in categories –

(i) supplier quality appraisal
(ii) tool/process equipment appraisal
(iii) in process and final appraisal

Depreciation cost of capitalised equipment.
Costs of the gauge calibration service.
Cost of outside calibration/maintenance service.

Departmental account codes

17314   Quality assurance depreciation
           Test/teamdown equipment depreciation
           Dye penetrant equipment depreciation
           Metallurgical laboratory depreciation
           Quality assurance calibration service (standards room)
17124   Outside calibration/maintenance

Quality cost category – rework costs

Total cost (labour, material, burden) of all rework, fault finding, or repair work done to manufactured or assembled product.
Salary and associated costs of staff performing fault finding and troubleshooting activities.

Costs incurred due to –
(i) incorrect design
(ii) defective purchased item (unless charged to vendor)
(iii) incorrectly performed manufacturing operations

Cost of material review board co-ordinator.
Do not include costs of unplanned extra operations due to lack of capability.

Departmental account codes

17   Material review board co-ordinator
        Job card recorded rework

A popular view amongst quality management practitioners is that quality cost reports should indicate the origin of failure costs by department (e.g. design, production, engineering, purchasing and marketing), in the hope that adverse publicity will provoke remedial action. Unfortunately, it may also antagonize departmental managers so that they become unco-operative in providing information for the report. It may even result in the deliberate obscuring of quality performance evidence and other counter-productive actions. Proclaiming the sins of others is not guaranteed to win co-operation and support. It could also stifle the internal customer–supplier relationship. Emphasis on improvement opportunities rather than attribution of failures may help to avoid such difficulties. It is also important to emphasize that the data will not be used for rationalization exercises and downsizing operations. For those organizations which have been engaged in a process of continuous improvement for some years and a 'blame-free' culture is in place, this method of reporting quality costs is a reality and can be effective. On the other hand, for those organizations just starting out on the TQM journey it will almost run into objections, 'resistance to change' and 'fear' problems. This is especially the case if staff suspect that a large part of their day-to-day tasks are non-value adding. The reporting system should not be such that people become defensive and spend more time arguing about the data than they do about taking improvement action.

It should go without saying that the purpose of a quality-related cost report is not primarily to promote the interest of the quality assurance department. Neither is to display the quality cost contributions of other departments. Such analyses are secondary objectives and should only be stated in the context of actual and achievable performance and the known real constraints as, for example, in a project format.

For maximum impact quality costs should be included in a company's cost reporting system. In the main, reporting on quality costs is a sub-section of the general reporting of the quality assurance department activities so that cost data can become entangled and buried with failure data and other quality statistics and as such loses their impact. For maximum impact quality costs should be included in a company's overall cost-reporting system. They could even be considered as the subject of a separate management report. Unfortunately, the lack of sophistication of quality costs collection and measurement is such that it does not allow quality cost reporting to be carried out in the same detail and to the same standard as, for example, the production/ operations, and marketing functions. Often quality reports do not separate out costs as an aspect of quality worthy of presentation and comment in its own right. This usually results in cost information not being used to its full potential. Separating costs from other aspects of quality and discussing them in the context of other costs would improve the clarity of reports and help to provide better continuity from one report to the next.

Senior managers are like everyone else in wanting easy decisions to make. Having costs, which are the bases of business decisions, tangled up with a considerable amount of technical and quality information makes the data less clear than they could be and often provides an excuse to defer a decision. The problem for senior managers should not be to disentangle and analyse data in order to decide what to do, it should be to decide whether to act, choose which course of action to pursue, ensure provision of necessary resources and, by comparing the quality costs to those budgeted, assess the effectiveness of the planned improvements. Problems, possible solutions and their resource requirements should be presented in the context of accountability centres which have the necessary authority, if not the resources, to execute the decisions of the senior management team.

The influence of senior management is vital in the reporting of quality costs. If there is no pressure to reduce costs against mutually agreed targets then the reporting will become routine and people, quite naturally, will devote their efforts to what they believe are the more important events. It is important that senior management develops a quality cost reduction strategy.

Quality costing in a multi-site operation involves the development of a standard reporting method to compare costs and establish best practice. This is especially important when the sites are based in different countries with different accounting conventions. In developing such a system consideration needs to be given to basic definitions, outlined in Chapter 3.

Overall, the standard of reporting of quality costs in European companies is poor. Good standards are essential if reports are to counter management indifference to TQM, make an impact and provoke action. However, it should be noted that putting costs on quality-related matters and reporting them is only a first step towards drawing the issue of quality more into the business arena.

5.4 REPORTING FORMATS

As might be expected, organizations use a variety of quality cost reporting formats and methods of presenting the data.

Presentation of costs under prevention, appraisal, and internal and external failure, is the most popular approach for reporting quality costs, albeit with different cost elements appropriate to different industries as discussed in Chapter 4. This format is favoured by quality assurance managers, perhaps because, on the face of it, it forms a balance sheet for the quality function with prevention equivalent to investment, appraisal to operating cost, and failure to (negative) profit. However, in some industries the time lag arising between action and effect are such that concurrent expenditures on, say, prevention activities and external failure such as warranty claims, bear no relation whatsoever to each other.

An important consideration in the presentation and communication of quality-related costs is the needs of the recipients and it may be worth presenting information in several different formats according to particular interests and likely use of the information. In all cases the cost information should be presented in a form that is immediately accessible and useful and that the recipients can identify with. The reporting format should be standardized. Typical of the questions which need to be kept in mind in deciding the reporting format are: 'What are we trying to communicate?'; 'What will people understand from the data?'; 'Will it encourage people to address problems?'; and 'Will the data facilitate improvement action?' For example, weekly reports of costs of scrap and rework are of greatest value to shop floor supervisors, and monthly reports of total costs, highlighting current problems and

Cost of Quality Report   Division: Local currency
(Equivalent to schedule VOR-16)   Month: July 93   exchange rate 1.65

	Current month			Year to date		
Quality costs category	Quality cost	% of sales	% Conv. cost	Quality cost	% of sales	% Conv. cost
1. Prevention costs						
a. Quality Engineering	32	0.4	1.19	224	0.5	1.4
b. Quality Training	-	-	-	-	-	-
Total prevention costs	32	0.4	1.19	224	0.5	1.4
2. Appraisal costs						
a. Supplier quality	15.6	0.19	0.58	116.6	0.27	0.7
b. In-process & finished product	49	0.61	1.8	380	0.9	2.3
c. 100% Insp. + VSR + gas stand	13	0.16	0.49	102	0.23	0.6
d. Appraisal equipment	12	0.15	0.45	86.1	0.2	0.5
Total appraisal costs	89.6	1.11	3.32	684.7	1.6	4.1
3. Internal failure costs						
a. Rework	3.4	0.04	0.13	23.4	0.05	0.14
b. Scrap	49.5	0.6	1.8	307.5	0.7	1.86
c. Substandard product	-	-	-	-	-	-
d. Extra operations	9	0.1	0.34	68	0.16	0.4
e. Other int. failure expense	22	0.27	0.8	159.4	0.37	0.97
Total internal failure costs	83.9	1.01	3.07	558.3	1.28	3.37
4. External failure costs						
a. Customer returns	4.5	0.06	0.17	30.5	0.07	0.18
b. On-site Insp. & test	-	-	-	-	-	-
c. Warranty expense	32	0.4	1.19	154	0.36	0.9
d. Other Ext. Failure Exp.	1.6	0.02	0.06	11.6	0.03	0.07
Total external failure costs	38.1	0.48	1.42	196.1	0.46	1.15
1993 Actual quality costs	243.6	3.0	9.0	1663	3.84	10.02
1993 Plan quality costs	273	3.4	10.2	1456	3.4	8.8
1992 Actual quality costs	226	4.18	9.91	1541	3.6	9.91

References	Current month		Year to date	
	Actual	AFP	Actual	AFP
Sales	8007	6945	12814	42531
Conversion cost*	2678	2469	16517	16440

*Conversion Cost-Labor and manufacturing overhead necessary to convert material to available form

Figure 5.1 Quality cost report form (prevention-appraisal-failure).

COST OF QUALITY: 1992			
	Product Type 1	Product Type 2	Total

	Product Type 1	Product Type 2	Total
Sales Volume	193,497	204,293	397,790
Annual Number of Products Rejected	21,973	26,781	48,754
% of Output	10.9%	12.2%	11.6%

	£000	£000	£000
Material Costs	568	275	843
Processing Costs	536	432	968
Short Shipments			105
Heat Treatment			158
Annual rework cost	184	262	446
Outside Inspection	233	181	414
Intermediate Inspection	225	71	296
Brinell	63	45	108
Final/Customer Inspection	540	385	925
Hydraulic Test	271	192	463
Dip Weigh	63	45	108
Special Products			158
Laboratory			143
Test House			146
Quality Control			195
Customer Complaints/Product Liability			68
TOTAL QUALITY COSTS			5,544

Figure 5.2 Quality cost report form (by product type).

progress with quality improvement projects, would be most suitable for middle management, while total costs, costs to act on and adverse trends or deviations from the norm are needed by the Chief Executive Officer and members of the senior management team. While selective reporting of this type has its merits, it should be done against a background of the total cost of quality. Ideally quality cost reports should show opportunities for cost savings leading to increase profits or price reductions.

Figures 5.1 and 5.2 show formats used by two different companies for reporting quality costs to senior management. Both companies are involved in the manufacture of high integrity products where failure in service can be catastrophic. The first format uses the prevention, appraisal and failure format and tracks costs by month and cumulatively to year end. The second format is by the company's two major product types and relates yearly costs to major cost elements.

An assembler of trucks takes a global approach to quality cost collection and reporting. They use the usual three quality costs categories – prevention cost, verification costs (appraisal costs) and failure costs. Failure costs and verification are collected on a monthly basis by department. Figure 5.3 shows an example of the assembly department quality costs. The figures from each department are then compiled into a monthly quality loss cost summary report for senior management (Fig. 5.4). A similar format (Fig. 5.5) is used by a manufacturer of packaging which used a spreadsheet format to present to the managing director and production director a monthly quality cost report. The data is categorized using PAF and costs are attributed by function.

An example where quality cost reporting is kept simple and clear is a company involved in graphics-related products. Details of the reporting are shown in Figs 5.6 and 5.7.

The first of these (Fig. 5.6) shows expenditure for one month against what are perceived to be the major quality-related cost topics. The report is business oriented by using the data to produce projected annual costs and by expressing these as percentages of anticipated turnover. It is interesting to note that in the earlier of the two examples the arithmetic is not precise. Figures are rounded and summed such that the month-to-year factor of 12 does not apply uniformly throughout the report. It is also noticeable that there is no warranty cost and that an item for which there had been no expenditure in the month being reported contains an entry in the anticipated annual expenditure. Total quality costs of 33% of annual sales turnover seem an horrendous sum (scrap is costed at sales value). Nonetheless the company is a successful competitive company which has 'seen off' a number of its competitors. It is in a business which makes technologically complex products which have very stringent visual standards applied to them by customers who are large, powerful, technically expert and quality conscious. High scrap levels are intrinsic to the technology. Perhaps the relatively high expenditure of 3% of annual sales turnover on prevention costs is a better guide than failure costs are to the company's standing

Assembly Dept Q-costs

Failure costs

F No	Description	Number of times (admin)	Man hours used (H)	Charged at (£)	Q-cost (H) × (£)	
F11	Line reject scrap (part cost)					
	Line reject scrap (administration cost)					
	Rework to line rejects					
	Rework on assembly line				Total failure cost (F11)	
F13	Production errors (production on line)					
	Rectification area corrections (not including insp & test)				Total failure cost (F13)	
F16	Assemble wrong truck due to wrong order (job sheet)				Total failure cost (F16)	
F17	Design incorrect (fitting time ie TM)				Total failure cost (F17)	
					Total failure cost	

Verification costs

F No	Type of verification	Number of times (admin)	Man hours used (H)	Charged at (£)	Q-cost (H) × (£)
V4	Assembly line inspectors, equipment and testing				
	Audit bay & auditors				
	Clerical support				Total verification cost (V4)

Figure 5.3 Assembly department quality costs.

Date _____

Quality loss cost summary report

Department responsible for Q.L.C.	Failure cost Internal — Design	Purch	Mat cont	Prod eng	Assy	External — Service	Verification cost — Design	Purch	Mat cont	Prod eng	Assy	Total quality loss cost — Current month Quality costs	% of sales	Year to date Quality costs	% of sales
Cost control															
Administration		F19	F18												
Prod. planning															
Product planning	F1	F2	F3	F4											
Prod. dev/design	F5	F6	F7	F8	F17		V1								
Procurement		F9	F10		F11				V3						
Production				F12	F13					V6	V4/5				
Sales/marketing		F14	F15		F16										
After sales supp.															

TQLC expressed per truck	Month	Year to date
Number of trucks produced		
TQLC/trucks		

Warranty claim costs	Year to date
	F	FL
Warranty claims/truck	

Quality loss cost report pages

QLRC1 Front page summary report
QLRC2 Failure costs definitions
QLRC3 Appraisal costs definitions
QLRC4 Design quality costs
QLRC5 Purchasing & projects quality costs
QLRC6 Goods in & stores quality costs
QLRC7 Assembly quality costs
QLRC8 Production/plant engineering quality costs

Quality loss cost verification costs and failure costs come under the joint heading of quality loss costs. Both arise either because we failed to get it right first time or are not sure that we got it right first time.

Verification costs are the costs required to verify and follow up that a job or a product has been done 'right first time'.

Failure costs are all the costs that the company must bear when things are not done 'right first time'.

Figure 5.4 Quality loss costs summary report.

CATEGORY   **DEPARTMENT**

CATEGORY			Sales Office	Material Control	Production Control	Corrugator	Conversion	Warehouse	Laboratory	Accounts	Marketing	Total	Category Total	Category (%)
A1	time	Q. Systems	–	–	–	–	–	–	240.00	–	–	240.00		
A2	time	Control Equip.	–	–	–	–	–	–	–	–	–	.00		
A3	time	Calibration	–	–	–	–	–	–	240.00	–	ins.	240.00		
A4	time	S.Q.A.	–	ins.	–	–	–	–	160.00	–	ins.	160.00		
A5	time	Training	ins.	ins.	10.00	ins.	5.00	ins.	20.00	–	–	35.00		
A6	time	Audits	ins.	ins.	ins.	ins.	ins.	ins.	200.00	–	–	200.00		
A7	time	Improvement	ins.	ins.	10.00	ins.	ins.	ins.	240.00	–	–	250.00		
A8	time	Admin.	800.00	–	200.00	–	200.00	–	30.00	–	50.00	1280.00	2405.00	8.5
B1	time	I.M.C.	–	–	–	–	–	–	280.00	–	ins.	280.00		
B2	time	P'cess Insp.	–	–	–	200.00	400.00	–	360.00	–	–	960.00		
B3	time	Final Insp.	–	–	–	–	–	–	480.00	–	40.00	520.00		
B4	material	Test Mats.	–	–	–	–	–	–	waste	–	–	.00		
B5	time	Test Data	–	–	–	–	–	–	40.00	–	–	40.00	1800.00	6.3
C1	material	Xs. waste	–	–	–	19604.52	see Corr.	80.00	–	–	ins.	19604.52		
C2	time	Rework	–	–	–	160.00	240.00	n.r.	80.00	–	–	560.00		
C3	time	Re-test	–	–	–	n.r.	n.r.	n.r.	80.00	–	–	80.00		
C4	time	Faulty Mats.	–	40.00	–	30.00	ins.	80.00	40.00	–	–	110.00		
	material		–	no loss	–	–	ins.	–	–	–	–	.00		
C5	material	Concessions	see C1 / .00	–	.00	ins.	ins.	–	10.00	–	–	10.00		
C6	material	Up-grading	–	230.18	618.82	–	–	–	–	–	–	849.00		
C7	time	Defect Analy's	40.00	ins.	40.00	40.00	–	ins.	120.00	–	–	200.00	21413.52	75.5
D1	time	Admin.	136.00	–	.00	850.00	96.00	43.00	–	30.00	9.00	1164.00		
D2	material	Claims	.00	–	–	1509.00	.00	80.00	–	–	.00	1589.00		
D3	time	Rework	–	–	–	–	.00	–	–	–	–	.00		
	material		–	–	–	–	–	–	–	–	–	.00	2753.00	9.7
												28371.52		100.0

Notes: (1) All costs in (£)
              (2) ins. = insignificant
              (3) n.r. = not recorded

Time per Hour – £10.00

Figure 5.5 An example of a monthly quality cost report.

COST OF QUALITY REPORT

		Month	Projected yearly total	Percentage turnover
Failure costs internal				
In-house rejects	(Product X)	34 700	416 400	18.4%
	(Other)	11 700	14 700	6.2%
Rework–remake		1 060	12 700	0.6%
Rework–re-inspection		130	1 500	0.1%
Give away–excess material		355	4 200	0.2%
Extra operations–excess time (total)		48	600	–
Down time – Lost time (total)		1 604	14 400	0.6%
	Total	49 600	590 500	26.0%
External				
Customer service (Quality reasons)		–	9 000	0.4%
Customer rejects		3 675	44 100	1.9%
	Total	3 675	53 100	2.3%
Appraisal costs Inspection				
	Total	3 980	47 000	2.1%
Prevention costs				
Laboratory (60% total)		1 290	15 500	0.7%
Quality admin.		2 410	28 900	1.3%
Patrol inspection		1 850	11 900	0.5%
Other		950	11 400	0.5%
	Total	6 500	67 700	2.9%
	Overall total	63 755	758 300	33.4%
	Turnover	180 600	2 267 800	100%

Figure 5.6 An example of a monthly quality cost report.

COST OF QUALITY REPORT

First quarter

	Months 03, 04, 05	Percentage of quarter's turnover	Projected annual total	Percentage annual turnover
Failure costs				
internal				
In-house rejects (Product X)	270 554	31%	1 082 216	–
In-house rejects (Other)	33 125	4%	132 500	–
Rework–remake	1 690	–	6 760	–
Rework–re-inspection	–			
Give away–excess material	2 480	–	9 920	–
Extra operations–excess time (total)	300	–	1 200	–
Down time – Lost time (total)	6 976	1%	27 904	–
Total	315 125	36%	1 260 500	–
External				
Customer service (Quality reasons)	2 000	–	8 000	–
Customer rejects	23 189	4%	92 756	
Total	25 189	3%	100 756	–
Appraisal costs				
Inspection Total	22 840	3%	91 360	–
Prevention costs				
Laboratory (60% total)	8 990	1%	35 960	–
Quality admin.	182 530	2%	74 120	–
Patrol inspection	4 500	1%	18 000	–
Total	32 020	4%	128 080	–
Overall total	395 174	46%	1 580 696	–
Turnover	866 205		3 464 820	

Figure 5.7 Three-month quality cost report.

respect to quality performance and attitudes, although some quality practitioners would not accept that patrol inspection is a prevention activity.

The second report (Fig. 5.7) reports costs approximately one year later and shows a slightly amended format. The contribution of one product line to scrap costs is formally acknowledged by featuring it separately. The costs for the quarter are accurately scaled up to a projected annual total. Percentage figures have been rounded to the nearest whole number and individual items costing less than 0.5% of annual sales turnover have been omitted from the proportioning exercise.

One of the best examples of quality costing witnessed is from a manufacturer of high technology generating equipment. It has been measuring quality costs for 10 years. During the last five years these costs have become a permanent part of the management information system. Information is appropriately presented to meet the different needs of directors, managers and supervisors. What is to be included in the report, how costs can be measured, and how to improve presentation of the data, are constantly under review. Costs are produced or endorsed by the accounts department. Evidence of the status of quality-related costs as an important business expenditure is shown by expressing them as a fraction of the work's recovered cost.

Presentation of the data is excellent. Wordage is kept to a minimum. The cost summary is kept simple, featuring only 12 cost elements but providing

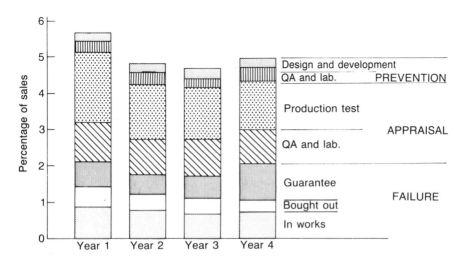

Figure 5.8 Quality costs.

Table 5.1 Quality costs

Activity			Unquality costs			
Failure	In-works	Scrap	287 335	286 537	324 655	304 784
		Rework	47 455	149 142	140 129	157 385
	Bought-out	Scrap	251 530	240 053	259 488	182 524
		Rework	34 000	34 400	34 273	19 771
	Guarantee	MG & C.	341 855	288 631	390 688	604 596
	Total failure		£1 062 175	£998 763	£1 149 233	£1 269 060
	Percentage of sales		2.00	1.65	1.65	2.02
Appraisal	Quality assurance		521 800	561 304	638 588	577 482
	Laboratory		30 000	33 050	35 310	36 934
	Production test		1 001 500	670 000	957 940	804 991
	Total appraisal		£1 553 300	£1 464 354	£1 631 838	£1 419 407
	Percentage of sales		2.93	2.42	2.35	2.25
Prevention	Q & R programme		0	8 039	3 727	17 159
	Quality assurance		100 058	123 213	180 114	162 880
	Laboratory		40 000	44 015	47 080	49 246
	Design/development		125 000	150 000	160 5000	175 000
	Total prevention		£265 058	£325 267	£391 421	£404 285
	Percentage of sales		0.50	0.54	0.56	0.64
	Total unquality costs		£2 880 533	£2 788 384	£3 172 492	3 092 752
	Percentage of sales		5.43	4.61	4.56	4.91

historical data for comparisons to be made (Table 5.1 and Fig. 5.8). An interesting feature of the report is the isolation of failure costs owing to bought-out materials and components as a separate cost element (it would have been expected that the costs of scrap owing to suppliers fault would be recoverable from the suppliers). It is evidence of the company's recognition that the quality of goods purchased is an important factor in its own attempts to achieve high quality, and ensures that supplier quality assurance remains a high-priority prevention activity.

Subsidiary data are presented in the form of histograms and pie charts. A noticeable feature is that all cost data are presented on charts with standard ranges and scales. Thus the relative magnitude of cost elements plotted on separate charts is kept in perspective, making comparisons and judgements easier. The first (or highest-ranking) set of subsidiary data presented in this way contains the following information.

- *Chart 1.*   Three-period average percentage of works recovered cost versus cost periods over four years for (a) in-works, (b) bought-out, and site defective costs, plus quality assurance department costs, and (c) in-works and bought-out (net) defective costs (scrap and rework).
- *Chart 2.*   In-works scrap and rework costs. Actual costs and percentages of works recovered cost by period, and average cost per period for the preceding three years.
- *Chart 3.*   (a) Summed in-works scrap costs of parts supply division; assembly, test, packaging; and others, by period. Average cost per period for each of the preceding three years is also indicated. Pie charts show contribution of work centres to current period costs.
- *Chart 4.*   In-works rework costs broken down as in Chart 3.
- *Chart 5.*   Total bought-out defective costs: (a) as credit and net cost by period, and average per period for each of the preceidng three years, (b) as percentage of works recovered cost, before and after credit (Figure 5.9).
- *Chart 6.*   Bought-out defective costs of scrap. (a) Histogram of summed contributions from raw materials, sub-contracted work and proprietary goods, by period, and average per period for each of the preceding three years. (b–c) Pie charts of 20 individual suppliers' contributions to the total. (Fig. 5.10)
- *Chart 7.*   Bought-out defective costs of rework broken down as for Chart 6.
- *Chart 8.*   Site defective costs. Actual and percentage of works recovered cost, by period, and averages per period for each of the preceding three years.

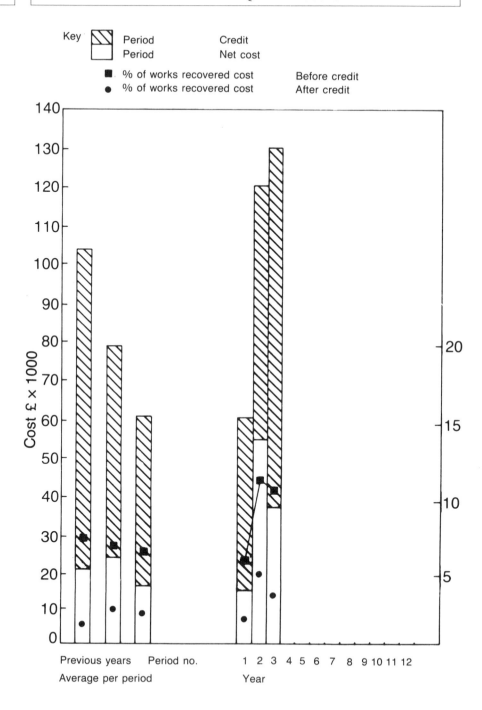

Figure 5.9 Bought-out defective costs.

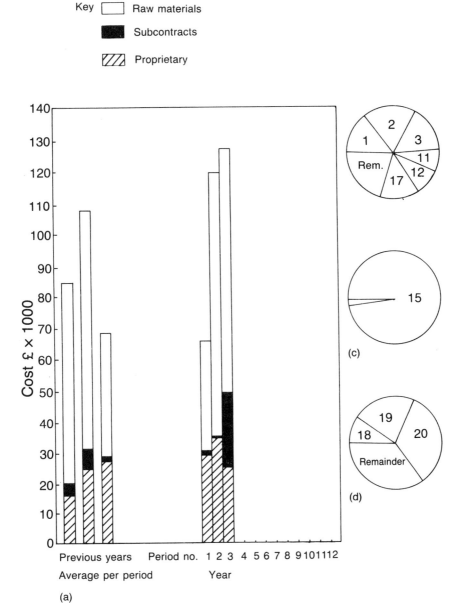

Figure 5.10 Bought-out defective costs (scrap).

- *Chart 9.* Quality assurance department and materials tests. Actual and percentage of works recovered cost, by period, and averages per period for each of the preceding three years.

All the summarized data referred to above is backed by detailed information – especially the failure costs. There is adequate documentation available to indicate that none of the major cost areas is likely to have been overlooked. For example, the consequential costs of defective materials/parts and scrap, and of design errors, are stressed in the company's reports.

One of the best examples of reporting quality costs to line operators is from a supplier of automotive safety components including seat belt restraints and air bags. The accumulated reject performance along with the cost of internal scrap is visibly displayed for each product line – safety belts, buckles, window regulators and door locks. The accumulated reject performance for all products is also provided to each line. Examples from the door locks and restraints product lines are given in Figs 5.11 and 5.12, respectively.

Consideration should also be given to displaying quality cost data as part of an organization's visual management system. In this way information is diffused rapidly and it is a valuable method of encouraging everyone in the organization to assist in reducing the costs of non-conformance. Attention should be given to the use of histograms and pie charts with standard ranges and scales. This ensures that the relative magnitude of cost elements plotted on separate charts is kept in perspective, thus making comparisons and judgements easier.

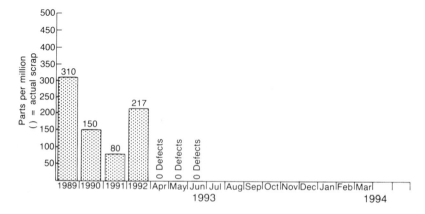

Figure 5.11 Accumulated reject performance (door locks).

Other areas of quality cost reporting which need consideration, include the following.

- There should be clarity and simplicity of reporting, with minimum use of words.
- A summary of the action taken should be given.
- The cost data must be complete. Consideration must be given not only to monthly figures but perhaps moving annual totals to assist with the identification of trends.
- The summarized data should be supported by detailed information, especially the failure costs.
- The data should give guidance and encouragement to people on how the costs may be reduced.

Some organizations employ a two-tier quality costing reporting system. Each department identifies the major costs of non-conformance which are specific to them and the department manager is responsible for activating improvement projects to reduce these costs. The key non-conformance costs on a company-wide basis are identified and individual executives made responsible for their reduction. The reporting of both departmental and company key quality costs is carried out on a monthly basis.

When reporting costs at regular intervals it is important to ensure that sets of data remain comparable with one another. If additional cost elements are

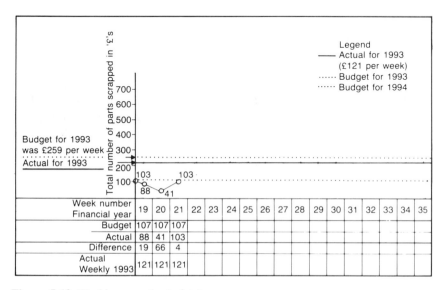

Figure 5.12 Weekly scrap (restraints).

included as an organization becomes more experienced in quality costing these must be reported separately until an appropriate opportunity arises to include them. It is also worth coding each cost element to indicate its source and status (e.g. accounting records, calculation from standard data, calculation through surrogates, average rates, estimates) and various other cost apportionment.

Many manufacturing companies make goods for stock and it may be many months or possibly years after manufacture that a product goes into service. This raises the issue of comparability (or even relevance) of categories of one cost with another. Much has been written about definition, categorization, and reporting of quality costs, and the implication is always that the reported costs are concurrent and relevant to each other. Clearly prevention costs should have a bearing on appraisal and failure costs, and expenditure on appraisal may influence the magnitude and distribution (between internal and external) of failure costs, but not necessarily concurrently. In some industries the time lag arising between action and effect are such that concurrent expenditures on, say, prevention and warranty, bear no relation whatever to each other. Reporting only concurrent costs in isolation can be misleading and it is perhaps worth considering in some cases contemporary costs as well as concurrent costs.

The time-lag between manufacture, the sales of the product and warranty claims and payment is often so long that warranty costs should not be reported in the same context as current quality costs. In some cases the warranty and guarantee period may not be initiated until several years after the sale of the product to the customer. Such a time lag can considerably distort the quality performance of the organization as depicted by the level of quality performance of the organization as depicted by the level of quality-related costs. Warranty costs in any period may bear no relation to other quality costs incurred in the same period, and should not be reported in the same context. To include them can distort considerably the quality performance of the company or department as depicted by the levels and ratios of quality-related costs. The delays may also mean that the causes underlying the failures leading to the claims may no longer be a problem. If the effects of the time lag and the effects of price changes, inflation and exchange rates, are added, there can be no doubt that warranty costs ought to be reported as a separate category of quality cost and not considered in the context of current quality costs. In the context of other (non-quality) costs it should be reported as a loss, and related to other losses (and profits).

5.5 'ECONOMIC COST OF QUALITY' MODELS

It is apparent that the costs and economics of many quality-related activities, including investment in prevention and appraisal activities, are not known.

It is perhaps surprising therefore to find in the literature a number of diagrammatic representations of quality-cost models which purport to show relationships between the major quality-cost categories. Many discussions of quality costs in the literature feature such a model, but many quality management practitioners are doubtful about the representations and feel that they can be misleading.

The general suppositions underlying all these notional models are that investment in prevention and appraisal activities will bring handsome rewards from reduced failure costs, and that further investment in prevention activities will show profits from reduced appraisal costs. However, despite these common principles there are wide differences between some of the models.

Plunkett and Dale [5] have examined in detail these various 'cost of quality' models; the main findings of this piece of research are now summarised.

- There is a striking dissimilarity between the notional models (e.g. Besterfield [6], Harrington [7] and Juran [8] and those based on actual data (e.g. Campanella and Corcoran [9], Huckett [10] and Hagan [11]), see Plunkett and Dale [5].
- The notional models conveniently, and in some cases inexplicably, combine major quality-cost categories. Some of the models do not distinguish between internal and external failure costs; some combine prevention and appraisal costs, thereby suggesting that reduction of failure costs by increasing the combined expenditure on prevention and appraisal is the prime strategy for reducing quality costs. In fact, reduction of appraisal costs by increasing preventative measures may be a reasonable and worthwhile alternative. Indeed in some cases it is the easiest and quickest way to achieve substantial reductions in quality costs. However, expenditure on appraisals, above a certain threshold level, tends to move costs from external to internal failure categories and savings derive mainly from detecting faults sooner. The combination of cost categories is dependent upon the objective of the quality costing exercise. If, for example, the objective is to reduce failure costs, there may be little point in distinguishing between prevention and appraisal costs. If, on the other hand, the objective is to reduce failure and/or appraisal costs, then it may be unimportant to separate them. Combining different categories of costs together obscures the relationship between categories of activity and between their associated costs.
- There is a diversity of measures of quality used as the abscissae in indicating the relationship between the major quality cost categories. The models based on real data are plotted against a linear time base rather than against some measure of quality performance.
- Some of the models imply nonsensically extravagent returns on investment in prevention and/or appraisal. Indeed, it is noticeable that whenever investment in prevention expenditure is discussed there is an

implicit expectation of a large return on the investment. Investments in prevention through capital or resources often involve stepwise increases because of the generally low level of expenditure on prevention, but are never represented as such by the models. While recognizing that companies are in business to make profit, and that there may be competition for limited resources, the payback expected (and sometimes proffered) from investment in quality improvement activities seems unusually high, and since high returns are usually associated with high risk, one wonders whether, as a general rule, the benefits from investment in prevention are seen in business circles as being problematical.

● There is little hard evidence to support the notion that quality-cost curves are exponential and give rise to cost minima.

● The view that many of the widely publicized quality economics models are inaccurate, and may even be of the wrong form, is widely supported by quality managers. Everyone would like to have a valid model which they could use to assess their present situation and predict the effects of changes. Companies are always keen to learn by how much their quality costs might be reduced through quality improvement activities. So far as is known there are insufficient data available to construct such a model, though there should be enough collective experience available to make a reasonable hypothesis as to the shape and the relative proportions of the constituent costs in the diagram. For example, there are reasonably good grounds for believing that optimum quality, if it exists, is near to the highest attainable standard of quality. The model should take account of the fact that investments in prevention through capital or resources often involve relatively large stepwise increases. It should also reflect the often considerable time lag to be expected between investment in prevention and/or appraisal and reduction in failure costs, and especially in warranty costs.

5.6 SUMMARY

Presentation of costs under prevention, appraisal and internal and external failure is the most popular approach. Companies should not be blinkered by this categorization and need to examine the best ways of reporting to suit their own particular circumstances.

An important consideration in the presentation of quality costs is the needs of the recipients and it may be worth presenting information in several different formats. This chapter has examined the merits of a number of methods of selective reporting, but such reporting should always be done against a background of the total costs. Ideally quality cost should show opportunities for cost savings leading to increased profit or price reductions.

Good standards of reporting are essential if the cost figures are to make an impact and provoke action. Quality cost reporting should become a regular practice but it must not become a chore. The key points to be considered in the reporting of costs in order to reduce them have been examined in the chapter.

For maximum impact quality costs should be included in a company's cost reporting system. Quality cost reporting is not yet widely accepted as one of the normal activities in reporting quality performance. Quality cost collection and measurement lacks sophistication and cannot be carried out in the same detail and to the same standard as, for example, the collection of production operations and marketing functions costs. In the last few years, a number of organizations have started to address these two issues.

REFERENCES

1. Chartered Institute of Management Accountants (1991) *Managing Accounting – Official Terminology*, The Chartered Institute of Management Accountants, London.
2. Innes, J. and Mitchell, F. *Activity Based Costing: A Review with Case Studies*, The Chartered institute of Management Accountants, London.
3. Bailey, J. Implementation of ABC systems by UK companies. *Management Accounting*, February, 30–31.
4. Eldridge, J. and Dale, B.G. (1989) Quality costing: the lessons learnt from a study carried out in two phases. *Engineering Costs and Production Economics*, **18** (1), 33–44.
5. Plunkett, J.J. and Dale, B.G. (1988) Quality costs: a critique of some 'economic cost of quality' models. *International Journal of Production Research*, **26** (11), 1713–26.
6. Besterfield, D.H. (1979) *Quality Control*, Prentice Hall.
7. Harrington, J.H. (1976) Quality costs – the whole and its parts – Part 1. *Quality*, **15**(5), 34–35.
8. Juran, J.M. (1988) *Quality Control Handbook*, McGraw Hill.
9. Campanella, J. and Corcoran, F.J. (1983) Principles of quality costs. *Quality Progress*, **16** (4), 16–21.
10. Huckett, J.D. (1985) An outline of the quality improvement process. *International Journal of Quality and Reliability Management*, **2** (2), 5–14.
11. Hagan, J.T. (1986) Quality costs, Chapter 7 of *Quality Management Handbook* (eds L. Walsh, R. Wurster and R.J. Kimber), Marcel Deker.

Uses of quality costs | 6

6.1 INTRODUCTION

The majority of writers on the subject of quality costing focus on the use of quality costs. Indeed there is no point in collecting costs information if it is not to be used. Its usefulness is the only justification for its collection and clearly this is one of the most important criteria in setting up a cost collection system. The collection of cost information should not be the final objective; it should be to facilitate improvement action. Most organizations are looking to quality cost data to show things that their other quality-related data does not reveal. This requirement raises two interesting points. First, in requiring cost data to be more useful than other data, it is implicit that use or usefulness is the principal criterion in collecting data. Second, it may not be necessary for cost data to actually add anything to other data on which it is based. Its usefulness may lie solely in being expressed in monetary terms. In general, companies tend to identify situations they would like to achieve through the use of cost information. By and large, questions about uses do not elicit answers which are specifically cost oriented (e.g. set cost reduction targets and establish cost efficiency measures).

The uses of quality costs are numerous and diverse, reflecting organizational needs and situations. However, they may be grouped into four broad categories. First, quality costs may be used to promote quality as a business parameter; second, they give rise to performance measures and facilitate improvement activities; third, they provide the means for planning and controlling future costs, and fourth, they act as motivators. The chapter discusses these four broad areas of usage.

6.2 PROMOTING QUALITY AS A BUSINESS PARAMETER

This first use – promoting quality as a business parameter – is usually expressed as attracting the attention of the board of directors and the senior management team by using their language (i.e. money) in order to help shock them into action in relation to quality improvement. However, Eldridge and Dale [1] warn that if the costs collected are substantially less than the typical 10–20% of annual sales turnover figure, which by now most managers are familiar with, it could work in the opposite manner and help to convince senior managers that the quality performance of the organization is satisfactory, when it is not. They also point out that if 'the costs uncovered are not of the magnitude anticipated, it may result in a search for something that was not there'.

There is little doubt that costs help to keep quality aspects of the business in the spotlight – but only if featured in the regular management accounts and reporting system. In promoting quality as an important business parameter some organizations go even further. Costs are used to illustrate that everyone's work does impinge on the quality of the product and/or service and to promote ownership for quality improvement. The success of gatherers and presenters of quality-related costs in promoting quality by means of costs is difficult to gauge. So far as is known there has been no formal study to determine how Chief Executive Officers who are aware of the importance of quality became so. It is clear that many executives got the message without having quality cost information to hand. Indeed, in some cases it is the other way around, in that a belief in the importance of quality to corporate health has prompted a quality costs investigation.

The situation has been encountered where the nature of the technology and processes is such that scrap and rework account for one quarter of a company's total costs. Some organizations once having identified their major quality costs become very concerned about the magnitude of the cost of scrap and rework. They often have no reason to suppose that their competitors are significantly less efficient than they themselves are, and recognize that such high scrap and rework costs could make them uncompetitive if their competitors achieve substantial breakthoughs in their process management and subsequently improve their yields. This must surely engender very different behaviour and attitudes to quality than in those organizations where the situation is not so severe. The same is true in the case of organizations who have to scrap all non-conforming products.

There is little doubt that high direct expenditures on quality-related matters seem to be acceptable to companies whose quality standards are necessarily very high and determined by mandatory regulation. For companies in these types of situations, quality is not just about saving costs and improving profitability, it must be fundamental to all their business vision, mission, objectives and activities. Hence, for them quality costing should be akin to business accounting.

Knowledge of quality-related costs enables business decisions about quality to be made in an objective manner. It permits the use of sensitivity analyses, discounted cash flow and other accounting methods and techniques for the evaluation of expenditure projects as in any other area of the business. In this way it helps companies to decide how, when and where to invest in prevention activities or equipment. This is a most valuable use of cost data. But even if full cost data are available it may not be useful for this purpose, because in many organizations the fundamental economics of prevention and/or appraisal do not seem to be well understood. Indeed, it is noticeable that whenever investment in prevention expenditure is discussed there is an implicit expectation of a large return on the investment. Progressive companies are always looking for profitable ways to invest in quality improvement activities, but their task is made very difficult by the lack of data and understanding of the economics of investment in such activities.

Scrap, rectification and rework costs and fault finding are collected and reported in most companies and are regarded as important costs which feature in companies' business decisions. Most companies would confidently claim that the decision whether or not to do corrective work or to scrap a product or batch is taken on economic grounds. Not so. The economics of scrapping or rectification are by no means clear in many companies. A major difficulty encountered in this is the valuation to be placed on scrapped goods. Some popular views encountered are that the value should be the selling price, the market price, the raw material's price or the materials' cost plus the cost of processing to the point of scrapping. These different bases will obviously give rise to very different valuations, which may not matter if the costs are not to be used in deciding courses of action. However most companies claim that the decision whether to scrap or rectify is taken on economic grounds. So if the real cost is not known, how can sensible economic decisions be made? If the true economics of rework are known why is there so much difficulty in putting a value on scrap? To complicate matters further, the decision about whether to scrap or rework is often taken by personnel who do not have access to the financial information necessary to make an economic choice. And in any case the economics will vary depending on workload, schedules, customer pressure, contractual requirement and urgency of delivery. In many organizations the scrap versus rework decisions are based primarily on the ease of rework, engineering/technology knowledge, available capacity, production output, delivery targets and overtime policies against a background of a general feel for costs, than by the true economics of the situation.

Continuing on this theme it should also be noted that recouping scrap and costs from suppliers is not as efficiently done as might be expected, even though it is written into the purchasing agreement. Most companies are successful only in recovering materials costs. Rectification costs incurred owing to supplier faults are not usually recovered. An anomaly uncovered at one company studied was that management claimed to agree possible sorting and rework charges with suppliers before starting work on the raw materials, but did not know its own in-house economics of scrap and rework. Perhaps there are *ad hoc* methods of estimating costs to be charged back to the suppliers which are unsuited to estimating in-house costs because they would be incompatible with other in-house methods and costs.

Despite this, there are many opportunities for investment in prevention, with consequential real cost savings. Employing qualified experienced staff, encouraging study, facilitating the education of all employees, and providing training are examples of investment in prevention. Investment in supplier quality assurance and assistance through supplier partnerships and development, assessment, auditing and rating, training and joint improvement activities through teamwork is claimed by many companies to pay handsome dividends.

Of direct interest to production engineers and technical specialists are the possibilities of effecting savings through investment in tooling, processes, equipment and mistake proofing devices. Poor standards of tooling are frequently responsible for excess work and the extra costs of improved production tooling are often a worthwhile investment. Quality considerations also enter into the selection of machinery inasmuch as a premium is paid for machine tools with the potential to achieve a capable process, thus avoiding failure costs, and perhaps some appraisal costs. At one company studied, the quality assurance manager noted that operator gauging time was interfering with the machining operation. Investment in electronic gauging equipment was comfortably justified on grounds of increased productivity. The extra data available from the equipment have also been of value in assessing controlling and improving machine and process capability. In the same company a design change was introduced to improve the robustness of the design. This involved a new specification for surface finish requirements. To achieve the new specification, additional operations were needed which increased the direct labour content by six operators. This cost was featured in the quality costs reporting. Management subsequently invested in capital equipment to automate these extra operations.

Kaplan [2] takes this line of argument when he suggests that if manufacturing costs decrease as quality increases (and there is evidence of this) then the financial justification for new capital equipment, including robots, should include the savings in manufacturing cost from achieving a lower incidence of defects.

It is often found that a knowledge of quality costs is of considerable benefit in the education of staff in the concept of TQM as a key business parameter and gaining their commitment to a process of continuous quality improvement. The level of quality costs is often fed back to staff in the form of diagnostic reports and surveys and this opens up dialogue on what are the major areas for improvement. This knowledge of quality costs helps to justify and reinforce the need for TQM and reduces scepticism as to why the organization is setting out on the TQM journey.

Looking forward, aspects of quality that will need to be developed if the business aspects of quality are to be raised from the level of *ad hoc* cost reports and occasional cost reduction exercises to the level enjoyed by other major business parameters are the following:

1. *Quality cost performance indicators*. Quality assurance managers are keen to use cost data to monitor internal quality performance in cost sensitive areas and to establish bases against which to gauge overall quality cost performance.

2. *Investment criteria*. While it may be axiomatic that prevention is better than cure, it is often difficult to justify investment in prevention activities. To some extent such investments are regarded as blind acts of faith. Little is known and nothing has been published on the appropriate levels and timing of investments, payoffs or payback periods.

   The relatively low level of expenditure on prevention activities (appraisal and failure) is stressed by every quality cost analyst. The majority of managers would like to deploy a greater proportion of quality-related expenditures on prevention but have no data to support their arguments. It is even doubtful whether the true economics of investment in appraisal versus failure costs are known in many companies.

3. *Quality efficiency indices*. Business efficiencies are commonly analysed and expressed using a variety of criteria (most financial). Maintenance and improvement of quality are not among the criteria used. Quality assurance managers' efforts to persuade fellow managers and directors of the value of quality to an organization's corporate health are often frustrated by a lack of well-known and accepted indices or standards. Some companies have developed measures for the purpose of internally monitoring quality improvement but no general guidelines or methods of calculation exist which would readily allow a company to assess its standards against a norm or against other companies' performances.

4. Specific problems of quality costing requiring attention are:
   (a) costs of equipment downtime,
   (b) the economics of machine and process capability versus higher capital cost of equipment,
   (c) extra costs incurred due to order splitting,
   (d) costs arising from concessions, modifications, design/engineering and document changes.

6.3 FACILITATING PERFORMANCE MEASURES AND IMPROVEMENT ACTIVITIES

The second use – giving rise to performance measures – is a most popular one. Whilst there is a wide variety of specific uses they can conveniently be categorized under a few headings. Costs may be expressed as absolute costs (including costs per unit of output or sales turnover) or as relative costs (i.e. as indices or ratios to other business costs). These cost measures are used for three main purposes:

1. comparison with other parts of the business or with other businesses,
2. decision making, and
3. motivation.

There are serious limitations which constrain the usefulness of absolute cost data. It would be misleading to compare absolute cost data since there are likely to have been, during the intervening period of the comparison, changes in output levels, product/service mix, method, processes, technology and people.

Indices and ratios are used to facilitate comparison and show changes and trends over time. The coverage of indices and ratios in the quality costing literature (apart from some general advice on making sure that the factors used to derive the index are related to each other and that single ratios often do not tell the whole story and will always need to be considered alongside other ratios) is disappointing and lacks conviction. AS2561 [3] recommends that at least three comparison bases should be used and urges care and caution in the selection of bases. Other useful guidance is contained in BS6143 Part 2 [4] and Campanella [5]. Perhaps indices are too specific to particular situations to make general writing on the subject easy or worthwhile, or perhaps they are just not very telling. Relating quality costs to other costs which are well known and are always under scrutiny for reduction may cause quality costs to become so, too. When quality costs are presented in such a way that they are seen as a way for increasing company profitability executives' attention automatically becomes focused on them.

Whilst quality are useful, they need to be supplemented with other, non-cost, data when making specific decisions. It should not be forgotten that important differences between individual companies' costs are reflected not by how much is spent, but by how it is spent. The most popular comparative measure against which quality costs are measured is gross annual sales turnover, followed by manufacturing or operating cost value added. Other useful bases are hours of direct production labour, units of product, raw material usage, and processing cost. The expression of quality costs as a percentage of the works recovered costs is a particularly good example of a ratio because the level of overhead is always under the organizational spotlight. Another useful ratio is failure cost expressed as a percentage of profit instead of, as usual, as a percentage of annual sales turnover; it is found that this ratio has a considerable impact on senior management.

The same care and caution as applied to the selection of ratios need to be exercised in the analysis of trends. Take for example the total quality costs/sales turnoveer ratio. If in a particular month a considerable percentage of sales is despatched from finished stock in the warehouse this ratio will show a significant decrease for no improvement in quality performance and reduction in costs.

Hesford and Dale [6] reporting on this ratio make the point:

It is somewhat artificial, in that it is driven by financial targets rather than from actual measured values and costs of products sold. The figures are 'adjusted' by the accounts department in such a manner to ensure that the phasing satisfies the corporate accounting targets on annual sales turnover and profits. It did, however, provide a reasonable measure of effectiveness and improvement in productivity terms and it had the advantage of being a baseline for company targets.

Any ratio involving warranty costs could also lead to misleading results. Eldridge and Dale [1] reporting on changes in a series of ratios make the following point:

The ratios relating to internal quality show an improvement, whilst the two ratios influenced by warranty costs and the casting returns from the major customer showed a deterioration. The normal practice of this particular customer is to hold the non-conforming castings until they have accumulated a full lorry load, before returning them to the company. It is this practice, rather than a deterioration in the quality of supplied castings, which has resulted in the adverse change in these two ratios. This finding also highlights the dangers of trying to assess changes in quality performance based on measures relating to warranty costs; one needs to understand the underlying practices.

Despite the many warnings against making comparisons, there is no escaping the desire for data for comparison purposes to assess performance. Companies are keen to know if their quality performance in terms of quality-related costs is good, bad or indifferent. However, it is dangerous to compare quality cost data between different companies, industries and service situations unless the accounting practices used and how the costs were computed are known and comparable. At present, every company's method of calculation is probably unique to that company. Internal comparisons are fine but it is external comparisons which should be treated with caution. Comparisons between sets of quality cost data from different sources should be discouraged and restricted to examining costs before and after specific quality improvement projects and activities have been completed, and improvement with time (though this also can have many pitfalls).

Confidentiality of cost information is often the greatest barrier to its publication and accountants are much more reluctant to reveal cost information than their quality assurance, engineering or technical counterparts. In the authors' research it has been noticed that on a number of occasions company personnel who clearly were being very frank in their answers to questions, became hesitant and uncertain when it came to discussing costs. Contacting accountants to seek clarification on data did not help. Indeed, in some cases it seemed to have the opposite effect to that intended and respondents became even more reticent, almost as if they had been 'warned off'. The case for confidentiality of some costs is questionable on a number of counts.

- Published costs need not be current data.
- Quality costs are perhaps only 10–20% of selling price.
- The nature of quality costs is such that no indication of a company's most important or sensitive costs is likely to be gleaned from analysis of them. Management accountants could do their profession and quality assurance managers a service by examining just how confidential quality costs need to be instead of labelling them 'Confidential' perhaps because they have not taken the trouble to think about them. Making cost information more freely available would provide considerable assistance to those managers trying to get their board of directors to invest in a process of quality improvement; it could also be used within the company for motivational purposes.
- For many standard products a competent production engineer/technical specialist could probably construct a fairly accurate manufacturing cost profile anyway.
- Confidential costs could readily be disguised by multiplying them by an arbitrary factor.

Perhaps confidentiality was the problem when Sullivan and Owens [7] tried to collect quality cost information from an ASQC survey. Perhaps many fewer companies collect costs data than would be expected. (Surveys in the UK by Duncalf and Dale [8] and in Ireland by Roche (9) suggest about one-third of companies collect quality-related costs of any kind.) Perhaps ASQC members were not interested enough to respond. Whatever the reason, the response rate of c. 0.1% to 35 000 enquiries does not provide grounds for optimism that costs for comparison purposes are likely to be freely available in the near future.

The cross-industry surveys of Gilmore [10] and the journal *Quality* [11] contain limited amounts of data which are interesting. Both sets of data show clearly that there are large industry-to-industry variations. Although the editor of *Quality* specifically warns against making comparisons there are strong grounds for suspecting from their data that companies which have a more sophisticated system of quality costing appear to have a better quality performance (or is it vice versa?) Gilmore [10,12] attempts to extract more out of his data than is really warranted and is relatively rash compared to other writers on the subject of quality costing in his assertions on the comparability of his data.

To be of real value data should be accurate and complete. Lack of qualification of much of the published data makes it difficult to take anything but a circumspect view of it. Many figures are so similar (especially the divsion of costs between prevention, appraisal and failure) that one wonders whether they all originated from the same source. Similarities in the distribution of costs within categories of industry also prompts the thought that there may, possibly, be quality cost structures which are characteristic of particular industries (i.e. in the same way that different industries have characteristic materials, wage and overhead cost ratios).

Use of quality costs for decision making is mostly restricted to choices between competing cost-reduction or quality-improvement projects and management time and resources, initiating corrective action and setting targets for cost reductions. In a study of quality-related decision making, Duncalf and Dale [8] found no evidence of other uses.

Quality costs are also used to identify products, processes and departments for investigation, to allocate resources, to set cost-reduction targets, and to measure progress towards targets. The data can also be used to assess the effect of management actions (i.e. to reduce scrap) on costs of any planned changes made to processes. However, just because high costs are being generated say on a particular product does not make them a logical starting point, there are other criteria to consider. The lack of routine quality costing information does not hinder an organization from pursuing quality improvement projects which have been identified from technical and/or quality assurance data. It is, however a handicap in setting overall cost reduction targets. Hesford and Dale [6] reporting on the development and use of quality costing at British Aerospace Dynamics Ltd describe a selection of improvement projects generated by the quality costing exercise. They say:

> Many of the high costs identified by the quality costing exercise have now attracted quality improvement efforts. For example, improved methods of printed circuit board (PCB) assembly led to a substantial reduction in reject rates due to the provision of more accurate information to operators, together with improved training. Operators participated with enthusiasm and the level of inspection support required was reduced by 50 per cent. Another example of improvement resulted from investigations into the methods and rules for applying calibration and standards which were carried out by a working party. Members of the group identified inconsistencies in the rules for deciding on calibration periodicities and pinpointed the need for improved information on measurement capabilities at each site.

The ranking of competing improvement projects by different cost bases and by numbers gave very different indicators. The preferred base depends on factors and circumstances that may change with time or with a company's business situation. Different indicators may require very different amounts and types of resources. They may be used to evaluate the cost benefit of individual quality-related activities (e.g. quality system registratation, SPC, and supplier development and partnership sourcing). Quality costs are clearly a useful tool for initiating improvement projects and levers for uncovering quality problems. They highlight errors and local problems previously unconsidered and requiring attention and serve to pinpoint concerns. They also help to question costs seen as inevitable and part of the way of doing things. Quality improvement projects appear to offer the quickest route to useful exploitation of cost data. Utilization of total quality costs takes much longer.

Another possible use of costs in the broad category of improvement activities is that quality costing might focus attention on the chronic problems for which compensations had been built into the system. The argument (which is an integral part of Juran's [13] teaching) goes that sporadic problems can be, and are, readily picked up by other means (e.g. SPC) but that the results of chronic problems are built into the base values, against which judgements are made. Obvious examples are allowances for material loss and average scrap levels built into standard costs, but there must be many other examples (e.g. personnel and equipment on standby, additional supervision and extra stocks). To expose all such costs and reduce and eliminate wastage would require a very wide view of TQM along the lines of world class companies, and a ruthless and relentless pursuit of truth and continuous and never-ending improvement, to be adopted.

Quality cost data may also be used to assist with vendor rating. Winchell [14] lists 'visible' and 'hidden' quality costs. Indeed in the visible quality costs category are the following:

- receiving or incoming inspection;
- measuring equipment calibration;
- qualification of supplier product;
- source inspection and control programme;
- purchased material reject disposition (material review);
- purchased material replacement;
- rework of supplier-caused rejects;
- scrap of supplier-caused rejects.

The visible costs, if tracked, are perhaps most significant because they can be good indicators of problem areas.

Hidden quality costs include:

- those that are incurred by the supplier at his plant (i.e. the sorting of conforming from non-conforming product in a delivered batch);
- those incurred by the buyer in solving problems at the supplier's plant; and
- those costs which usually are not allocated to suppliers, but are incurred by the buyer as a result of potential or actual supplier problems – including loss of business from customers who don't come back.

In much of the foregoing it is implicit that placing costs on activities and quality management data somehow enhances the underlying data and shows something which might otherwise not be revealed. While enhancement of data in this way may be useful it may not always be necessary. Sometimes only translating numbers into costs is sufficient to provoke action (e.g. Richardson [15]. Similarly, the mere collection of data may provoke investigative action.

6.4 PLANNING AND CONTROL

The use of quality costs as a means of planning and controlling quality costs against targets and standards is widely mooted in the literature. Costs are the bases for budgeting and eventual cost control. Many writers on the subject of quality costing list budgetary control as the ultimate objective. Despite this, there is a lack of convincing arguments or examples to support the objective. In general, the use of budgetary control of quality-related costs, though popular in concept, is not well examined in the literature. One example, found at Bridgeport Machines, is described by Dale and Plunkett [16] as:

> At the beginning of each financial year a quality plan and budget is drawn up for quality assurance, supplier quality assurance, capital investment, training and reliability of their machines in service. All of these costs are reflected in the level of quality costs. For example, if the projected reliability level for a machine (as indicated by its reliability index) is not achieved, then warranty and external failure costs will be higher than anticipated and the result will be a failure to achieve budget.

Contributions from the quality assurance fraternity tend to see establishment of quality cost budgets for the purpose of controlling cost as the ultimate goal which may be achieved after accumulating a lot of data over a long time in pursuit of quality improvements for specific cost reductions. Morse [17], on the other hand, sees the prime purpose of a quality cost system as presenting management with a means of planning and controlling quality costs. Other accountants seem to go along with this view but Cox [18] qualifies it when he points out that there are instances where product and service quality cannot be a matter for compromise and that only in those situations where the only result of failure is a loss of profit can trade-offs be made. Balancing Cox's [18] circumspection is Claret's [19] optimism about the level of sophistication that may be achieved in planning and controlling quality costs. Unfortunately no one shares his optimism, if they do, they are reluctant to say so in print.

Whilst the theme of planning and control is popular with writers, there are surprisingly few examples in the literature of its application to quality costs. With the exception of Burns [20] who describes the use of costs to predict warranty expenditures it seems to be assumed that conventional expenditure control is the main purpose. An example uncovered from the authors' research was the use of quality costs to provide information on future quotations for products or contracts having onerous quality and manufacturing conditions.

In terms of planning and control it must again be stressed that the fundamental economics of appraisal are not known in most companies. High costs of failure are apparently used to justify inspection and its frequency, without any attempts being made to determine the true economic balance. It is somewhat surprising that the economics of inspection are not well established and widely known in view of the fact that inspection oriented approaches to quality control have predominated in manufacturing industry for many decades. There is evidence of the potential for cost reductions by drastic reductions in inspection forces apparently without loss of quality. It is expected that there would be little change in first-off inspection unless the capability of equipment and tooling to sustain tolerances was improved, but that the patrol and final inspection activity could be reduced through the effective use of SPC.

As already mentioned, organizations manufacturing products on a one-off basis with long manufacturing lead times have little opportunity to build up an historical file of meaningful cost data for use in planning and control. Companies in these kinds of situations are often restricted to the use of costs in the context of improvement projects.

6.5 MOTIVATIONAL PURPOSES

Quality costs can be used for motivational purposes as regards improvement at all levels in a company. It is often found that people do not know what and how to improve and need to be provided with clear direction.

Costs have traditionally been used to motivate senior managers to become interested and take part in the promotion of quality. That is they have the potential to improve profits without any increase in sales. Costs also enable them to see whether or not there is a major opportunity for waste and cost reduction and if so, where this lies. In this way they provide tangible proof of the need for quality improvement, and top level leadership in the process.

As companies move towards TQM the use of costs as a motivator becomes more widespread. Uses for motivational purposes include display to shop floor workers of scrap costs arising within their department, and to emphasize to middle managers their department's contribution to total quality costs. Both are examples of the principle of accountability and ownership being used. Thus, for example, costs of scrapped goods are displayed to line supervisors, operatives and clerical staff because they can see the relevance of them to their work. It is found that this group of people respond positively in terms of increased quality awareness, improved handling of the product and housekeeping disciplines. Although the costs may be relatively small in company terms they are usually large in relation to operatives' salaries. Thus a strong impact is made, in particular, when poor trading conditions result in restrictions being placed on salary increases and even freezes or reductions being imposed, without disclosing sensitive cost information.

6.6 SUMMARY

According to Morse [17]:

The potential uses of the information contained in such a (quality cost) report are limited only by imagination of management.

Many of the uses can however be grouped into four broad categories.

1. Quality costs may be used to promote quality as a business parameter.
2. They give rise to performance measures.
3. They provide the means for planning and controlling quality costs.
4. They act as motivators.

This chapter has examined in detail these four categories of use.

Whilst it is clearly important to make good use of quality costs information it is equally important to avoid misuse of it. For example:

- In some industries quality costs ae not susceptible to conventional cost reduction techniques and quality may not be compromised to save money, e.g. where there is a possibility of severe loss of life or ecological disaster. Only in those situations where the consequence of failure is merely loss of profit is a manufacturer in a position to trade off quality expenditure against potential loss of profit resulting from product failures (Cox [21]).
- Costs alone must not be used to determine an optimum level of quality as suggested by 'economic cost of quality' models which appear everywhere in the literature (Chapter 5). While there is no objection to trying to optimize quality costs, quality should not be compromised. Quality should be determined by customer requirements, not optimum quality costs.
- Comparisons with other cost data should be avoided. Comparisons should only be made after it has been shown that the data are genuinely comparable (i.e. sources, computation, accounting treatment, and reporting methods are identical).

REFERENCES

1. Eldridge, S. and Dale, B.G. (1989,) Quality costings: the lessons learnt from a study carried out in two phases. *Engineering Costs and Production Economics*, **18** (1), 33–44.
2. Kaplan, R.S. (1983,) Measuring manufacturing performance: a new challenge for managerial accounting research. *The Accounting Review*, **58** (4) 686–705.
3. AS2561 (1982,) *Guide to the Determination and Use of Quality Costs*, Standards Association of Australia, N. Sydney.
4. BS6143: Part 2 (1990) *Guide to the Economics of Quality-Prevention, Appraisal and Failure Model*, British Standards Institution, London.
5. Campanella, J. (ed.) (1990) *Principles of Quality Costs: Principles, Implementation and Use*, ASQC Quality Press, Milwaukee.
6. Hesford, M.G. and Dale, B.G. (1991) Quality costing at British Aerospace Dynamics: a case study. *Proceedings of the Institution of Mechanical Engineers*, **205** (G5), 53–7.

7. Sullivan, E. and Owens, D.A. (1983) Catching a glimpse of quality costs, today. *Quality Progress*, December, 21–24.

8. Duncalf, A.J. and Dale, B.G. (1985) How British industry is making decisions on product quality. *Long Range Planning*, **18** (5), 81–8.

9. Roche, J.G. (1981) *National Survey of Quality Control in Manufacturing Industries*, National Board of Science and Technology, Dublin.

10. Gilmore, H.L. (1983) Consumer product quality control cost revisited. *Quality Progress*, April, 28–32.

11. Anon. (1977) Quality cost survey. *Quality*, June, 20–2.

12. Gilmore, H.L. (1984) Consumer product quality costs. *Proceedings of the World Quality Congress*, Brighton, 587–95.

13. Juran, J.M. (ed.) (1988) *Quality Control Handbook*, McGraw-Hill.

14. Winchell, W.O. (ed.) (1987) *Guide for Managing Supplier Quality Costs*, ASQC Quality Press, Milwaukee.

15. Richardson, D.W. (1983) Cost benefits of quality control, a practical example from industry. *BSI News*, Oct.

16. Dale, B.G. and Plunkett, J.J. (1990) *The Case for Costing Quality*, Department of Trade and Industry, London.

17. Morse, W.J. (1983) Measuring quality costs. *Cost and Management*, July/August, 16–20.

18. Cox, B. (1982) The role of the management accountant in quality costing. *Quality Assurance*, **8** (3), 82–4.

19. Claret, J. (1981) Never mind the quality? *Management Accounting*, May, 24–6.

20. Burns, V.P. (1970) Warranty prediction: putting a $ on poor quality. *Quality Progress*, December, 28–9.

21. Cox, B. (1982) Interface of quality costing and terotechnology. *The Accountant*, June 20, 800–6.

Case study, company 1 | 7

7.1 INTRODUCTION

Company 1 is a member of a large group of companies engaged in metal refining and fabrication of a very diverse range of metal products. It is a fully integrated manufacturing unit making products from refined and prepared raw materials. The headquarters of the division in which the company is located are sited at a sister factory some 40 miles away. The company's products are supplied to vehicle and traction equipment manufacturers via a holding and warehousing operation which also supplies a network of agencies and service centres with spares and replacement products.

At the factory where the quality costing research investigation was carried out the company manufactures heat exchange ancillaries for automotive and traction equipment. Its operations include casting of aluminium alloys, machining castings, sheet metal cutting and forming, tube joining, component assembly, welding, brazing and soldering. It employs 150 people and has an annual sales turnover of about £5 million per year.

Prior to the study the only costs collected and identified as quality costs were the costs of operating the quality control department, expenditure on warranty, and the costs of scrap and defective products.

The research approach in this case study was to examine the company's operations against the model elements of BS6143 [1] (the 1981 version of the Standard) and to put costs on them.

The company's quality costs for the first quarter of the current year in which the study was carried out (hereafter referred to as Year 1) were measured. Then using these costs a projected quality cost report was prepared for the full year. The work was carried out in the third quarter of Year 1 by which time all the first-quarter transactions and accounting were complete.

In this study a deliberately ingenuous approach was adopted to try to ensure that all the major obstacles to the collection of quality costs in the company were discovered. Before attempting to gather costs, knowledge of the company's operations and practices was gained by studying the company's procedures and reports, supplemented by discussions with staff from quality control, inspection, personnel, work study, production and accounts departments.

Attempts were then made to detect and measure costs against each of the cost elements listed in the BS6143 guide [1] (the 1981 version of the Standard). A list of abbreviated elements, their coding and the corresponding coding

Table 7.1 Corresponding sections in BS6143 and ASQC categorization of quality-related cost elements

BS6143	ASQC	Elements
A1	1, 1a, 1b	Quality control and process control engineering
A2	2	Design and develop control equipment
A3	3	Quality planning by others
A4	–	Production equipment for quality – maintenance and calibration
A5	–	Test and inspection equipment – maintenance and calibration
A6	1a*	Supplier quality assurance
A7	4	Training
A8	5	Administration, audit, improvement
B1	2	Laboratory acceptance testing
B2	1, 3	Inspection and test
B3	4	In-process inspection (non-inspectors)
B4	5	Set-up for inspection and test
B5	6, 17	Inspection and test materials
B6	7, 8, 16	Product quality audits
B7	10	Review of test and inspection data
B8	11	On-site performance testing
B9	12	Internal testing and release
B10	13	Evaluation of materials and spares
B11	15	Data processing, inspection and test reports
	14	As A4
	9	As A5
C1	1	Scrap
C2	2	Rework and repair
C3	3	Trouble shooting, defect analysis
C4	4	Re-inspect, re-test
C5	5	Scrap and rework: fault of supplier
C6	6	Modification permits and concessions
C7	7	Downgrading
D1	1	Complaints
D2	2	Product service: liability
D3	3	Products returned or recalled
D4	4	Returned material repair
D5	5, 6, 7, 8	Warranty replacement

*Supplier quality assurance prior to order placement only.

used by the ASQC [2] is shown in Table 7.1. Each element given in Table 7.1 is fully defined in the body of this chapter. It should be noted that some revision of the cost elements has been made in BS6143: Part 2 [3].

7.2 COMPANY QUALITY CONTROL AND ACCOUNTING SYSTEMS

The company, which is an approved supplier to the Ministry of Defence, has a comprehensive quality manual clearly setting out the responsibilities of quality, production, engineering and other personnel for quality-related matters. The manual contains no reference to quality costs other than warranty. There was, however, a clear acknowledgement of the existence of quality costs in the company.

The company accounting system divides the company into 21 indirect cost centres, covering its manufacturing facilities. There are also 188 financial codes, of which, apart from the routine administrative codes applied to the quality control cost centre, only sales of scrap material, indirect materials, inspection equipment, research materials and warranty repairs were readily recognizable as being quality related. Another potential source of quality cost information – labour bookings – was equally disappointing, having only 'defective material' as an obviously quality-related code, though it was learned later that bookings to 'prototype' might also contain some quality costs. The accounts department does, however, produce a monthly scrap report analysed across production cost centres and displaying material, labour and overhead costs.

It is fair to say that so far as quality-related costs are concerned the accounting system lacked sophistication and the availability of data failed to meet expectations. Some idea of the situation may be gauged from the fact that only four of the 188 financial codes referred to quality-related matters, and perhaps even more telling, there was only one labour-booking code for work concerned with defective products. As a result, the costing relied a great deal on estimates. The extent of estimation was such that only 50% of the total quality costs were derived from data specifically noted in accounts under headings identifiable as being quality related.

7.3 DETECTION AND MEASUREMENT OF QUALITY-RELATED COSTS

7.3.1 Prevention costs

In many ways, and as already discussed in this book, prevention is the most difficult of the categories to cost. This is because prevention activities are made up of a number of disparate elements carried out on a part-time basis by people from different departments. The cost depends heavily on estimates of apportionment of time by personnel who do not usually record how they spend their time.

A1a   Quality engineering – planning the quality system and translating product design and customer quality requirements into manufacturing quality controls of materials, processes and products.

      This work is carried out exclusively within the quality control department and the cumulative effort input is estimated (by the quality control manager) to be equivalent to 30% of the time of one of the senior staff* in the department.

A1b   Process engineering – represents those costs associated with implementing and maintaining quality plans and procedures.

      This work is also carried out exclusively within the quality control department and is estimated to take the equivalent of 30% of the time of one of the senior staff in the department.

A2   Design and development of quality measurement and control equipment.

      The cost sources for this element are: 1. staff time inputs from the quality control department and production engineering department, estimated to be 5% of a senior member in each case; 2. research and development work carried out at headquarters on behalf of the local factory; and 3. (possibly) charges collected under the financial code for research materials.

      It is worth noting that in discussions with company personnel a view was expressed that it would be more appropriate to include this element under the category of appraisal instead of prevention.

A3   Quality planning by functions other than the quality control department.

      BS6143 lists possible inputs from laboratory, manufacturing, engineering and sales personnel, none of which applies in this company, according to the quality control manager.

A4   Calibration and maintenance of production equipment used to evaluate quality.

      The only item of expenditure under this heading is the calibration and maintenance of pressure gauges, estimated at half a man-day per month. It is arguable that maintenance of water baths used for detection of leaks in soldered joints should be included under this heading or indeed that this type of expenditure properly belongs in the appraisal category as is recommended by the ASQC.

*In the interests of confidentiality of salary information, and because some tasks may be undertaken by any or all of the three senior people in the quality control department, a 'senior man' with, at the time of the study, an employment cost of £10 000 per year was invented.

It is worth noting here that whilst, overall, there is generally close agreement between BS6143 and the ASQC on the content and categorization of cost elements, the British Standard classifies calibration and maintenance of production equipment use to evaluate quality (element A4) and maintenance and calibration of test and inspection equipment (element A5) as prevention activities, whereas the ASQC regards them as appraisal activities (appraisal elements 14 and 9 respectively).

A5   Maintenance and calibration of test and inspection equipment.

Sources of cost data for this element are: 1. the financial code for indirect materials – inspection equipment; 2. invoices for calibration services from outside the company; and 3. staff time input, estimated as being 5% of a senior man's time.

It is noteworthy that a £12 000 capital investment in calibration equipment has reduced the cost of purchased calibration services from approximately £7500 per year to £2000–£3000 per year.

A6   Supplier assurance.

The costs of this element are wholly within the quality control department. The involvement of purchasing and material control staff with suppliers or sub-contractors is not seen as incurring any quality-related costs. The staff time input from the quality control department is estimated to be 8% of a senior man.

A7   Quality training.

Quality-related training is not identified separately within the training function of the personnel department. Training schedules for new workers emphasize the necessity for doing work of the correct quality but no specific quality training is given. In the quality control department an estimated 2% of a senior man's time is devoted to quality training activities.

A8   Administration, audit, improvement.

Administration costs such as travel, telephones, post and printing are collected under individual financial codes but not by cost centre. Costs could be allocated on proportional bases but it has been found that the allocations vary widely, depending on the basis used, so that it is difficult to arrive at an agreed equitable allocation, much less an accurate one. Depreciation costs of the capital assets of the quality control department are available.

Auditing and improvement costs, mostly incurred within the quality control department, are estimated as equivalent to 15% of a senior man's time. It is recognized that staff from other departments became involved in major audits but no estimate of their involvement, or the cost, is available.

The prevention costs and findings are summarized in Table 7.2.

Table 7.2 Prevention costs

Cost element		Recorded costs (£) Jan.	Feb.	Mar.	1st qtr	Projected annual cost (£)	Source	Notes
A1	Quality control and process control engineering	–	–	–	–	6000	Estimated time	
A2	Design and develop control equipment	–	–	–	–	1000	Estimated time	Charges in respect of headquarters. R & D work not included
A3	Quality planning by others	–	–	–	–	nil	–	
A4	Production equipment for quality – maintenance and calibration	–	–	–	–	200	Estimated time	
A5	Test and inspection – maintenance and calibration	215	205	30	450	1800 2500 500	Materials External services Estimated time	External services from sub-contractor estimated '£2000–£3000 per year'
A6	Supplier quality assurance	–	–	–	–	800	Estimated time	
A7	Training	–	–	–	–	200	Estimated time	
A8	Administration, audits, improvements	–	–	–	–	1500 4000	Estimated time Capital depreciation	Travel, telephones, post, printing, etc. all collected under single cost centre
Total						18 500		
Projected annual sales turnover (%)						0.37		

7.3.2 Appraisal costs

These are defined as the costs of assessing the quality achieved and are broken down into 11 cost elements. The largest items of cost can be determined readily and accurately because they involve full-time activities by specific personnel. Less certain is the extent of involvement of quality control department senior staff and of production operators in appraisal activities.

B1   Laboratory acceptance testing (of purchased production materials).
         These are costs of tests to evaluate the quality of purchased materials which become part of the final product or that are consumed during production operations. It was expected that these costs might have been readily traceable as research materials, cost transfers from headquarters services, and invoices for outside services. In the event it was found that there was no expenditure against the financial-code-designated research materials in the first quarter of Year 1 and only £56 by the design section of the engineering department in the whole year. Payments for purchased laboratory services are said to be small and infrequent. Cost transfers from headquarters (about £3000 per year) for thermal performance testing of products may contain charges which are appropriate to this element.

B2   Inspection and test (including receiving inspection).
         This element covers the inspection activity from within the quality control department (but does not include testing, work carried out by production operators). It is the cost of 10 full-time inspectors, plus 70% of the time of a supervising foreman/manager.

B3   In-process inspection (by personnel other than inspectors).
         This element can be complicated because in engineering manufacture operators are frequently required to carry out inspections as part of their normal work. Measurement of the cost of this kind of inspection activity is not usually practicable and probably was not intended by the committee who were responsible for preparing the BS6143. However, in company 1 a major activity is testing the airtightness of soldered joints, repairing them if necessary, and retesting them. The first testing operation is inextricably linked with repair and retest operations, which are cost elements C2 and C4 respectively under the internal failure cost category.
         The costs involved are substantial and, depending on the repair rate and the view taken about whether the 'repairs' are part of the manufacturing process or are the result of failures, the costs could be divided between the appraisal and failure categories – see C2 and C4.
         In the period under review there were nine skilled workers employed full time on test and repair work. Because their work is carried out in five different maufacturing areas the amount of direct supervision their work attracts is difficult to estimate and may give a spurious

impression of rigorousness which is clearly unwarranted in view of the complexities in this element. It is presumed that as direct workers, test and repair men's time costs normally attract overheads.

B4   Set-up for inspection and test.

This is the payroll cost of setting up equipment or products for inspection and function testing. Whilst it is known that time is booked in the machine shop for set-up and test of machines, and that costs must be incurred in setting up products for thermal testing, it is probably not worth separating them out. The element is clearly intended for industries which manufacture large, heavy or complex products for which it can be a substantial cost item.

B5   Inspection and test materials (i.e. materials consumed or destroyed in the control of quality).

Material usages for this purpose are small and most costs have been included under element A5. Material usages arising from destructive test (e.g. temperature cones) are included in the company's scrap costs.

B6   Product quality audits.

These are estimated to take up 2% of the time of a foreman/manager in the quality control department.

B7   Review of test and inspection data.

If, as believed, this means checking that all the inspection and test schedules (usually associated with heavy engineering projects) have been met, the practice of 100% final inspection and test of all products obviates the need for regular review of test and inspection data before release of the product for shipment.

B8   Field (on-site) performance testing – costs incurred in testing for product acceptance on customers' premises.

This activity, which may involve representatives of the quality control and design departments, is not large and neither staff time nor travelling expense is separated out.

B9   Internal testing and release – the cost of setting up and in-house testing of the complete product for customer acceptance.

Such work would normally be covered under B3 in company 1. Occasionally special arrangements may be made for a customer to witness tests. The level of staff involvement in this activity is estimated to be 2% of a senior man's time.

B10   Evaluation of site material (field stock) and spare parts – the costs of evaluation, testing or inspection of site material, resulting from engineering changes, storage conditions or other suspected problems.

Because much of the company's production is made for stock by distributors and users there is often a considerable delay between manufacture and the product going into service. Hence problems arise from deterioration during storge, changes to specifications, etc. It is estimated that attention to these problems takes up to 5% of a senior man's time.

Table 7.3 Appraisal costs

Cost element		Recorded costs Jan.	Feb.	Mar.	1st qtr	Projected annual costs (£)	Source	Notes
B1	Laboratory acceptance testing	–	–	–	–	–	–	Possibly £3000
B2	Inspection and test	–	–	–	–	80 000	–	Employment cost of full-time inspectors
						7 000	Estimated time	Supervisor/manager part-time
B3	In-process inspection (non-inspectors)	–	–	–	–	67 500	–	Full-time test and repair men; overheads not included; including overheads £396 000
B4	Set-up for inspection and test	–	–	–	–	–	–	Not applicable
B5	Inspection and test materials	–	–	–	–	–	–	Included under A5 and C1
B6	Product quality audits	–	–	–	–	200	Estimated time	
B7	Review of test and inspection data	–	–	–	–	–	–	Not applicable
B8	On-site performance tests	–	–	–	–	200	Estimated time	
B9	Internal test and release	–	–	–	–	200	Estimated time	
B10	Evaluation of materials and spares	–	–	–	–	500	Estimated time	
B11	Data processing	–	–	–	–	2 000	Estimated time	
Total						157 600		May be much higher; See notes at B1 and B3 above
Projected annual sales turnover (%)						3.14		

B11   Data processing inspection and test reports – the costs incurred in accumulating and processing test and inspection data used in evaluation work.

Ｔhe bulk of this work is carried out within the quality control department and involves data from service centres as well as the manufacturing operation. It occupies an estimated 20% of the time of a senior man in the department. The cost of accumulating data by production personnel and inspectors is not known.

The results of the examination of appraisal costs are shown in Table 7.3.

7.3.3 Internal failure costs

These are defined as the costs arising within the manufacturing organization of the failure to achieve the quality specified (before transfer of ownership to the customer). The major items of cost are scrap and rework. The cost elements comprising internal failure costs, according to BS6143 are as follows:

C1   Scrap – all scrap losses incurred in the course of meeting quality requirements. This element includes only that scrap arising through the fault of the manufacturer; that which is the fault of a supplier is included under element C5.

Costs are generated from inspection/rejection reports and standard costs. They comprise the cost of materials and direct labour to the point of scrapping. The direct labour costs include overhead charges. Inclusion of overheads in this way has the effect of inflating some failure costs relative to other quality costs which do not attract overheads. It is not clear whether allowance is made for parts recovered from scrapped products.

An interesting and expensive source of scrap which is quality-related arises at company 1. It is that scrap which is described as 'natural wastage' and arises mainly from setting-up and offcuts. The offcuts arise from stamping out components from metal tubes. Clearly every effort is made to minimize such wastage, but some is unavoidable. Similarly, although scrap materials are used whenever possible in setting up machines there is inevitably some waste when good new material has to be used for the final checks before producing components for use. The value of such materials could only be construed as quality costs if the amount of scrap produced in this way could be shown to be greater than was necessary.

Non-ferrous scrap is segregated into various categories (copper, brass, clear and tinned) and sold. Despite the BS6143 guidance to the contrary, the income from these sales should not be deducted from the costs of scrapping products because: 1. it makes the quality performance appear to be better than it really is; 2. the type and quantity of scrap sold at a particular time may bear no relationship to the current output; and 3. the inclusion of 'natural wastage' in the scrap sold would, in effect, subsidize non-conforming product. It is interesting to note that the income from sales of scrap in the first quarter is approximately equal to the materials' value of products scrapped in the same period.

Staff time from the quality control department is estimated as 10% of a senior man's time and there is some input from the accounts department in preparing cost data. However, in view of the fact that scrap costs include overheads, it would be wrong to add on these costs.

C2 Rework and repair – the cost incurred in meeting quality requirements where material can be restored for use.

As mentioned earlier under B3, the apportionment of costs between elements B2, C2 and C4 is complicated because of the test and repair activity. However, irrespective of the outcome of any consideration given to such apportionment, there are other costs which clearly should be included under this element. The company's quality manual prescribes a system by which the direct hours and issue of the necessary excess materials is formally recorded and passed to the accounts department. So far as is known, these costs are not formally reported and the best information that could be gleaned was the half-time involvement of a welder on castings and the record of hours claimed under the heading of 'defective materials'. In order to be consistent with the accounting practice used to calculate the cost of producing scrap, it is of course necessary to add overhead charges to these costs.

C3 Troubleshooting or defect/failure analysis (to determine causes).

This work is carried out within the quality control department and is estimated to take 10% of the time of a senior man in the department.

C4 Re-inspection, re-testing (of products which had failed previously).

As discussed under B3 and C2 above, the involvement of test and repair workers in the production process complicates apportionment in this heading. Re-inspection and re-testing of rerouted rework is not identified separately from first inspection and tests. Because initial failure rates can be as high as 50% (albeit with easily repairable minor defects) the costs of the activities under this element could be fairly large.

C5 Scrap and rework; fault of supplier; downtime.

Suppliers are expected to reimburse the full purchase price of any supplies which are unusable owing to the supplier's fault. Any other costs incurred up to the point of scrapping are not recovered. On the matter of rework, it is either carried out by the supplier or by the company at the supplier's expense. On some occasions attempted rework of faulty supplies may cause some lost time, materials or manufacturing capacity. Overall there is little net cost to the company, but records are worth keeping for supplier assessment purposes.

Table 7.4 Internal failure costs

Cost element		Recorded costs (£)				Projected annual costs (£)	Source	Notes
		Jan.	Feb.	Mar.	1st qtr			
C1	Scrap	10 885	11 945	15 710	38 540	154 160	Accounts	Scrap valuation includes overheads
C2	Rework and repair	6 700	7 584	7 363	21 647	86 588	'Defective material' hours	
						15 000	Estimated time	Welder part time plus overheads
						1 000	Estimated time	Supervisor/manager part time
C3	Trouble shooting and defect analysis	–	–	–	–	1 000	Estimated time	
C4	Re-inspect, re-test	–	–	–	–	–	–	Included under B3
C5	Scrap and rework suppliers' fault	–	–	–	–	–	–	Negligible net cost
C6	Modification permits, concessions	–	–	–	–	1 000	Estimated time	Assumes all 'design charges' are related to modifications
						33 000	Engineering department	
C7	Downgrading	–	–	–	–	–	–	Not applicable
	Total					291 748		Without overheads this total reduces to £106 000
	Projected turnover (%)					5.8		

C6 Modifications, permits and concessions – the costs of time spent reviewing products, designs and specifications.

Modifications are usually covered by concessions – usually from the
engineering department or (occasionally) from customers. No estimates
of the time or costs involved were obtained from the engineering department, but it was learned from the accounts department that there is
a substantial monthly design charge, much of which could be related
to design changes. The input from the quality control department is
estimated to be 10% of the time of a senior member of the department.

C7 Downgrading.

It is not the practice of the company to sell 'seconds' at a reduced price.

These considerations and findings on internal failure costs are summarized
in Table 7.4.

7.3.4 External failure costs

These are defined as the costs arising outside the manufacturing organization
of the failure to achieve the quality specified (after transfer of ownership to
the customer). Interpretation of the definition is not as straightforward as it
appears, inasmuch that 1. the point of transfer of ownership is not unequivoc-
ably defined; and 2. in the case of this company's products, the warranty
period may not be initiated until several years after the sale of the product
to the customer.

D1 Complaints administration – the costs of administration of those
complaints which are due to quality defects.

Complaints being handled by the maufacturing company (as distinct
from the distribution service and agency outlets) are dealt with wholly
within the quality control department. It is estimated that the time spent
on such matters is 5% of the time of a senior member of the department's staff.

D2 Product or consumer service; product liability.

Costs arising within the manufacturing company are likely to be
included under D1 above.

D3 Handling and accounting of products rejected or recalled.

Costs of these are not measured or estimated. They are probably
negligible.

D4 Returned material repair.

Repair work is carried out under one cost centre and covers: 1. work
which is chargeable back to the customer; 2. work done under
warranty; and 3. repairs carried out free of charge. It is important
here to distinguish between 2 and 3. Work done under warranty is
work relating to products which have failed in service whilst under
warranty (other warranty costs are included under D5 by virtue of

Table 7.5 External failure costs

Cost element		Recorded costs (£) Jan.	Feb.	Mar.	1st qtr	Projected annual costs (£)	Source	Notes
D1	Complaints administration	-	-	-	-	500	Estimated time	
D2	Product service, liability	-	-	-	-	-	-	Covered under D1 and D5
D3	Returned product handling and accounting	-	-	-	-	-	-	Included in D4
D4	Returned products' repair	2 896	2 816	3 709	9 421	37 684	Accounts	Inclusion of overheads uncertain
D5	Warranty replacement	1 744	1 612	2 217	5 573	22 292 6 500	Accounts Estimated time	Uncertain if all costs included
Total						66 976		
Projected annual sales turnover (%)						1.34		

work carried out by retail service outlets). Work done free of charge on products returned by customers is work relating to products which failed on test or were damaged on receipt or corroded. It is this latter cost which is to be collected under this element. It is identified in the accounts as 'Company Liability'. The quality control department staff effort input to this activity is inseparable from that going into element D5.

D5 Warranty replacement – the costs of replacing products which have failed within the warranty period.

Charges arise from several different sources: 1. payments made to service centres for repairs carried out under warranty; 2. replacement products issued free of charge to service centres or customers in exchange for failed products which are repairable; and 3. staff time input dealing with warranty claims and payments – 65% of a quality engineer's time.

Whilst simple in principle, the actual method of achieving the objective of satisfying customers may render the collection of costs difficult. Some customers deal directly with the factory. Faulty products may be repaired and returned to the customer at a certain cost, or they may be replaced in the stock by stripping and refurbishing the returned unit, but at a different cost. Service centres are recompensed at agreed rates for warranty repair work, but the same rates do not appear to apply to similar repairs carried out at the factory. Replacement units issued by service centres when a faulty unit is irrepairable are billed at the service centre stock valuation, which, of course, is far higher than the factory issue price. Free-of-charge replacements of products found to be faulty before going into service are more straightforward but the valuation and crediting of the returned damaged products is unclear.

The external failure costs are summarized in Table 7.5.

7.4 DISCUSSION OF FINDINGS

In carrying out the costing exercise points have been raised and discussed briefly in the context of the element or category. It is intended here to discuss each category in the broader context of the cost collection exercise as a whole.

7.4.1 Prevention costs

In a small company, where the many disparate preventive activities are not sufficiently large to occupy the whole or even a large proportion of an employee's time, it is necessary to record or estimate the proportions of time spent on each activity in order to obtain a prevention cost analysis. Estimates of the proportions of time spent on various activities tend to be highly subjective and may be 'average' or 'typical' observations not necessarily specifically relating to the period under review. It has been found in this case study and the others discussed in the chapters which follow that estimates tend to be based on medium- or long-term experiences and may not reflect current experiences. Furthermore, estimates tend not to change. Once a considered view has been arrived at the estimator tends to stick with it.

In the present case some 55% of the prevention cost is derived from the estimated time coupled with an average employment cost. With the foregoing remarks in mind, this might be expected to yield a fairly inaccurate estimate of prevention costs, especially when coupled to uncertainties about charges in respect of research and development work at headquarters and other outside services. However, when it is realized that the whole prevention activity cost amounts to only around 5% of the estimated total quality-related cost and less than 0.4% of projected annual sales turnover the case for accurate time apportionment and costing takes on a different perspective. Furthermore, if one takes the view that only those costs which are subject to change, or are sensitive to some business parameter, should be collected and analysed accurately, there seems little point in gathering detailed information about how much time people devote to various prevention activities. Thus, it is important to keep cost elements or categories in perspective and not agonize over the accuracy of minor cost elements in the prevention category. On the other hand, over the quality-related cost spectrum the full-time activity of three employees at a total employment cost of about £30 000 per year is being apportioned by subjective estimates. It may be that the size of activity is worth monitoring by recording the time spent on the major elements of quality activities. It is suggested that noting half-day increments once weekly against those topics which this study has shown to be the most important would adequately meet the need.

As already noted, for the purpose of ascribing costs to staff time, whilst maintaining confidentiality of individual salaries, and owing to the fact that some of the activities may involve any or all of the senior staff in the quality control department (i.e. quality control manager, quality control engineer, quality control foreman), a hypothetical 'senior man' was invented. If further justification is needed, it is suggested that the validity of the assumption is at least as great as the validity of completeness of the underlying data.

7.4.2 Appraisal costs

Clearly the costs of inspection and testing are far greater than all the other appraisal costs put together. Indeed some of the elements listed in BS6143 attract no costs at all, and several others which together account for less than 10% of a manager's time might usefully be combined. In fact, apart from charges incurred for laboratory acceptance testing, the appraisal costs are the employment costs of 10 inspectors, nine test and repair men and one foreman/manager from the quality control department.

Problems of estimating apportionment of a foreman/manager's time are rather more straightforward under this category because 90% of it is divided between only two elements. None the less it is felt that it could be beneficial to record broad uses of time as suggested earlier.

Under this category two problems of definition of quality-related costs arise. The first is whether all or part of the activities of test and repair workers should be classified as being quality related, and the second is whether quality-related direct work should attract overheads for the purpose of measuring quality-related costs.

One view taken of the first problem is that the whole of the test and repair activity is a normal production cost and not a quality-related cost. Another view is that first-time test and repair is a normal production activity but that any subsequent tests and repairs are quality-related costs. Yet another view is that all the costs are quality related but that the tests are appraisal costs and the repairs are failure costs. The sum involved is the employment costs of nine workers, i.e. about £67 000 (without overheads).

The effects on quality cost distributions and ratios of omitting this cost are shown in Table 7.6. The effects of splitting the cost between production and quality, or between quality cost categories, have not been evaluated. As metioned in Chapter 3, there is often no 'right' answer to the problem; it is a matter to be decided by people knowledgeable about the industry, the technology, the products and the processes.

The second problem, whether direct worker costs should attract overheads when measuring quality-related costs, is fundamental to the whole exercise of quality costing. The high overheads which exist in manufacturing industry can grossly distort the level and distribution of quality costs. If overheads are included, the costs of those elements involving direct workers are going to be grossly inflated in comparison with those involving indirect workers. For example, in the context of appraisal cost, assuming for the moment that the costs of test and repair direct workers are quality-related costs, the employment costs of 10 full-time inspectors who are indirect workers is £80 000 whilst the cost of nine test and repair workers, including overheads, is approaching £400 000. Hence it is clearly ludicrous to include overhead charges in quality-related labour costs. In any event, because staff and indirect worker costs are being ascribed directly to quality cost elements, adding overheads to direct worker costs at the standard rate must necessarily involve some double-counting. Overheads which may sensibly accrue to quality-related costs are those included in charges from other parts of the company because they are analogous to invoice from outside companies.

The matter is discussed further below in the context of failure costs.

7.4.3 Internal failure costs

Scrap and rework charges together with design changes account for almost the whole of the cost under this category.

Although the system for collecting costs of scrap is well established, other costs in this category were difficult to obtain. The problem of overheads arises again, and whilst it is conceded that it is entirely appropriate for overheads to be added to direct labour charges for the purposes of stock valuations and records, it is again contended that it is not appropriate for the purpose of collecting quality-related costs. The problem arises only because of the practice of recovering overheads on a direct labour basis. If a basis of, say, units of saleable products was used, there would not be a problem. The effects on the quality costs report of omitting overheads can be seen in Table 7.6.

A noticeable feature of scrap reports is the significantly large weights of nonferrous scrap (1 tonne per month) accruing under the heading 'natural wastage' which arises mainly from material used during set-up and from offcuts or surpluses from stamping operations. Such scrap is a production materials loss. Its value is not a quality-related cost and care must be taken that it is

Table 7.6 Projected annual quality cost ratios: effects of overheads and 'test and repair' operations

Cost category			Omitting test and repair		US survey data*	
		As collected	Less overhead	As collected	Less overhead	FMP†	MIG‡
Prevention	Projected	18 500	18 500	18 500	18 500	–	–
Appraisal	costs (£)	157 600	157 600	89 900	89 900	–	–
Internal failure		291 748	106 000	291 748	106 000	–	–
External failure		66 976	66 976	66 976	66 976	–	–
Total		534 824	349 076	467 124	281 376		
Prevention	Quality	3.4	5.3	4.0	6.5	10.5	10.3
Appraisal	costs (%)	29.5	45.1	19.3	32.0	34.5	26.0
Internal failure		54.5	30.4	62.3	37.7	39.0	43.0
External failure		12.6	19.2	14.4	23.8	16.0	20.7
Total		100	100	100	100	100	100
Prevention	Sales	0.37	0.37	0.37	0.37	0.51	0.6
Appraisal	turnover (%)	3.14	3.14	1.8	1.8	1.67	1.5
Internal failure		5.8	2.12	5.8	2.12	1.90	2.5
External failure		1.34	1.34	1.34	1.34	0.77	1.2
Total		10.65	6.97	9.31	5.63	4.85	5.8

*Quality costs survey. *Quality*, June 1977, pp. 20–2 [4].
†FMP, fabricated metal products sector of industry.
‡MIG, manufacturing industries in general.

Table 7.7 Projected annual quality costs: comparison of findings on scrap, rework and warranty with US survey data

Cost category		Company 1	US survey data*	
			FMP†	MIG‡
Scrap	Projected costs (£)	154 160	–	–
Rework		101 588	–	–
Warranty		28 792	–	–
Total		284 540		
Scrap	Quality costs (%)	54.0	32.4	41.0
Rework		35.7	64.0	38.5
Warranty		10.3	3.6	20.5
Total		100	100	100
Scrap	Sales turnover (%)	3.08	3.6	3.2
Rework		2.03	7.1	3.0
Warranty		0.58	0.4	1.6
Total		5.69	11.1	7.8

*Quality costs survey. *Quality*, June 1977, pp. 20–2 [4].
†FMP, fabricated metal products sector of industry.
‡MIG, manufacturing industries in general.

not counted as such. The approval of BS6143 of the practice of deducting income from sales of scrap from scrap costs is surprising for the reasons already given under C1 earlier.

The definition of rework and repair costs is complicated by the test and repair situation as discussed earlier. Leaving aside that complication, even in those cases where the definitions and procedures to product rework costs appear to be straightforward, difficulty was experienced in obtaining them. The figures quoted in Table 7.6 were the best that could be obtained at the time but they appear to be small in comparison with other reported data (see Tables 7.6 and 7.7).

Similarly no firm data were available for the costs of modifications, concessions and the general impact of design engineering on quality-related costs. Without more detailed enquiries there is no way of gauging whether the figure quoted in Table 7.6 is anywhere near correct. It would appear that the costs to be included under this element appear to be very specific to the industry/company.

In the context of internal failure costs it is interesting to speculate whether the true economics surrounding the scrap or rework decision are known for each product under different conditions of output rate, manufacturing capacity, production schedule, urgency of delivery and materials supply, or whether the decisions are really made in the light of engineering knowledge and experience.

7.4.4 External failure costs

The major costs incurred under this heading are for repair of products which have been returned by customers because they were found to be faulty before being put into service, and replacement of products which have failed in service during the warranty period.

Although superficially it should be a simple matter to determine the magnitude of these costs, in practice it is complicated by some business and accounting practices. The systems are described under D4 and D5. Examples of the complications which arise in ascertaining quality costs are replacement of a defective unit from stock and replenishing the stock by refurbishing (as distinct from repairing) the faulty unit, and the obscuration of in-house warranty work carried out in the repair section of the factory. However, the figures quoted in Table 7.5 are as supplied by the accounts department and have, presumably, been properly disentangled.

7.5 PRESENTATION AND USES OF QUALITY-RELATED COSTS

The only presentation and uses of quality-related costs in company 1 are the monthly reporting of the quality control department costs for budgetary control purposes and reporting of gross costs of scrap and warranty in management accounts. Although ratios are used as performance indicators in some aspects of the business, gross values are preferred. Quality costs do not feature in any of the ratios used. These typically involve measures of labour, sales and manufacturing cost. Costs do not appear to feature specifically in the day-to-day decisions about quality matters though it must be said that there is a very cost-conscious atmosphere about the factory. On the other hand, dealing with warranty claims is a very cost-oriented activity. The basic documentation for which is a list of product applications, normal warranty limits, exceptions, warranty reimbursement costs, and agreed labour rates for agencies and service centres.

7.6 OVERALL REVIEW AND COMPARISON WITH OTHER DATA

Table 7.6 summarizes the costs collected in this study and shows their distribution and ratio to projected annual sales turnover (£5 million). The table also shows distributions and ratios determined from a US survey [4] of quality-related costs. Although the industries surveyed were very diverse, and even the fabricated metal products sector of industry covers a wide range of products, it is interesting to observe some of the comparisons.

Clearly, omitting the test and repair costs and overheads from the company's quality costs yields distributions and ratios similar to those found in the US survey which, although the details of the computation of the data are not known, and it would be unwise to infer too much from the comparison, suggests that even with all the limitations discussed above the costs determined in this case study are not grossly in error and the company performance may be close to average.

Table 7.7 shows the company performance compared with that of another set of respondents to the US survey. This set of respondents measured only failure costs under the headings of scrap, rework and warranty. Again, without reading too much into the figures, it appears that the company's failure costs may be lower than might be expected, but there is also a suggestion that estimates of rework costs may be low and that the distribution of cost between scrap and rework is abnormal. However, it cannot be stressed too strongly that these are merely interesting observations and are not a basis for conclusions leading to any kind of action.

The costs are also shown graphically in Figs 7.1 and 7.2. These show clearly that the major costs are internal failure costs and that 95% of costs are ascribable to seven of 28 elements. It appears unlikely, even allowing for the uncertainties, errors and lack of information, that the picture grossly misrepresents the situation in the company. It also puts into proper perspective the subdivision of categories into many elements and the pursuit of accuracy in costing minor elements. A feature of the analysis was that one could readily obtain marked changes in proportions of annual sales turnover and of quality costs depending on the view taken about inclusion of test and repair work as a quality cost, and of overheads.

Aspects of quality costs not uncovered by the BS6143 checklist approach, but which were revealed in discussions with company personnel, are an arbitrary 10% excess materials allowed for 'headers' of casting moulds, and a 2.5% allowance for scrap in computing product costs. It is also normal practice to allow for losses by planning for 3% more production than is required.

7.7 MISCELLANEOUS POINTS ARISING FROM THE STUDY

Although it is believed that most of the major quality-related cost sources have been identified and reasonable estimates of the cost magnitudes of the different elements have been made, it is worth touching briefly on a few of the difficulties met with in trying to evaluate costs. These may be of value

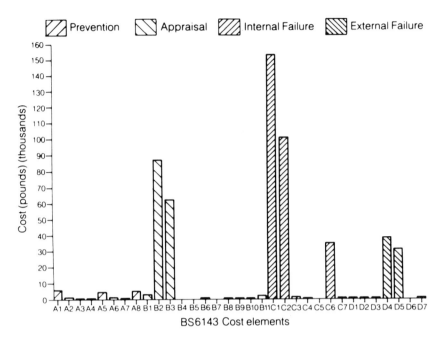

Figure 7.1 Quality costs.

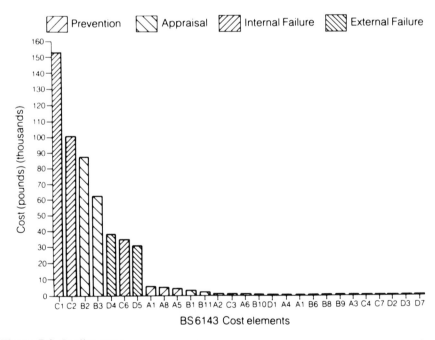

Figure 7.2 Quality costs.

to other quality cost collectors. It is accepted and understood that various practices in a company come about for good and sensible reasons, nevertheless some practices complicated and hampered the exercise to the extent that some costs were never properly resolved. These include the following:

- Different words and headings are used for the same thing in different departments.
- Different departments use different dates for the same transaction of activity.
- Calendar months are used in some departments and week numbers and accounting periods in others.
- The word 'scrap' is used loosely to mean or include rejected products, production waste rectification and rework.
- Retesting after repair is booked as testing.
- Unmeasured work is booked to 'prototype'.
- There is a minimum bonus rate for skilled workers doing non-productive tasks. Hence their time is booked to high-bonus codes irrespective of the task. Unskilled workers book to the correct code.
- There is only one rework code. It is sometimes used for booking time spent on inspection and sorting, thus combining appraisal costs with failure costs.
- A worker may properly book time to several cost centres but the 'home' cost centre carries the cost.
- Some costs lose their identity because bonus claims of the same value are lumped together for wage calculation purposes.
- Some different types of claims are combined because of an eight-column limit on the computer analysis display and print-out.
- Internal informal reporting does not always distinguish clearly between free-of-charge repairs and warranty costs.

REFERENCES

1. BS6143 (1981) *The Determination and Use of Quality-Related Costs*, British Standards Institution, London.
2. ASQC Quality Costs Committee (1974) *Quality Costs – What and How*, American Society for Quality Control, Milwaukee WI.
3. BS6143: Part 2 (1990) *Guide to the Economics of Quality: Prevention, appraisal and failure model*, British Standards Institution, London.
4. Anon. (1977) Quality cost survey. *Quality*, June, 20–2.

Case study, company 2 | 8

8.1 INTRODUCTION

Company 2 is engaged in the manufacture of ancillary equipment for reciprocating engines used mainly for powering trucks and cars. It produces some 300 000 units per year in a variety of sizes and configurations to suit different applications. It makes a precision product which operates under difficult service conditions. The manufacturing operations are essentially machining, forming, assembly and test and are carried out on a two-shift small-to-medium batch production basis. It is one of six manufacturing divisions and has an annual sales turnover of some £72 million and is part of a diversified major US corporation.

The fact that its customers are few in number, technically expert, commercially powerful and extremely competitive has considerable ramifications for the company, especially as engine and vehicle manufacturers feel that poor performance from the company's products may adversely affect their own reputations in the marketplace and thus market share. Company 2's products feature strongly in the customers' promotion of the image and performance of their goods. It is probably true also that the rapid rate of growth of the market means that customer loyalty has not yet become established to the point of being a major factor in the placing of orders. Add to this ownership by a company with its roots in aerospace technology, and international competition from both within and outside the company, and the result is a dynamic operation with an aggressive attitude to continuous quality improvement. The managing director makes an analogy between poor quality and friction in machines – one should be trying always to eliminate them. But quality was not its only crusade. Quality topics have to compete with manufacturing system development, advanced machining systems, manufacturing resources planning, total productive maintenance logistics, just-in-time, energy-saving and other cost-saving topics for money and resources.

The company's earliest attempts to collect quality costs were very rudimentary – scrap and rejects in the plant, and warranty claims from customers.

The availability of quality cost information has developed with the quality system itself, such that many important quality costs are now available on a weekly computer print-out. In the beginning the company used the quality management and costing systems of the parent company in an informal manner. It took the combined pressures of a sharp increase in production requirements and a particularly exacting customer to force the company into formalizing its methods of working. It was a traumatic exercise in which the company looked closely at what it was doing. It found that making people do what they really should be doing was not easy. However, it resulted – among other things – in a five-year vision, strategy, objectives and plan for the development of Total Quality Management, the formation of a quality assurance (as opposed to inspection) department with a senior manager in charge, and considerable capital expenditure on quality-related equipment. The quality system has continued to be developed such that current emphasis is on vendor development and on providing the best total value to the customer in terms of overall excellence of performance and quality. This is not just in terms of hardware delivered but also in terms of total product and service over the complete life cycle of the product. Tangible evidence of the developments is seen in the regular detailed reporting of quality and cost information to functional managers and of scrap and reject costs, by departments, to shopfloor workers. The conference sessions held by management also indicate the importance attached to quality matters with cost-reduction meetings held monthly and product quality review meetings daily.

Whilst the company acknowledges the general usefulness of quality-related costs in everyday decision making, it had at the time a deeper purpose for establishing a rigorous system for collecting and presenting costs. It also had a considerable obstacle to overcome to reach its ultimate objectives. The company manufactures for a rapidly expanding market and the parent company intended to expand the manufacturing facilities at some of its sites. Thus, the six manufacturing divisions are in competition with each other for a large capital investment. Company 2 is confident that its quality record is superior to that of its group competitors and wishes to devise a rigorous system of cost definition, collection and presentation to be adopted by all the manufacturing divisions so that its superiority shows. The obstacle to this objective is that the headquarters manufacturing division uses a different cost system to the other competing divisions. The headquarters division uses a project-costing system whilst the others all use standard-costing systems. A further objective was to try to use costs to indicate how, where and when to invest in prevention.

The company was indeed successful in demonstrating to its parent company that it was competitive in terms of quality, cost and delivery, and additional capital investment has been made available to the site in question.

8.2 IDENTIFICATION OF SOURCES OF QUALITY COSTS

In this second case study a more flexible approach was taken to the identification of sources of quality costs than in the first case study. Briefly, the approach used was to study the quality management and costing functions in action, without prejudice, and to make comparisons later. As a first step, the company's systems and procedures manual was closely studied for any time which might be construed as relating to quality. This generated a list of topics and questions which were raised and discussed with the quality manager and other staff as seemed appropriate. A similar exercise was then carried out on the company's costing system. Only when these studies were complete was any attempt made to make comparison with BS6143 [1] and, later, to draw up a quality-related cost report.

8.3 SOURCES OF COST IDENTIFIED FROM SYSTEMS AND PROCEDURES

Copies of the company's systems manual are held by departmental heads who have the responsibility of ensuring that all their staff are aware of new or revised systems which affect the running of the respective department. The systems are drawn up by a full-time systems administrator in conjunction with the heads of the departments involved in operating the system. Each system sets down the objective and the procedure to be followed. The titles and position of personnel responsible for actions in the procedure are indicated together with the appropriate form reference numbers. Managers with responsibility for operating the systems are signatories to the system. Thus, the company view of what are quality-related systems is immediately apparent because the quality manager is a signatory to them. The following systems were identified as being quality related:

1. goods receiving – production material;
2. goods receiving – tooling, gauges;
3. internal quality control and assurance procedures;
4. manufacturing quality review;
5. coding for scrap parts;
6. product specification, serial numbers;
7. suppliers' sample approval;
8. assembly release;
9. disposal of in-process scrap;
10. in-process scrap control;
11. inspection test and product stripdown;
12. request for tool store service;
13. engineering concessions;
14. engineering orders;

15. engineering instructions;
16. release of work to manufacturing areas;
17. outside processing of components.

It might have been expected that control of engineering and manufacturing specifications, tool control, foundry scrap for set-up, and issue of replacement parts for assembly would also have borne the quality manager's signature, but this was not the case.

Amongst the topics and questions generated from the survey of procedures and systems were those shown below. They are given here as examples of issues which have to be resolved in a quality cost collection exercise and are aspects to be considered by would-be quality cost collectors.

- Is the preparation of systems and procedures in itself a quality-related activity? (Especially as no fewer than 17 of the company's 50 procedures are related to topics that are clearly quality oriented.).
- Can quality awareness by stores personnel (e.g. by stock rotation, suitable storage, careful handling) be considered as a quality cost?
- Among the codes to which direct workers may book non-productive time are some (e.g. sorting) which may involve them in quality-related work without it being apparent from their job cards.
- When it is not possible to identify the department responsible for the loss of hours, the rework/excess work account must be specified.
- The time spent on the rectification of supplier faults is booked to the materials control department (presumably with the intention of recovering the cost from the supplier) but it is given a quality tag by noting the inspection reject report number on the time return.
- A system which requires all systems to be audited periodically is not itself classified as a quality-oriented system – at least as judged by the affiliations of the authorizing signatories.
- Instructions relating to the receipt and handling of products for service and repair do not suggest these activities are quality related.
- Is the movement of inward goods to a bonded area to await inspection a quality-related activity?
- Are the costs of purchasing and accounts departments dealing with rejected supplies quality related?
- The process of gauging may cause quality-related costs to arise. If gauging frequency is low it may be achieved within the standard machining time. If it is high, it may interfere with the rate of production. How should the costs of gauging be classified in these two cases?
- The necessity for resetting machines is a quality-related matter. Is downtime for machine resetting a quality cost?
- What is the cost of machine downtime?
- What are the economics of improved machine capability versus the higher capital cost?

- The time at which a machine is stopped by an inspector (on the grounds of product non-conformance) is logged but the time of restarting is not.
- Testing of products under simulated operating conditions is the responsibility of the quality assurance department.
- The disposition of rejected components or assemblies involves personnel from outside the quality assurance department in unmeasured quality activities (e.g. marking and segregating scrap, defining rework, scheduling rework on to the shopfloor).
- Codes for scrap and reworkable parts contain definitions such that the value of the scrapped part may not be a quality-related cost (e.g. parts no longer useable due to customer and/or engineering changes or errors).
- Some definitions of codes for scrap and reworkable parts imply that the economics of reworking and of salvaging parts are known and are the basis of the decisions whether to scrap or rework components.
- Non-working time codes on operator job cards contain two codes which are quality-related: 1. stopped by inspection and 2. waiting first-off and others. Are the costs quantifiable and, if so, are they appraisal costs? It should be noted that reasons for non-working not covered by other codes is added to 2 above.
- Excess codes cover rework and extra operations and are generally regarded as quality costs. However, one code – extra machining operations – may be used for reasons unconnected with quality (e.g. poor tooling).
- Drawing and print control are usual activities in engineering manufacture and are a quality safeguard. Is a quality-related cost incurred in this activity?
- Completed parts are stored in a clean area and protected from dust settlement. Can these precautions be considered as quality-related costs?
- Is the use of expensive packing materials to protect the product in transit a quality-related cost?
- Materials and contracts personnel get involved in dealing with non-conforming items received from overseas suppliers.
- The process route traveller requires the point of scrapping to be noted on the form.
- What are the costs incurred due to order-splitting because of rejection? There appears to be some difficulty in getting a disposition decision before the next processing operation.
- The quality assurance department is involved in agreeing fixed manufacturing costs. Does this include the opportunity cost of losing capacity during machine set-up?
- Although primary responsibility for engineering concession authorization lies with the product engineering department, quality assurance and production control departments become heavily involved.
- When traceability of parts released on concession is considered necessary, the sales engineering department also becomes involved and the work related to the maintenance of records increases considerably.

- Is the preparation of engineering instructions with mandatory status a quality-related cost?

8.4 SOURCES OF COSTS IDENTIFIED FROM ACCOUNTS LEDGERS

The company's costing system is the use of cost centres based on functions, cost topics and operating departments. Each cost centre is broken down into a number of cost elements each of which carries an account number and an indication of the account type (e.g. asset, liability, income or expense). It is the listing of these account numbers and titles, covering all the elements of all the cost centres, which was scrutinized for potential quality-related cost sources. This of course could only be done sensibly in the light of the knowledge gained earlier from studying the company's operations and systems.

A list of titles of accounts which it was thought might be relevant to the quality cost collection exercise and some other pertinent points uncovered are shown below. Again these may be helpful to people undertaking a quality costing exercise:

- provision for stock loss;
- obsolescence;
- laboratory equipment;
- office furniture and fittings;
- product component cleaning machinery
- provision for warranty payments;
- PAYE, superannuation, holiday pay;
- product transfers to other divisions;
- resale of refurbished products;
- spares;
- transfer of spares to other divisions;
- repairs;
- after-sales service;
- refurbishing returned units;
- rework;
- scrap materials;
- scrap sales;
- warranty costs;
- reject materials;
- stock loss provision;
- redundant stock scrapped;
- customer exception costs;
- depreciation;
- administration (salaries, travel);
- product technology;

- repairs to machinery and equipment;
- operating supplies;
- field test supplies;
- quality assurance department;
- customer engineering department;
- product support department;
- production department;
- works engineering department;
- manufacturing engineering department;
- industrial engineering department;
- standard costs derived from materials and labour costs and the recovery of overheads include an allowance of 5% for scrap losses;
- scrap is valued at the materials cost plus half the direct labour and overhead costs which would have been incurred if the item had been processed to completion;
- scrap sales records include allowance made to the customer on returned products which cannot be repaired;
- Rework costs include the cost of sorting rejected batches;
- the value of products returned by customers before being put into service is collected in a separate account and added to rework costs;
- special accounts are set up to deal with abnormal warranty situations;
- 'customer exception costs' are costs of the company's quality assurance staff based at a customer's works dealing with an exceptional problem;
- suppliers are debited with the value of faulty goods supplied;
- there is, possibly, some double-counting taking place when items are scrapped after rework;
- rework costs do not include overheads;
- not all the sort and rework claims are accepted by the accounts department. Owing to the fact that rework and other non-productive hours of direct workers are deducted from total hours before production efficiency is calculated based on the remaining hours, it may be in the production department's interest to claim as many non-productive hours as it can.

The company operates over a thousand active accounts across 33 cost centres. Hence the 30 or so accounts identified as possibly being directly relevant to a cost collection exercise seem but a small fraction of the total. However, it must be pointed out that the same account titles recur under different cost centres. It is also the case that there is a proliferation of cost centres, especially in those activities closest to the manufacturing operation. Since cost centres suffice for departments/functions such as administration, finance, personnel, purchasing, production control, sales administration, customer engineering. On the other hand, works engineering, manufacturing engineering and quality assurance have four cost centres each (one administration and one for each factory site), and production has five cost centres through which to control its costs. In the case of the quality assurance department, four cost centres for 35 personnel (at least 80% of whose costs must be remuneration) is surely an accounting extravagance. However, it is by no means unusual for there to be closer scrutiny and analysis of costs the nearer one gets to the manufacturing operation. Perhaps this is because the manufacturing function is the easiest activity to measure.

8.5 APPLICABILITY OF BS6143 AT COMPANY 2

The study also examined the applicability of BS6143 [1] (the 1981 version of the Standard) in the company. Hence, just as in company 1, the applicability of each of the elements listed in the standard was checked against the working practices in the company. However, in this case, owing to the fact that the company is US owned and that it is seeking to set up a cost reporting system which sets a style and standard acceptable to its sister companies, it made sense to keep the ASQC lists [2] and definitions in mind. In doing so differences between the ASQC and BS6143 lists and definitions emerged and are noted. These differences are important to quality cost collectors in transnational organizations.

8.5.1 Prevention costs

Definitions of prevention costs differ slightly between the British Standard (BS) and the American Society for Quality Control (ASQC) recommendations. The principal differences are as follows.

1. The BS definition of prevention costs permits a wider range of quality-related activities (and hence costs) to be included than does the ASQC definition.
2. The BS document separates out supplier quality assurance as a specific cost element whereas the ASQC document includes only vendor surveys prior to placing an order, other dealings with vendors being classed as appraisal activities.
3. The ASQC sees the maintenance and calibration of test and inspection equipment used in the control of quality, and production equipment used to evaluate quality, as being appraisal activities rather than prevention.

Apart from these differences there is close agreement between the two authorities.

The main prevention activities identified from a study of the company systems manual and discussions with a number of quality assurance department staff are matched against the model as follows:

A1   Quality engineering – planning.

The quality system and translating product design and customer quality requirements into manufacturing quality control of materials, processes and products. Implementing and maintaining quality plan and procedures.

This work is carried out exclusively within the quality assurance department. It absorbs most of the effort of two quality engineers. There is some input from the quality manager and from the quality engineering manager, and possibly from the quality assurance department foremen and inspectors.

A2   Design and development of quality measurement and control equipment.

This work falls wholly within the quality assurance department.

A3   Quality planning by functions other than the quality assurance department.

This is an area where there may be significantly large inputs from other departments (e.g. purchasing, production engineering, manufacturing engineering and customer engineering) via such activities as the test house, gauge tables, planning inspection levels and engineering concession authorizations.

A4   Calibration and maintenance of production equipment used to evaluate quality.

As defined this element does not match the situation at company 2. Such work as is done on this equipment is appraisal work (and hence in line with the ASQC categorization of this type of work).,

A5   Maintenance and calibration of test and inspection equipment.

This work is carried out by calibration room staff and by external service laboratories. It should be noted that the ASQC categorizes this type of work under appraisal activities.

A6   Supplier assurance – the cost of personnel engaged in preventive activities of the supplier quality assurance programme.

This element is an important part of the preventive activities at company 2. It occupies a significantly large proportion of one quality assurance foreman's effort and there are inputs from purchasing, production engineering and metallurgical services on the site.

A7   Quality training.

The company is not active in providing outside training, but if it should become so, the costs should be easy to collect.

A8   Administration, audit, improvement and other costs.

Administration includes costs of secretarial services, telephones and travelling. Audit costs are the costs of personnel engaged in planning, documenting, implementing and maintaining audits on the quality system. Improvement costs are the costs of the quality improvement process and motivational activities.

Administration costs are within the quality assurance department's control, and the audit and improvement activities are mostly from the audit inspector and the quality engineering manager respectively.

(a) Comment

Activities of people within the quality assurance department which are substantial in terms of time consumed and must have a preventive content. These activities, which are difficult to quantify and which may not be identified under the elements listed above are the daily review meetings, work aimed at changing from a corrective approach to a prevention-based/process control approach, involvement in reliability work, and post-warranty performance analysis. Similarly, the involvement of personnel from other functions (e.g. purchasing and production engineering) are difficult to quantify and cost.

However, overall, much of the activity is concentrated within the quality assurance department so that a good approximation of the prevention costs may be gained from estimates of man-hours spent on prevention activities and from the departmental budget.

If a cost breakdown under the different elements is desired, it is probably that estimates of time spent on the different activities would be so conflicting that one could have little confidence in them. This problem can only be overcome by requiring staff to keep records of how they spend their time. A weekly return accounting for activities in 10% (i.e. half-day) increments would be sufficient for the purpose. Secretarial and other costs could be allocated in direct proportion to the levels of the different activities, and outside services may be costed directly from invoices.

8.5.2 Appraisal costs

The definitions of appraisal costs used by the BSI and the ASQC are similar in intent despite differences in wording (e.g. BSI's costs of assessing the quality achieved compared with the ASQC's costs incurred to determine the degree of conformance to quality requirements). With the exceptions noted earlier under prevention costs (A4, A5) the elements are almost identical. Some of the elements, however, clearly relate to large-scale heavy engineering and are not applicable to the operations of company 2. The remaining categories cover appraisal activities reasonably well.

B1   Laboratory acceptance testing (of purchased materials).
        This includes an input from production engineering which may be difficult to quantify, but costs of external testing should be easy to determine from invoices.

B2   Inspection and test (including goods inwards inspection).

This is probably the largest single cost element, including as it does the cost of all the inspection staff together with a substantial proportion of their supervisors' time, material review board time, and some management time.

B3   In-process inspection by personnel who are not inspectors by job description.

This may also be a fairly substantial cost, part of which may readily be measurable (e.g. production personnel engaged full time on testing) and some of which may be very difficult to measure (e.g. gauging by operators which may add to the time of the operation).

B4   Cost of setting up equipment or products for inspection or functional testing is largely covered in this case by B3 above (e.g. testing in service-like environment and subsequent stripping down for post-test inspection).

B5   Inspection and test materials include crack detection fluids, paper for machines, plaster of Paris, and losses of castings and shafts in reliability testing. The items and sources of cost are very diverse and whilst some materials costs specific to quality or metallurgical functions may be relatively easy to collect from invoices, the costs incurred from production materials may be difficult to determine. This is not because material items costs are not known, but because the usages are not recorded.

B6   Product quality audits are a part-time activity of the audit inspector and could be costed from their time allocation data.

B7   Review of test and inspection data.

The practice of 100% inspection obviates the need for regular reviews of test and inspection data before release of the product for shipment.

B8   Field (on-site) performance testing.

Not applicable as defined.

B9   Internal testing and release.

Not appropriate as defined.

B10   Evaluation of field stock and spare parts.

Not appropriate as defined.

B11   Data processing inspection and test reports.

This activity occupies a significant fraction of the senior quality engineer's and the audit inspector's time, and there is a *pro rata* input from the quality manager.

(b) Comment

Important appraisal cost elements not accounted for above are the depreciation cost of capital equipment used for inspection, gauging and balancing, and the costs of items needing frequent replacement. Presumably inventories and costs of all inspection and gauging equipment are available and should make these costs easily determinable.

8.5.3 Failure costs

(a) Internal failure costs

There is good agreement between the BSI and ASQC publications on the definition of internal failure costs (i.e. the costs arising within the manufacturing organization of the failure to achieve the quality specified – before transfer of ownership to the customer). There is also good agreement on the definitions of individual cost elements. The elements and their relevance to internal failure costs at company 2 are as follows.

C1   Scrap – all scrap losses incurred in the course of meeting quality requirements (scrap caused by overruns, obsolescence or design changes requested by customers are not included).

         Although the points in the process at which parts are scrapped is noted on the process route traveller, no attempt is made to calculate the value at that point. The current practice is to cost scrap parts as material cost plus half the direct labour and overhead costs which would have been incurred if the item had been processed to completion. Periodic analysis of data from travellers and reject notes should demonstrate the aptness of the present practice, though some weighting should be applied to account for the segregation, marking and handling of scrap by indirect workers. A comparison between the numbers of replacement parts issued and the records of parts scrapped should indicate the amount of scrap which is not accounted for.

         It is the practice in some companies to deduct the value of scrap parts from the scrap failure costs before presenting the quality cost statement. This, of course, is an understatement of failure costs and should be avoided.

C2   Rework and repair – the costs incurred in meeting quality requirements when material can be restored for use.

         Rework is recorded but is not analysed and costed, though it is claimed that the decision whether to scrap or rework is taken on an economic basis. Clearly the distribution of rejected parts between scrap and rework should change with the economics of production at that time. The sensitivity of the economics under various conditions of production is not known in company 2.

         In addition to the direct costs of rework there are costs for sorting and checking rejected batches and the costs of the involvement of production control and other personnel in replanning for rework. The cost of provision and use of equipment for carrying out rework, which cannot be accommodated on production line machines, should not be overlooked.

         A complicating factor in the cost of rework is the practice of specifying the rework/excess work account when it is not possible to identify a particular department as being responsible for the machine time lost.

C3   Trouble shooting or defect/failure analysis.
      There are inputs from the quality assurance department and the product engineering department.
C4   Re-inspect, re-test.
      These activities are not noted directly but presumably could be estimated, if necessary, from knowledge of the amount and type of rework as a fraction of the total processing activity.
C5   Scrap and rework through fault of vendor.
      Costs of material are recovered from the vendor but the costs of processing material to the point of rework/scrap, and the costs of idle facilities and labour, are not recovered.
C6   Modification permits and concessions – the time spent reviewing product designs and specifications.
      Because there are inputs from a number of people in many functions this cost may only be estimated. If the element is interpreted in the wider sense of the whole activity of obtaining qualifications, modification permits and concessions, together with the effects of delays and batch splitting, the cost must be considerable and very difficult to quantify without detailed records of time inputs from all the staff involved.
C7   Downgrading.
      This is usually taken to mean reclassification as 'seconds'. The company does not market 'seconds' though some components which are substandard for normal products may be able to be used satisfactorily in remanufactured units. Remanufacture or overhaul is not a quality-related cost and it is doubtful whether it is worth considering the difference in value between standard components in normal production units and the downgraded components in the remanufactured units which are sold more cheaply.

(b) Comment

Because scrap and rework costs are collected and probably amount to an impressive sum of money, there may be a tendency to assume it is the whole cost (or indeed a reluctance to investigate more closely in case it turns out to be even bigger). Nevertheless, the process economics used to decide whether to scrap or to reject are probably worth investigating because they may enable savings to be made. Similarly the booking of lost machine time to quality-related codes on spurious grounds may warrant investigation to make sure that the quality-related cost account is not being debited unfairly. In the matter of modification permits, discussed under C6 above, it may be worthwhile doing a 'snapshot' costing to determine the magnitude, sources and causes of these costs. To attempt to collect them on a regular basis appears to be a horrendous task, even though the costs may be relatively large.

(c) External failure costs

External failure costs are defined as the costs arising when products fail to meet quality requirements (after transfer of ownership to the customer). This is not an entirely satisfactory definition because it implies that all costs, irrespective of who incurs them, should be included. The BSI definition, though slightly differently worded, has similar implications. Such costs may be of value to students of life cycle costing and reliability studies, but in this case the costs to be considered will be those quality-related costs incurred by the company.

D1   Complaints administration.

Complaints reach the company via several routes, e.g. customer service, marketing, production engineering and quality assurance. Unless complaints are formally channelled through rigorous procedures and dealt with by a small number of people, it is difficult to see how such costs could be collected separately.

D2   Product or customer service, product liability (i.e. the costs of product services directly attributable to correcting imperfections, including any liability costs).

Costs incurred through the customer service organization of the company for products which, for example, fail on test or cause problems with fitting (as distinct from failure in service) could be collected under this heading. Isolating this element of expenditure would require a great deal of cooperation from customer service and other departments outside the control of the quality manager. In these circumstances, a decision about whether or not to gather these costs depends largely on the relative magnitude of the costs.

On the matter of product liability, the cost is probably carried by the vehicle manufacturer. If not, the costs incurred (which should be easily retrievable) or the requisite insurance premium costs should be included under this heading.

D3   Products rejected and returned, recalls, retrofits, the cost of handling and accounting for rejected products including any recall and retrofit costs.

It is unlikely that the handling and accompanying costs of this limited activity are sufficiently large to warrant them being identified separately.

D4   Returned material repair – the costs associated with analysing and repairing customer-returned material.

Such costs should be readily identifiable because of their non-routine nature and because of the external customer's involvement. Recovered material or components should not be credited to this account.

D5   Warranty replacement – the cost of replacing failures within the warranty period.

This cost should relate strictly to the replacement cost of the faulty item. Other costs incurred (e.g. investigation of warranty claims) should be included under D1 above.

The BSI and ASQC documents suggest that these costs may be sub-divided to show the warranty costs incurred from errors arising in different departments, e.g. marketing, engineering, production and quality assurance. Analysis of warranty claims may reveal sources of error but it is debatable whether quantifying blame by allocating costs is helpful in eliminating errors, or is worth the effort.

The value of material or components recovered from failed pro-ducts should not be credited to the warranty account.

(d) Comment

This category probably incurs the same type of problem that arises with internal failure cost, i.e. because a substantial cost is already known, there is little incentive to refine it further. Refining the costs may be difficult because the activity at the company–customer interface is not within the sphere of direct influence of the quality manager and hence would require an extremely high level of commitment and cooperation from the customer service and marketing functions. The costs involved may not warrant the effort, especially if there is little potential to reduce them.

8.6 DISCUSSION OF FINDINGS

In assessing the applicability of BS6143 it appeared that the costs of most of the elements which are applicable could be ascertained without too much trouble. However, it was surprising to learn that only five elements of costs were available directly from the accounts department without having to analyse cost data. This suggests a weakness in the matching of quality elements, as defined in BS6143, with the kinds of cost data usually available in companies.

The difficulties of whether activities should be classified as being quality related, which arose at company 1, also arose at company 2. Examples here are provision of 'clean areas' and 'protection' for components and assemblies. Clearly cleanliness from abrasive dirt is important in the manufacture of high-speed delicately balanced machinery, but is the cost of ensuring it a quality-related cost? Other examples are the segregation, marking and handling of scrap, movement of goods for inspection purposes, the activities of purchas-ing and accounting personnel in dealing with rejected supplies, and the effects of order-splitting (for quality reasons) on planning and manufacture. From a quality viewpoint it may appear that these activities are quality related and should feature in quality-related costs. However, an accountant might argue that they should be omitted on grounds of difficulty of quantification alone.

Activities which are clearly quality related are those concerned with products passed on concession, and modifications. The feeling gained at company 1 that these are large, costly, but unmeasured activities was reinforced at company 2, perhaps because, although it is sensibly autonomous in its production operations, qualifications or changes to specification must be approved by the parent company in the United States, so that relatively minor matters can become quite protracted. This is the case with most companies whose headquarters are outside the country in which they have a manufacturing facility.

A quality cost which company 2 has no difficulty in defining (if only because it has been decisive about it) is the valuation of scrapped goods. Many quality management practitioners and accountants have some difficulty with this and opinions on the matter range from purchased materials costs to full selling price. Company 2 takes the view that it should be the full materials cost plus half the combined direct labour and overhead cost. Although the point in the process at which the item is scrapped is noted on the manufacturing route card, the company does not feel it is worth calculating the labour and overhead costs at every stage in the manufacturing process. It has settled on half of what these costs would have been if the item had been processed to completion. Because of company 2's relatively high materials costs, there seems little point in trying to refine it further.

Other minor points on costing worth noting from the work at company 2 are:

1. although scrap valuation includes overheads, rework costs do not;
2. apparently US tax law encourages companies to value all scrap at full sales value;
3. although there was good agreement between the accounts department and quality assurance department on scrap costs, there was no evidence of an independent check from a materials balance.

A noticeable feature of the accounting system at company 2 and that at other companies is the greater accountability the nearer one gets to the manufacturing operation. This has implications for the cost collection exercise because the bulk of quality costs are incurred close to the manufacturing operation. Hence, the accountability bias is in the quality cost collector's favour. A factor working in the opposite direction is the involvement of personnel from a wide spectrum of functions. It is not usual for personnel in functions such as purchasing and accounting to make returns of how they spend their time. Indeed, it is the general lack of information about how people, other than direct workers, spend their time which presents a considerable obstacle to the collection of quality costs.

A pitfall waiting for the unwary was the reporting of changes in provision (e.g. for warranty) as opposed to actual expenditure in the period. According to the Chartered Institute of Management Accountants' [3] official terminology, provisions for liabilities and charges are:

Amounts retained as reasonably necessary to cover any liability or loss which is either likely, or certain to be incurred but uncertain as to amount or as to the date on which it will arise (Companies Acts).

Although this seems perfectly straightforward, problems can arise for cost collectors because the provision for a particular liability may be topped up with arbitrary amounts of money from time to time. Hence to determine the true expenditure it is necessary to know about the topping up as well as the change in provision. A more familiar trap met with was the reporting of net costs of scrap. The errors which may be unwittingly introduced by this practice are quite large in the case of company 2, because many of its components are made of expensive alloys which have a high scrap value.

The use of costs as motivators to shopfloor workers in company 2 was interesting. The costs displayed were the costs of scrapped goods, because shopfloor workers could see the relevance of them to their work. Further, although the scrap costs are relatively small in company cost terms, they are large in relation to the wages of operatives on the factory shopfloor. Thus a strong impact is made without disclosing sensitive cost information.

8.7 COST REPORT AND COMPARISON WITH OTHER DATA

At the time of the study, by pure coincidence, there was a company-wide initiative in collecting quality costs taking place and the quality manager was preparing a quality cost report. The quality-related costs collected are listed by element and category in Table 8.1. They amount to £1.65 million, equivalent to 6.1% of the annual sales turnover in the year the study was conducted. The distribution between categories is broadly as expected and, also, within categories there are a few elements which account for a large proportion of the cost.

When a first cost report is complete it is natural to wonder whether the performance it reflects is good, bad or indifferent. In a company like this, with a number of competing manufacturing divisions, it should be possible to make inter-divisional comparisons of quality performance using, for example, numbers of rejects, warranty claims, supplier assessment and customer sastisfaction index, as well as costs. This comparison is one of the methods employed in internal benchmarking. Unfortunately, the company has not yet developed its quality-related costing systems to such a state that meaningful comparisons may be made. Indeed, it is doubtful whether even the reporting of numbers is uniform enough for valid comparisons to be made. An alternative is to wait until another report is completed, perhaps a year later, and look for differences. Again, unfortunately, this would not give an absolute measure of performance. Hence a comparison has been made with published data despite the dangers of doing so which have been stressed on numerous occasions in this book.

Table 8.1 Quality-related cost report – company 2

	£000	%	Total (%)	Annual sales turnover (%)
Prevention				
Laboratory and other services	23	21		
Quality engineering	38	35		
Calibration room	26	24		
Supplier quality assurance	12	11		
Administration and other costs	10	9		
	109	100	6.6	0.38
Appraisal				
Quality control	430	61		
Test	200	28		
Product inspection	6	1		
Gauges	32	5		
Operating supplies*	12	2		
Laboratory services	7	1		
Quality audit	12	2		
	699	100	42.3	2.4
Internal failure				
Scrap*	276	52.5		
Rework*	135	25.8		
Materials Review Board (production)	45	8.7		
Materials Review Board (quality)	12	2.3		
Data processing	4	0.7		
Purchasing/manufacturing engineering/product engineering	53	10.0		
	525	100	31.8	1.8
External failure				
Warranty*	37	11.6		
Abnormal warranty*	116	36.4		
Rejected materials*	16	5.0		
Service/administration/other	150	47.0		
Total	319	100	19.3	1.1
Overall total	1652		100.0	6.1

*Total figures obtainable from accounts department. Other figures estimated.

Table 8.2 Company 2 quality-related costs compared with some industry sector costs

Comparison of company 2 performance with published data*	Formal programme for cost collection					Informal programme for cost collection		
	Total % Net sales billed (NSB)	Prev. % NSB	Appr. % NSB	Int. Fail. % NSB	Ext. Fail. % NSB	Scrap (S) % NSB	Rework (R) % NSB	Warranty (W)† % NSB
Company 2	6.1	0.38	2.4	1.8	1.1	0.95	0.47	0.52
Machinery manufacture	4.43	0.49	1.05	1.76	1.14	2.5	1.5	2.2
Instruments, etc. manufacture	7.27	1.20	2.12	1.78	2.15	3.6	2.8	1.8
Manufacturing industry in general	5.8	0.6	1.5	2.5	1.2	3.2	3.0	1.6
	Total Q. cost	Prev. %	Appr. %	Int. Fail. %	Ext. Fail. %	Scrap % S+R+W	Rework % S+R+W	Warranty † % S+R+W
Company 2	100	6.6	42.3	31.8	19.3	49	24	27
Machinery manufacture	100	11	24	40	26	40	25	35
Instruments, etc. manufacture	100	16.5	29	24.5	29.5	44	34	22
Manufacturing industry in general	100	10.3	26	43	20.7	41	38	21

*Quality costs survey. Quality, June 1977, pp. 20–2 [4].
†Warranty includes abnormal warranty.

The data used are those from a survey carried out by the journal *Quality* [4] in which are reported categories of quality costs as percentages of total quality costs and of net sales billed NSB (turnover) for several industry groups at two levels of sophistication of cost collection (Table 8.2).

Keeping in mind the limitations of the data, it appears that company 2 is more akin to companies with a formal programme for cost collection and engaged in the manufacture of instruments, than to any other group. Gross expenditure as a percentage of annual sales turnover is similar to other manufacturers but the prevention expenditure appears to be low in both absolute terms and as a proportion of quality-related expenditures. Appraisal costs are high, which is consistent with low external failure and slightly high internal failure costs.

8.8 PRESENTATION AND USES OF COST DATA

It was interesting to note the difference in the formats devised by the quality manager at company 2 and the proposed format from elsewhere in the company. The former reflects the day-to-day quality-related activities as the quality manager experiences them whilst the proposed format is a copy of the received wisdom on the subject, modified to suit the company's *modus operandi* rather than its needs (whatever these may be).

It is interesting to note that the quality manager's original listing of quality-related cost elements was not categorized under prevention-appraisal-failure headings. That came later, presumably, to fit in with the received wisdom. The point is important because the original intent was simply to establish a list of cost elements and an agreed method of calculation of costs so that valid inter-site comparisons could be made. Categorization of these elements into prevention-appraisal-failure costs adds nothing to the usefulness or value of the data for their intended purpose. Nor is the proposed format accompanied by any justification for that particular format. It does not appear to help the company in what it is attempting to achieve and indeed one of the dangers of picking up ready-made formats is that important elements may get left out simply because they do not fit conveniently into one of the prescribed pigeon-holes. While predetermined formats and checklists may have much to commend them in helping less knowledgeable people to compile reports, there is no substitute for experience. Nor does this form of reporting help to identify directly projects for quality improvement, though the subsidiary scrap numbers and cost report is useful for this purpose.

REFERENCES

1. BS6143 (1981) *The Determination and Use of Quality-Related Costs*, British Standards Institution, London.

2. ASQC Quality Costs Committee (1974) *Quality Costs – What and How*, American Society for Quality Control, Milwaukee, WI.
3. Anon (1991) *Management Accounting: Official Terminology,* The Chartered Institute of Management Accountants, London.
4. Anon. (1977) Quality cost survey. *Quality*, June, 20–2.

Case study, company 3 | 9

9.1 INTRODUCTION

Company 3 is engaged in the manufacture of diesel engines for powering trucks, buses, trains and pumping stations. The type of production is medium-scale batch machining and fabrication, assembly and test. It employs 1300 people and has a sales turnover of about £48 million per annum.

Although it is a subsidiary part of one of a large group of companies it is an autonomous business unit set up in 1981 with all the usual functional departments except engineering and sales, which are centralized functions of the parent company. Sister units within the parent company are important suppliers and customers of company 3, and a sister company to the parent company is also a major customer.

Since becoming 'independent', company 3 has achieved remarkable changes in its quality performance. In a little over three years it has, for example, reduced its inspection staff by two-thirds and reduced defects per engine, detected at audits, from 30 to three. However, there has been little corresponding evidence of cost improvement. Thus the development of cost measurement and reporting was lagging behind the improvements in product and service quality. It should also be mentioned that the company's products often do not go into service immediately after manufacture, and when in service they remain operational for a relatively long time (typically three to ten years). Hence it takes a long time (perhaps one to three years) for the effects of quality improvement, as measured at the factory, to be noticed in the marketplace. The improvements have been achieved in a climate of very difficult trading circumstances for their major in-house customers and the company is always actively seeking new customers and applications for its engines.

Inevitably the quality management objectives, strategies, behaviour and attitudes within the parent company will have their influence on daughter companies. The situation of the parent company with respect to quality costs is that they have, in the past, monitored costs but not used them. At the time the research was being conducted they were attempting to collate quality cost reports from the seven daughter companies. At the time of the study the headquarters quality function was trying to collate costs listed by activity from seven different operations under the usual prevention-appraisal-failure categories, as laid down in their quality policy manual. This was despite the fact that the policy manual is itself subdivided into functional activities and the only reference to categorization of activities under prevention-appraisal-failure is in the policy on costs.

The focus of the work reported and discussed in this chapter was to identify and analyse the available quality cost information and examine how it might be used.

9.2 IDENTIFICATION OF SOURCES OF QUALITY COSTS

In this case study the approach adopted to the identification of quality-related costs was initially that used in company 2, i.e. the company's operating procedures and costing systems were scrutinized to identify items which might refer to quality-related activities or costs. In addition, there was much information to be gleaned from monthly reports on quality-related activities. This was most notably in the fields of suppliers, in-house failures and warranty. The parent company quality policy manual also gave clues to where quality-related costs might be found. A paper on quality-related costs from a similar industry (Schmidt and Jackson [1]) added nothing to this part of the exercise. It merely served to endorse the information found in company 3's documents and records.

9.3 COST SOURCES IDENTIFIED FROM PROCEDURES AND SYSTEMS

The company's operating procedures are grouped under seven categories:

1. procedure information
2. finance
3. quality
4. production
5. manufacturing engineering
6. personnel
7. materials department

All the procedures were examined for leads to quality-related costs. The company's accounting systems and reports were also scrutinized with the same objective. Both of these searches were supplemented by discussion with company staff as appropriate. In the event this part of the exercise was not so fruitful as expected and much more was gained from studying quality cost reporting as practised in the company.

The principal points noted from this part of the exercise are offered without comment as potential pointers to other quality cost collectors, as follows:

- Instructions for booking direct labour hours, including excess hours (some of which are due to quality-related matters), are described under financial procedures.
- Some machine shop rectification work is done by setters and by apprentices.
- Measured excess time bookings are recorded on operation cards and authorized by the industrial engineering department.
- Performances and costings are derived from the data on operation cards.
- Of 15 excess time codes three are positively quality related (defective material, previous operation defective, rectifications), whilst others may be so (e.g. equipment defective or temporary, alternative material or method, fitting shortages) depending on the underlying reasons and the view of what is or what is not a quality-related activity.
- Labour-booking procedures for additional unplanned operations raise many questions about what is or what is not quality-related work even though only four of 12 categories are the responsibility of the quality assurance department and become the subject of a standard quality non-conformance report.
- Labour performance reporting is by weekly tabulation of analyses of booked hours. Among the many analyses carried out are excess and indirect bookings by direct workers, measured and unmeasured excess hours by type, part number, operation number and operator.
- Four of eight quality non-conformance liability codes are related to suppliers and customers.
- Procedures specify that 'agreed costs' for sorting and fitting should be recovered by the purchasing department from suppliers of defective parts.
- Manufacturing engineering supply estimates of additional costs which are incurred owing to defective material from suppliers.
- In-plant rectification costs of defects which are the supplier's liability are negotiated with the supplier prior to the work being done.
- Matters which are, or are likely to be, passed on concession do not become the subject of quality non-conformance reports.
- Procedures for production concessions and engineering design modifications make no reference to cost allocation of the activities involved.
- If rectification is not possible, the foreman will determine, in conjunction with inspection, if a concessionary procedure can be involved. This indicates that the concession is a second resort for the disposal of non-conforming parts and products.
- When non-conforming parts are the result of careless workmanship, the operator concerned is expected to rectify them without a time allowance being given. When the operator responsible cannot rectify the work for some reason, someone else does it and is recompensed for it.

- Rectification costs incurred on bought-out materials are net of recharge to suppliers.
- The quality assurance department analyses on a weekly basis the quality non-conformance reports and collates defect incidence against cost to produce a 'top-ten' machine shop scrap report.
- The finance department receives scrap analysis data from the quality assurance department as well as quality non-conformance reports to assist with the compilation of scrap costs analysed by manufacturing area.
- Scrap valuation for quality cost purposes is direct materials cost and direct labour (at base hourly rate) to the point of scrapping. For stock valuation purposes an overhead on direct labour is included.
- Parts downgraded for service use may incur unplanned additional work. This is not picked up as a quality cost.
- Finished parts found to be non-conforming after being passed to stores, assembly or goods inward are not the subject of a quality non-conformance report but costs of rectification are picked up by use of appropriate accounting codes on the operations card.
- Rectification costs are gathered under headings of bought-out material, made-in components, and rectification of incomplete assembly work. They are collected across the site and are not analysed by department.
- Modification work costs are also gathered on a site basis against modifications to rejected products and modification of components to new specifications.
- The quality circle programme costs are identified separately but quality training costs are not.
- The whole engine test operation is regarded as a quality cost and is under the control of the quality assurance manager.
- The purchasing department performance reports made no reference to their supplier quality assurance activities and related improvements.

9.4 QUALITY COST COLLECTION AND ANALYSIS

9.4.1 General

At company 3 an outstanding feature was the infectious enthusiasm of the quality assurance manager in leading a crusade for continuous and company-wide quality improvement. His views of what constituted quality cost, and in particular failure costs, were challenging, stimulating and enlightening. His philosophy focuses attention of management failures as well as shopfloor failures. Guilty managers could run but they could not escape from the logic of the cases against them.

The parent company's policy on quality costs and improvements states that the quality cost report must show prevention, appraisal and failure categories.

Company 3's procedures and accounting practices do not make any such specification. Nor are they set up to produce quality-related costs in that format on a routine basis.

In addition to the policy statement rather a curious memorandum which originated within the parent company describes the concept of total quality costs as follows:

Total Quality Cost is designed to identify all the costs of not getting the product right first time. It therefore includes the following major costs broken down into different categories where appropriate:

- the cost of employing the total quality function (hourly paid wages, salaries and all related benefits)
- the cost of all production workers' time booked to remedying quality defects (rectification, etc.)
- all obsolete stock provisions
- the costs of implementing engineering design modifications on current models
- all bookings to scrap (labour and materials)
- estimates for new model testing work
- warranty expenditure for the period (not the charge to the profit and loss account which would include the movement in warranty provision in addition, but the actual expenditure).

On the matter of measurement the memorandum goes on:

From the above categories it can be seen that the collection of relevant cost data needs to be done by recognising that all costs booked to certain cost centres or account codes are considered as quality costs, and are collected as such . . . .

The other way to approach the costing would be in terms of heads employed on quality which could then be adjusted by the appropriate wage or salary rate to give the cost of employing those heads. Additional adjustments could then be made for scrap costs, obsolete stock provision, warranty costs and product design costs . . . .

Obviously the first approach will give more accurate numbers if the costs are recorded in this detail. The second approach should give a method of producing a fairly accurate estimate of total quality cost if the cost centre/account code detail is not available. Either will represent a significant improvement over current practice.

The inclusion of obsolete stock provision is unusual on two counts because 1. a provision is not an expenditure and 2. (in company 3 at least obsolete stock is defined as material for which there is no forward requirement. The inclusion of new model testing work as a quality-related cost is also unusual. Most people would regard these costs as development costs. However, the points about the implementation of engineering design modifications and reporting of warranty expenditure are well made.

Notwithstanding the policies and guidelines of the parent company, company 3 reports quality costs on a routine basis in the ways which suit its own business, technology and processes. Hence its first-level expression of quality costs is through the scrap costs of its in-house machining operations in order to identify which of several quality problems to tackle. Monthly quality performance reports, using a presentation format similar to that used for cost control versus budget, show an array of appraisal and failure data together with a limited amount of cost data for each of 23 machining areas operating under separate cost centres. Part of the cost data is the cost of scrap, also expressed as cost per effective standard hour (ESH). (An effective standard hour is a standard hour's output of piece parts, assemblies or process operations, excluding all excesses, which are directly attributable to a finished product. The standard per piece multiplied by the quantity gives the total ESH produced.) The cost of rework and the inspection costs associated with it (including sorting) are also reported.

Data from these records for the year in which the study was carried out have been used to compile the bar charts and Pareto diagram shown in Fig. 9.1 to illustrate the change in perspective of problems which is brought about by presenting failure rate data on a cost basis instead of the usual number-of-failures basis. The effect is dramatic and is by no means uncommon. The implications of the change in perspective may also be dramatic because solutions to the major problems, as defined using the different bases, may call for very different amounts and kinds of resources.

The same kind of exercise cannot be done for rework (using the data as presented) because only cost, and not number, data for rework are presented in the report, though the numerical data must surely be known. However, if it is accepted that cost is the proper criterion against which to gauge the importance of problems, then the rework and associated cost data may also be used to identify problems warranting the allocation of high-priority limited resources. Figure 9.2 indicates the relative importance of problem areas using scrap value versus rework and associated costs, though it must be borne in mind that the magnitude of scrap costs are generally much greater than rework and associated costs. The changes in distribution which occur when translating scrap levels from numbers to costs, and then to costs per effective standard hour, are very marked. Such drastic changes are not uncommon, and whilst they may give immediate indications of which problems should be being tackled, it is worth noting that different ways of expressing the cost produce different indications. Hence it is important to try to determine and use the cost expression which is right for a company at that time. It should also be kept in mind that different problems may require quite different resources and have widely different timescales for solutions to be devised and implemented.

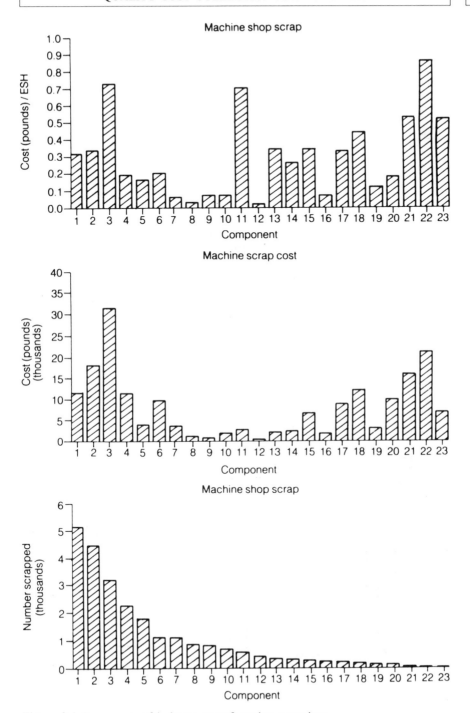

Figure 9.1 Scrap costs of in-house manufacturing operations.

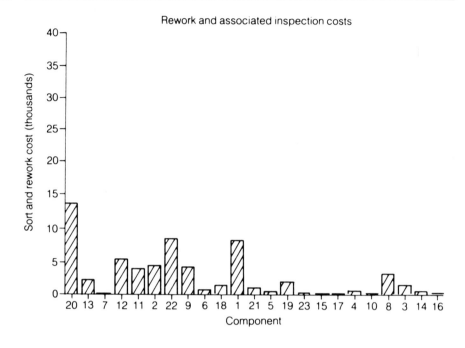

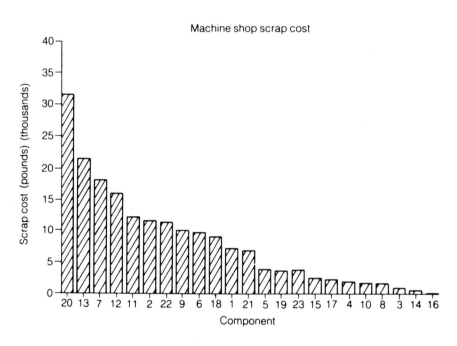

Figure 9.2 Rework, inspection and scrap costs analysis.

The prevention, appraisal and product testing activities of company 3 are executed under cost centres under the control of the quality assurance manager and the costs are reported routinely for budgetary control purposes. These costs together with the in-house failure costs discussed above comprise the majority of the in-house quality costs featured in the company's monthly quality cost reports. However, just as internal failure costs are the subject of close scrutiny and analysis to identify and rank problem areas, so, also, are the failure aspects of the company's external dealings with suppliers and customers given special attention.

9.4.2 Suppliers of rough and finshed goods

The quality performance of suppliers of bought-out finished goods is closely monitored. All goods go through the goods receiving section of stores. Some goods which pass goods inward inspection may be rejected from the production line. Rejections from either source are coded to indicate the reason for the rejection and the fact that it is the supplier's responsibility. Sometimes with certain suppliers the company is able to recover a nominal sum to cover associated costs such as removal of the component/unit, obtaining a replacement from stores, refitting and retesting. Costs to be recovered for sorting or correcting non-conforming goods are usually agreed with the supplier before the work is done.

Some finished materials failures do not show up until after they have been fitted to engines or at engine test. All defects detected during engine build and test are noted in the so-called 'Black Museum' report (including failures of parts made in-house). A very serious view is taken of items in this report because, clearly, the costs of correction at this late stage of manufacture can be very high, to say nothing of the effects on the production schedule and productivity. Interestingly this report does not deal in proportions or percentages; it reports absolute numbers on the grounds that the ultimate objective must be zero defects. Although the data are reported formally only monthly, the situation is monitored continuously and formal review meetings are held every week.

Requisitions are raised for the replacement of all rejected parts. Suppliers are charged for faulty goods supplied and, as mentioned above, in some cases additional associated costs may be recovered though this is unlikely to happen with in-house suppliers. The company does not have a simple inspect and reject relationship with its suppliers. It is in continuous negotiation with its suppliers and gives them considerable feedback on their products to try to get them to improve their performance.

Much of the cost associated with suppliers of defective finished goods is recoverable. The costs to the company are those of detection and handling of the goods and the administration costs of obtaining credit or replacements. These costs are not identified separately. The performance data are used to rank and classify suppliers. It is done using numbers and proportions of rejects, not costs, and is used to determine the inspection level and frequency to be applied to the suppliers' goods.

However, cost data are an important aspect of the data on failures to do with bought-out rough material. The reason for the greater importance of costs here is that a large proportion of the company's activities (and hence costs) are taken up with machining, finishing and treating components made from bought-out material. The costs are generated from standard costs and from information noted on the quality non-conformance report. They are produced as a monthly computer tabulation and are abstracted and featured as part of a monthly report in which suppliers are ranked by percentages of components scrapped, by scrap value, and by labour costs incurred in machining components subsequently scrapped due to faults ascribable to the supplier. It is the labour costs incurred which is the principal criterion in ranking suppliers. The data are presented for the current month and the year-to-date so that persistently poor performers are kept under the spotlight. The analysis is carried further to show, for each of the top-ten worst suppliers, a ranking of components (e.g. cylinder liner, cylinder head, crankcase) by number and percentage scrapped and the wasted labour costs incurred. Hence the company has a very clear picture of what problems it should be taking up, and with which suppliers. Equally importantly, the costs, which include overheads on direct labour, are also expressed in the report as costs per effective standard hour, thus making them comparable with other costs incurred by the company.

It is interesting to speculate whether companies take into account the different amounts and types of quality resources in bought-out finished material and bought-in rough material when pondering the make or buy decision.

It is also noteworthy that despite some good work on vendor development the purchasing department does not feature this topic in its monthly purchasing performance report.

9.4.3 Warranty and service reports

At the other end of the operation warranty costs and field service problems similarly receive close attention. Warranty cover is divided into four categories: 1. 'zero-month warranty' (i.e. defects discovered and corrected between delivery to the vehicle builder and delivery to the customer); 2. 'campaign warranty' which covers authorized campaigns to have specific known faults corrected free of charge even though they may not have caused problems on a particular vehicle; 3. 'in warranty' which is normal warranty work correcting failures which have occurred whilst the vehicle has been in service within the warranty period or mileage; and 4. 'out of warranty' which covers very exceptional situations where an engine has been in service for longer than 12 months, or in excess of 100 000 miles, but the company may still give warranty cover.

When a problem in the field is identified as recurring sufficiently often to warrant an investigation, a service problem report is prepared to initiate the investigation in either company 3 or in the engineering department of the parent company, depending on the problem. The criterion for deciding where to deal with the problem initially is whether the solution calls for an engineering design modification to be made. If not it goes to company 3, though their findings may well result in it going back to the engineering department. From these systems the company acquires a considerable amount of quality and reliability data to assist with planning its design and manufacturing quality assurance activities.

On the matter of quality costs, warranty claims from customers are settled by the vehicle builder who then attempts to recover, from company 3, costs relating to engines. As mentioned earlier, most of the company's products go into vehicles built by the parent company and fall into two groups. The feedback from the first of the groups contains a lot of detail about how costs are built up. Computer tabulations display costs of labour and materials, other charges (e.g. towing), handling/administration charges (10% of materials cost), and landing charges (import duties, etc.), together with details of the defect, engine, vehicle, customer and dealer. At one time there was a startlingly high incidence of false warranty claims arising from mistakes, deviousness, attempted deception and downright dishonesty. The automatic payment-without-question policy for settling small bills had contributed to this. The quality assurance department staff at company 3 now check the tabulations and separate out all claims over £400 and claims which look 'suspicious' because of wrong coding of defects and vehicle type. For example, in one month the company had 700 claims from this source. After examining the claims, 197 of them were resisted. This scrutiny of claims is reckoned to be saving the company 12–15% of claimed warranty charges. This indicates that the effort of analysing and scrutinizing claims has been handsomely rewarded and will be especially so in other large companies having automatic payment systems. Among the other data derived from the tabulations are defects per engine and corresponding data costs per engine versus time.

Data from the second outlet are not in the same form. These are data which have been processed by the quality assurance and reliability functions of the parent company. They are in the form of a warranty and service problem history of each vehicle from the day it is built to the expiry of warranty. Although these data also contain cost information it is not so readily retrievable as from the first set of data, though of course simple records of warranty payments without data about defects, etc. can be obtained from normal accounting records.

In the course of looking at warranty costs and discussions with the quality assurance department staff responsible for analysing the data a number of interesting points were raised:

- Warranty costs can be the sins of the father being visited upon the sons. In one case an engine went into service four years after being built. It failed in service and was rectified in the same year. The claim was not submitted until two years later.
- Some distributors have high incidences of particular problems which other distributors do not experience with the same engine type.
- Some individual vehicles are the subject of many small claims – usually for non-returnable parts.
- Some distributors' claims are frequently for sums just below the automatic payment-without-question limit.
- Analysis of the top 100 defects, as defined by claims (listing the top 100 faults corresponds to reviewing incidence of defects down to a level of 0.3 defects per 100 vehicles) on a set of 216 vehicles showed a different content and pattern from a similar analysis on a set of 868 vehicles of a different type, but having the same engine.
- Successful auditing of warranty claims requires a thorough working knowledge of the manufacturing and testing process, history and development, as well as the uses of the product. A knowledge of commercial practices and a suspicious mind are also valuable assets.

These points are worthy of note by organizations with a similar type of product and warranty claim system as company 3.

The third aspect of post-manufacture external failure costs is that of service problem reports. The immediate problem as it affects the customer will of course be taken care of under the warranty scheme but with frequently recurring or chronic problems raising a service problem report initiates further in-house work and costs. When the problem is dealt with by quality assurance and manufacturing people it usually involves a tightening up of procedures and practices and the cost is lost in the overhead, of which quality assurance and manufacturing engineering and supervision are a part. Problems directed to the engineering function (which is a headquarters department of the parent company) usually result in the production of an engineering design modification. Again, the cost is not measured. But it raises the whole question of costs arising from engineering design modifications and engineering concessions.

9.4.4 Engineering design modifications and concessions

Design modifications may be initiated by better design techniques, the opportunity or need to change materials used in the product's construction, better machining capability and persistent field failures. There are company procedures for controlling the modifications and rigorous systems for progressing requests for modifications through to acceptance and establishment.

It is not the intention here to give details of the system but rather to give an indication of the size and character of the activity.

For example, the company's imprest system permits expenditure of up to £10 000 per month and up to £5 000 on any single design modification proposal. Furthermore, the time taken to process modifications from proposal to acceptance indicates the depth of involvement. The fact of there being around 100 proposed modifications under consideration at any one time and 400 per year implemented show it to be a sizeable activity.

Concession to use components which do not meet specification may be sought for many reasons. Among them are the following.

- Materials already purchased and put into stock may be found not to conform to the purchasing specification.
- The vehicle assembly plant may be unable to build to specification and may seek to use alternative parts.
- Material shortages may force the company to switch to a new supplier at short notice.
- Components may be close but not exactly to specification.

Various uses of concession systems include overriding inspectors' decisions to reject components, seeking the engineering department's advice on matters not covered by specifications, and using concessions to bypass systems guarding against the too-ready introduction of modifications.

The disadvantages of concession systems are that their use sometimes induces lax attitudes towards quality such that the number of parts or the concession time period may be overrun in the knowledge that the concession can be renewed, and there may be a lack of urgency in tackling the cause of a problem for the same reason. Concession systems also proliferate paperwork since the subsequent disposal of every part of assembly should be the subject of a permanent record. Items which are passed on concession are really non-conforming items and the activities they generate are clearly quality related, as are many of those to do with design modifications, though neither is costed. Data have already been quoted to indicate the level of activity in design modifications. Add to these the fact that 9% of engines are passed on concession and one is left in no doubt that there is a sizeable quality activity slipping through the quality costing net. A contributory factor to failure to pick up modification and concession costs is that they are not the subject of a quality non-conformance report, which is the principal documentation for picking up failure costs.

9.5 QUALITY COST REPORTING

Details of the reporting and use of costs of scrap have been discussed in the preceding section. However, in addition to these reports the quality assurance

Table 9.1 Quality costs summary

	Period 12		Full Year	
	Actual	% Sales revenue	Actual	% Sales revenue
Prevention costs				
Quality planning	£29 788	1.0	£277 833	0.6
Quality audit	4 080	0.1	49 926	0.1
Maintenance and calibration	911	–	15 365	–
Total prevention costs	£34 779	1.1	£343 124	0.7
Appraisal costs				
Vendor inspection	£6 218	0.2	£71 859	0.1
In-process and final inspection	34 211	1.1	424 719	0.9
Engine test	57 495	1.9	619 135	1.3
Total appraisal costs	£97 924	3.2	£1 115 713	2.3
Failure costs				
Design change	£35 000	1.2	£420 000	0.9
Rework	15 732	0.5	253 277	0.5
Scrap	(48 775)	(1.6)	291 225	0.6
Warranty	197 000	6.5	2 215 000	4.6
Total failure costs	£198 957	6.6	£3 179 502	6.6
Total quality costs	£331 660	10.9	£4 638 339	9.6
Sales revenue base	£30 080 000		£48 233 000	

department and accounts department produce a quality cost report as part of the company's monthly operating review. All the costs which are used are taken from the company's standard accounting data. An example of the report as it appears in its final version is shown in Table 9.1.

The way in which the costs are built up is illustrated in Table 9.2. Down the left-hand side of this table are the accounting sources from which the costs are abstracted. The majority of them are cost centres using budgetary control, some are derived from labour-bookings to quality-related codes and the remainder are derived from invoices, stock records and quality non-conformance reports. Because the accounting system was not set up with the preparation of quality cost reporting in mind there are inherent problems in its use for that purpose. The limitations of the available data and their appropriateness for such a report are worthy of some discussion.

Quality assurance department staff salaries is a large sum which would probably justify being broken down into quality activities. Whilst the activities

Table 9.2 Quality cost synthesis

Item	Cost centre / Expense code	Quality cost elements	Prevention				Appraisal			Internal failure			External failure
			Vendor planning	Quality planning	Dual audit	Maint'ce & calibr'n	Vendor inspection	Process & final test	Engine change	Design	Rework	Scrap	Warranty
1	1630	Quality department staff costs	–	202644									
2	1634	Heat treatment – salaried staff	–	34400									
3	1630	Quality department materials, services, etc.	–	40020									
4	L5520	Quality circles		469									
5	1631	Audit inspection			49926								
6	–	Maintenance and calibration of quality fixtures				15365							
7	1635	Goods receiving inspection					62268						
8	I/L4301	Direct labour inspection					9591						
9	1632	Component machining inspection						130068					
10	1633	Component machining inspection						136969					
11	1636	Component machining and assembly inspection						16344					
12	1637	Engine assembly inspection						31357					
13	1638	Coppersmith's inspection						15684					
14	1639	Final inspections						59610					
15	–	Laboratory recharge						34687					
16	1683	Engine test – inspector's							37408				
17	1680	Engine test							263194				
18	1682	Pre- and post-test work							148069				
19	–	Engine test materials and purchased services							170464				
20	–	Obsolete stock								420000			
21	1681	Sick bay – Engine test									21919		
22	1866	Pre-test 'snagging'									159689		
23	–	Rectification and modifications (excl. item 22)									71669		
24	–	Scrap (materials and labour)										291225	
25	–	Warranty											2215000
		Total	–	277833	49926	15365	71859	424719	619135	420000	253277	291225	2215000
		% Quality related cost		6	1.1	0.3	1.6	9.2	13.3	9	5.5	6.3	47.7
		% Quality related cost		7.4				24.1			20.8			47.7
		% Sales revenue		0.7				2.3			2.0			4.6

of the quality assurance manager, engineers and technicians are mainly prevention oriented, they do not spend all their time planning for quality. For example, one technician is engaged full time on vendor-related activities and another on warranty matters. Nor does this section admit contributions to quality planning (or any other prevention activity other than quality circles) by persons outside the quality assurance department.

Quality audits here mean product audits on components and assemblies, not systems. These are presumably included in the staff salaries figure.

The costs gathered under the inspection headings are salary data abstracted from the budgets of each cost centre. Costs of inspection work by direct workers have overheads included. Inspection of their own work by operators is not costed. Nor are the involvements of production and engineering personnel in twice weekly scrap patrols, concession considerations, engine audits and other appraisal activities.

Engine test is an interesting inclusion. Some would argue that one cannot reasonably expect to build anything so complicated as an engine and not expect to have to make adjustments to it and run it before putting it into a vehicle; that this is all part of the manufacturing process; and that it is not a quality cost. However, the testing operation does much more than this. It is used to run-in engines, check pressures and flows, fuel consumption and exhaust-gas composition. The whole operation, involving a host of complicated mechanical, electrical, hydraulic and computing equipment, is under the control of the quality assurance manager, which clearly indicates the company view that it is a quality-related activity. Costs noted are personnel salaries and materials usages only. Maintenance, servicing, occupation costs and depreciation on this very expensive asset are not included in the costs.

The item 'Obsolete stock' is a curious one. In discussion with the appropriate accounts manager it was learned that obsolete stock is defined as stock in hand, at the annual stock check, for which there is no forward requirement of the next 12 months. Overstocking may come about by panic buying, purchasing supposedly economic batch quantities, or by speculative orders. The stocks become surplus to requirements because of design changes, even though request for engineering design modifications should take full account of existing stocks. Obsolete stock is not necessarily disposed of. The value of just-in-time purchasing becomes clear when situations such as this surface. The relationship between obsolete stock and quality-related costs is a tenuous one, unless one takes the view that 1. there is an implicit failure in being left with £420 000 worth of obsolete stock, and 2. all costs of systems failures are quality costs.

Costs of rectification of parts to new specifications derive from labour-bookings by direct workers, a data source not noted for its veracity or accuracy in most companies. To compound any inherent inaccuracy in the data the figures are inflated by a factor of five or more by the inclusion of overheads. It is noteworthy that in company 3 scrap costs are always kept under the spotlight and featured in so much reporting that there is a good chance they may be reasonably accurate.

Sources of cost data for the broad exercise of compiling the total quality costs are mostly cost centres or financial codes. There is little cost breakdown or cross-boundary analysis of the type which is usually necessary to trigger the uncovering of hidden costs. This, coupled with the known omissions noted above, probably means that the costs are underestimated by a considerable degree. The standard of reporting is poor. Reports do not separate out costs as an aspect of quality worthy of presentation and comment in its own right. This is a pity, because there is a lot of cost information available which is not being used to its full potential.

Overall the reporting probably understates the company's quality costs in those areas where the cost is reckoned only as salaries, but this may be counter-balanced by the inclusion of obsolete stocks and overheads on direct worker costs. However, if this is true, even the omission of costs of personnel from other departments involved in quality, of inputs from the parent company, and of quality ramifications of the concession and design modification systems means the report may understate the costs to a considerable degree.

A first inclination might be to vilify the accounts department for this. That would be unfair. Management accountants are usually willing to cooperate in collecting quality costs, but need guidance from quality people on what to measure.

9.6 COMPARISON OF PERFORMANCE WITH OTHER PUBLISHED DATA

The care which needs to be taken when making comparisons between sets of data from different sources has been strongly emphasized in Chapter 2 and has been reiterated in the earlier case studies. Nevertheless companies like to know how their performance compares with others. In this case, by good fortune, there are data published by a company in the same business. Also, of course, there are the US survey data [2] drawn upon in the other case studies. The temptation was too strong and the comparison was made, with the anomalous results now described which serve to reinforce the warnings about comparisons of quality cost data.

The data from the same industry are those of Schmidt and Jackson [1] from the Detroit Allison Division of General Motors in the United States. Although on a cursory reading they appear to claim that quality costs total 6.3% of sales revenue made up of 'prevention' 0.3%, 'remedial engineering' 1%, 'external appraisal' 1% and 'internal appraisal' 4%. They also provide data to enable their quality-related costs to be shown to amount to 11.8% of sales revenue made up as follows: prevention 0.3%, remedial engineering 0.9%, external appraisal 0.7%, internal appraisal 4%, warranty and policy 4%, scrap 1.8% and product liability 0.1%.

In attempting to compare the above data with those of company 3 and with the US survey data, there is an immediate problem with differences in terminology because Schmidt and Jackson do not use the conventional categorization of quality costs. Hence, if a comparison is to be made, some interpretations of the terminology is required. The terms 'prevention', 'internal appraisal', 'scrap' and 'warranty' present no difficulties. In the authors' view 'remedial engineering' equates with the simpler and more common 'rework'. 'Product liability' is an external failure cost and the use of the word 'service' in conjunction with 'external appraisal' in the paper suggests it too may be an external failure cost. It is suspected that 'policy' payments which are not included with warranty costs in the paper are not quality costs but there is no way of separating them out.

The comparisons are shown in Tables 9.3 and 9.4 using the format adopted by the journal *Quality* in presenting the findings from their survey.

Examination of the data suggests (even keeping in mind the earlier discussion about the limitations of the data) that the company's situation is closer to that in the Detroit Allison Division of General Motors than to the norms for the industry sectors in which they are grouped. Data compared under informal systems of quality cost collection (i.e. collecting only scrap, rework and warranty costs) suggest that the company not only spends a smaller proportion of its sales revenue on quality activities than does General Motors, but also that a greater proportion of its expenditure goes on warranty payments and

Table 9.3 Comparison of company 3 quality costs with published data

Cost category	Company 3	Quality costs (%)		Schmidt and Jackson†
		Quality survey data* (formal program)		
		Machinery	Transport equipment	
Prevention	7.4	11.0	8.7	2.5
Appraisal	24.0	23.7	45.3	33.7
Internal failure	21.0	39.6	33.2	22.8
External failure	47.6	25.7	12.8	41.0
Total	100	100	100	100
Sales revenue (%)				
Prevention	0.7	0.49	0.34	0.3
Appraisal	2.3	1.05	1.76	4.0
Internal failure	2.0	1.76	1.29	2.7
External failure	4.1	1.14	0.50	4.8
Total	9.6	4.44	3.89	11.8

*Quality costs survey. *Quality*, June 1977,pp. 20–2 [2].
†Schmidt and Jackson [1].

Table 9.4 Comparison of company 3 quality costs with published data

Cost category	Company 3	Quality survey data* (formal program)		Schmidt and Jackson†
		Machinery	Transport equipment	
Quality costs (%)				
Scrap	10	40	39	27
Rework	9	25	40	13
Warranty	81	35	21	59
Total	100	100	100	100
Sales revenue (%)				
Scrap	0.6	2.5	2.4	1.8
Rework	0.5	1.5	1.3	0.9
Warranty	5.7	6.2	6.2	6.6
Total	5.7	6.2	6.29	6.6

*Quality costs survey. Quality, June 1977,pp. 20–2 [2].
†Schmidt and Jackson [1].

and a smaller proportion on scrap and rework. These relationships are not illogical and are endorsed by the data in the comparison under formal programmes of cost collection (i.e. prevention, appraisal, internal and external failure costs). Further, these latter data could be interpreted as suggesting that the situation is brought about by the relative expenditures on appraisal. In short, General Motors may spend more on appraisal, giving them more scrap and rework, but allowing fewer non-conforming products to reach the customer. This of course is tantamount to inspecting-in quality, something which cannot be done. Piling heresy upon heresy, these data also suggest that company 3's proportionately greater expenditure on prevention activities is not paying off so far as the customer is concerned though it may be doing so for the company's gross quality costs.

Perhaps these apparent contradictions of the accepted wisdom only serve to reiterate and emphasize the imprudence of making comparisons between sets of data which are not fully understood. In seeking explanations of these apparent anomalies one is taken full circle back to definitions as discussed in Chapter 3.

Manufacturers who incur low external failure costs will enjoy a good reputation for customer-perceived quality, even though their in-house performance, with respect to making to specification first time, may be relatively poor, and costly. Among these may be manufacturers with ready outlets for seconds. It may also be true of manufacturers whose products happen to be in vogue among those to whom price (or even value) is not a prime consideration. It should not be imagined that only manufacturers of clothing for High Street outlets, children's toys, popular records, hula-hoops and skate boards come into this category. Many other items including watches, calculators, jewellery and motor vehicles are examples also. Hence, quite apart from the fact that the figures themselves may not be comparable, the market situations of different companies may make comparisons invalid.

9.7 PRESENTATION AND USES OF QUALITY COST INFORMATION

At the highest level of reporting, warranty charges are the only quality-related costs to feature in the profit and loss account of company 3. Because of the method of reporting to reflect movement in warranty provision there is a smoothing effect which obscures the actual month-to-month variation so it is unlikely to provoke any strong reactions. On the face of it, this may appear to be undesirable, but the situations leading to the warranty costs are so far behind the time of the report that they are unlikely to provoke useful action other than to extend the useful work already being done in auditing claims.

In the monthly operating review a quality cost summary, in the form shown in Table 9.1 is presented without comment. The quality performance summary is expressed in percentage rejects, defects per engine, performance against targets, and cataloguing of defects. Costs do not feature in the performance summary but are raised in the discussion on general quality topics in the report. Here cost is used as the measure of performance for non-conforming parts coming to light during assembly and test operations and also as the ranking criterion for suppliers of rough material. Total labour costs incurred due to non-conforming rough material are expressed as cash and as costs per effective standard hour. Machine shop scrap costs arising from operator errors, machine faults and jig faults are also expressed in this way. Scrap costs are used to rank cost centres and the components causing most problems. Period and year-to-date rankings are shown and scrap costs per effective standard hour accountable to operator error are charted for the year.

Despite the wealth of cost information and the way it is used the report does not pack a financial punch. The absence of comment on the total cost summary and a welter of technical details from which the cost figures do not stand out clearly from model numbers, numbers inspected, numbers rejected, and cost centre numbers diminish the financial impact of the report considerably. Its messages are more about problems than costs. The quality assurance manager's monthly report to the plant operations director and the parent company's quality director contains the same kinds of costs but does not emphasize them.

The underlying data leading to the rankings described above are published, as has been described earlier, in a useful quality assurance department report of scrap costs arising from bought-out rough material. In this report cost data are used to rank suppliers, company problems and suppliers' problems. It is surprising that this work or its effects does not somehow feature in the purchasing department's performance report.

Table 9.5 Example of component quality report sheet

Cost centre	Area Manager	Target	Full year	Location bay — Jan	Feb	Mar	Apr	May	Jne	Jly	Aug	Sep	Oct	Nov	Dec	Company 3 quality dept
	Cost £															Report no and reference no
Scrap	Cost/ESH £															Machine shop scrap; Brochure analysis of quality defect report by cost centre QDR Q/TO3
	Quantity															
Concessions	Total; No quantity; No – period															Concession; Record; Quality office
Samples (1st time perf)	Inspected; Passed; Failed %															Sample record book; Foreman log book
Final; Audit insp.; 1st time perf.	Inspected; Passed; Failed %															Final inspection; Record book; Foreman log book
Black museum rejects	Individual pt nos; Total quantity															Black museum report
Quality cost £	Rework; Inspection															Labour accounting report
Orders Guaranteed	No. of ord. qty; Period															Weekly scrap; Patrol report
Components audited	Jig test P/F; Audited P/F; Sample P/F															Audit report
Quality booking errors	No. of batches; Quantity short															Final inspection; Record book

Finally, it is the monthly quality performance report for the machining shop which promises to use cost data to make the greatest impact. A separate sheet for each work centre features various quality criteria (Table 9.5). Clearly displayed on the top line is the cost of scrap, which is also expressed as the cost per effective standard hour. Costs of rework and associated inspection costs are included in the report which also indicates target values. The report is updated monthly and there should be no escaping its message.

REFERENCES

1. Schmidt, J.W. and Jackson, J.F. (1982) Measuring the cost of product quality. *Automat. Eng.*, **90**, (6), 42–8.
2. Anon. (1977) Quality cost survey. *Quality*, June, 20–2.

Case study, company 4 | 10

10.1 INTRODUCTION

Company 4 is one of a subsidiary group of companies owned by a large multi-national company. It manufactures a variety of high-technology products but this case study was confined to a department making metallized polyester film capacitors for use in electronic circuits for blocking and coupling, bypass, and energy reservoir applications. Output is well in excess of 200 million units per year. Annual sales turnover is difficult to define because a large proportion of the department's output is used by sister companies and by the parent company and is transferred at the factory selling price. However, the total departmental 'turnover' is to be taken around £3 million per year.

The department operates on a two-shift system and employs approximately 120 people. It is essentially a production unit with some technical support under the control of the production manager but with most of its services coming from other departments.

The quality philosophy of the company is determined by the parent multi-national company with whom there is close liaison on technical, financial and quality matters. The philosophy followed is that of Juran [1] and there is widespread use of his videotape teaching package [2]. Despite this there are striking variations in the quality improvements achieved in different parts of the group of companies and it is noticeable that, in general, the greatest improvements have been made where there is direct competition from Japanese electronic manufacturers.

Quality costs had been collected in the department prior to the commencement of the research study. The objective of this study was to find out how the company had set about collecting quality costs of the department and how it used them. The company was looking for a monthly reporting system by which quality performance is measured in terms of real money, and in a way which is more useful than the underlying data and flexible enough to be applied company wide.

Juran's [1] philosophy on quality is that all improvement takes place project by project, so that, again, it is not surprising to hear in the company a great deal about 'the vital few and trivial many' problems and about quality improvement projects. However, improvement projects seem to have been identified, not from quality costs, but from production and quality control problems, and tend to be concentrated on process deficiencies. Hence quality improvement project teams often seem to be supplementing the technical services in firefighting production and technical problems rather than promoting quality.

The Juran principle of using a project by project approach to quality improvement is so deeply ingrained into the thinking of company 4 that some of its personnel see little merit in carrying out full quality costings, other than to get a 'snapshot' of total quality costs from time to time just as a reminder of their magnitude. The weakness of this is that such a use does not encourage refinement of costs and all that is produced is a copy of the original snapshot enlarged by inflation. There is also a tendency to fall into the trap of according an 'accurate' status to costs which have been derived from an intensive study carried out over a short period at some earlier date and to fail to revise estimates of technical and engineering inputs. Any snapshots carried out should also be compared with earlier ones to pinpoint areas of improvement.

Quality costs do not feature in the normal management accounting reports of the company. Apart from the various attempts at snapshot costing, the only other reports are those of the multi-discipline project teams and these leave much to be desired.

The research approach used was to become familiar with the technology and the process (which were very different from any of the earlier studies) and then to perform a critique of the existing quality cost collecting and reporting systems in the light of what had been learned from this and other studies. No attempt was made to match the quality cost elements identified by the company with those of BS6143 [3], though the omission of important types of cost is noted.

10.2 SOURCES OF QUALITY COSTS

Two sources of fundamental information on quality costs were uncovered. From the parent company there is a general definition and guidance on what should be included. This is shown alongside the departmental view of the constitution and categorization of quality costs in Table 10.1.

Quality-related costs are not specifically mentioned in the company's quality manual but it is interesting to note that the manual is by no means concerned only with the activities of personnel involved in quality assurance; it also acknowledges the contributions of administrative, production operators and supervisors, engineering, and technical service staff in its procedures covering topics such as:

Table 10.1 Parent company and departmental quality cost categorization

Company categorization	Departmental categorization
Definition: Quality costs are all costs and losses caused by defective products and the cost of special measures and effort to limit these costs and losses.	
Quality costs are divided into: – inspection costs – prevention costs – internal failure costs – external failure costs	
Inspection costs are related to: – material inspection – incoming inspection – product inspection by operators – product inspection by managers – product inspection by quality department personnel – environmental tests – costs of measuring and test equipment	Appraisal: – material inspection – product inspection by operators – product inspection by supervisors – product inspection by quality people – environmental tests – test-machines and operator hours – regular inspection on normal work
Prevention costs are the expenditures which have been incurred to reduce the chances of failures in the production process via – production and maintenance of manufacturing instructions – production and execution of the quality education plan – production of quality procedures – quality audits of internal processes – quality audits of external suppliers – execution of quality analysis	Prevention: – maintenance of manufacturing instructions – production of quality procedures – assessment of departmental quality –quality analysis – maintenance of test equipment – calibration
Internal failure costs are costs related to: – process disturbance due to bad material – rework of rejected products – damage during internal transport	Internal failure: – repairs and rework – scrap and losses – extra inspection due to failure – machine downtime – engineering repairs
External failure costs are costs related to: – handling of complaints – replacement of rejected products – service claims – man hours – materials	External failure: – customer complaint handling – extra inspection – rework – scrap

- specifications;
- documentation;
- work instructions;
- machine instructions (including setting and fault analysis);
- production supervisors' responsibilities (including training);
- inspection;
- disposition of non-conforming products.

Technical data for the department show materials loss allowances of 2% on all products and 2–5% processing losses, depending on the product type, for the basic cell preparation stage. There are further materials allowances and processing loss allowances of 1–5% for different materials and different processing/testing operations. Of course these losses will not necessarily all give rise to quality-related costs but some will, and the costs will be found to be included in the manufacturing cost and the factory selling price.

Discussions with accounts department personnel yielded stage-by-stage manufacturing cost analyses which confirmed the inclusion of 'loss' and 'scrap' allowances detailed in the technical data for the process. 'Loss' is defined as forerunnings, ends and dropouts, whereas process 'scrap' is defined as non-conforming product. Apart from these inclusions in the standard cost, and the quality assurance department budget, the only other obviously quality-related cost identified in the company's financial reporting is income from sales of 'scrap' metals. However, the company's technical engineering personnel work closely with the accounts department to produce cost analyses of products, operations and activities. One such analysis is the inspection/test content of the factory standard price of major product lines.

A survey of the manufacturing processes and the production operations also confirmed 'loss' and 'scrap' levels and the consequential need to plan for more output than is required. The by-now familiar problem of whether test operations costs are necessarily quality costs arose again at a particular processing stage at which the capacitance of cells is tested and they are sorted into tolerance ranges by machine. The reject rate from this test is of the order of 0.05%. The dilemma arises again at the final 'auto-test' stage at which the completed capacitor is electrically tested for capacitance, insulation resistance, high-voltage breakdown, and integrity of contact of leads. The only corrective work observed was overpainting of faulty printing prior to reprinting, and attention to rolls of taped-on capacitors when the number of gaps on the roll exceeded the specification. The taping process was, however, still under development.

An interesting fact which came to light during the study, and which shows the sensitivity of product quality to technological changes, is the effect of introducing a different type of coating on the product. It is also interesting to note that many of the quality problems encountered by the company derive from the metal spraying and resin coating operations (i.e. non-mechanical, non-electrical operations involving flame and powder technologies).

In-process inspection is carried out by personnel who report to the production foreman and the technical input on in-process quality-related matters comes mainly from the department's engineering resources. The role of the quality assurance department is a policing role at final inspection, and dealing with customer complaints. Thus, curiously, the quality assurance department does not include process yield and scrap levels among its measures of quality performance. Its internal measures of quality are numbers of rejected batches (currently 0.8% versus 4% four years ago) and defects per million which is an absolute measure of all defective capacitors reaching the final operation. External measures are provided by sister companies which inspect products before using them, and by two other customer companies which cooperate to the extent of detecting faulty components in circuits, and removing, packing and returning them with full information. Rejection rates for visual and electrical faults are about 30 per million for small capacitors and one per million for larger capacitors. When quality levels are of this order the feedback of data from customers is the only feasible means of quantification. Problems with packaging, labelling, etc. also become the subject of a customer complaint handling procedure.

Other activities which give rise to quality-related costs are quality improvement projects carried out part time by teams of three people, and the coordination of these projects. Special studies on quality-related matters are also undertaken by the company's technical service department. Thus whilst materials usage and appraisal activities appear to be well defined and analysed there are a number of unmeasured technical inputs from a variety of sources, which could make gathering quality costs difficult. However, an excellent thorough study of quality-related costs had been carried out by an engineer in the company two years prior to the work described in this chapter taking place.

10.3 MEASUREMENT OF QUALITY COSTS

The company has been measuring quality costs with progressively greater degrees of sophistication since 1970.

In the department which is the subject of this study a quality costing exercise was carried out during Year A. The investigator, from the company's quality engineering department, after a thorough study of the process listed 41 quality cost elements under the usual failure-appraisal-prevention categories. Further, he set down, for each element, how to calculate its cost, the data sources and named contacts for each data source. The most striking feature of this report is that the cost elements are particular to the company and the manufacturing operation. No attempt is made to fit elements to elements with generic titles.

A number of lessons can be learnt from this excellent quality costing exercise. First, there is no substitute for a detailed thorough examination. Modifications may be made later, if necessary, with hindsight and as experience of applying the model procedure grows. Second, people willingly adopt ready-made procedures if the procedure appears to fit their situation. Hence it is very important that the first-off should be soundly based. Third, procedures should be 'user friendly' (that is, the information needed should be readily obtainable from a relatively small number of sources). The costing was developed by examining the process in detail from beginning to end. Only later were cost elements, still operation based, grouped under the prevention-appraisal-failure categories. This grouping was probably done in deference to the received wisdom on the topic because the requirements of a costing system would not have produced elements which fell naturally into such groupings (though the words are useful as a primary checklist when examining activities to find if they are quality related). Indeed it is likely that only those costs which are easily measured and obviously reducible would have emerged (i.e. some failure and some appraisal costs).

This piece of work was built upon later by a quality assurance department engineer assigned to the production department. He carried out a similar exercise (based on three months' data) but combined some of the cost elements, isolated an important extra element and, most importantly, qualified the status of the cost data. Qualification was expressed in two ways. First, costs were labelled A, TD or E, indicating that they were derived from accurate data (i.e. from an exact amount of losses recorded over a reasonable period, or from booked time), from published technical data for the process, or estimated, respectively. Second, the cost report specifically highlights the dilemmas of cost allocation which occur at the heal and sort and autotest process stages, namely:

> The time included for operator inspection is the time spent on visual inspection only. There is no inclusion of time spent operating the machines in their test and sort capacity. However, the full machine hours costs have been used, despite healing being a necessary stage in manufacture, and the autotest machines doing manufacturing jobs such as cropping, unloading from strips and counting into boxes.

At the same time that the latter report was being prepared another quality cost report was being prepared by the department's technical services engineer. This report, which uses the elements defined for the first report (Year A), purports to apply the following year's (Year B) experience to the current year's (Year C) production levels to produce a forecasted expenditure or budget. A similar report has also been prepared by the same author in which Year C experience is applied to the forecasted production levels for Year D.

At company 4 it was noticed that many of the quality problems emanated from two parts of the process which involved flame technology and powder technology respectively. These are effectively foreign technologies in a manufacturing process which uses electrical and mechanical engineering in its principal technologies. When attempting to define quality cost elements, an implicit requirement is that the technologies must be fully understood. Failure to do so may result in the true causes of quality defects being missed, or to accepting lower standards of performance than should be achieved. This is not the case at company 4, which has a wide range of technological expertise available to it from the parent and sister companies, but it is a philosophical point worth noting.

10.4 COMPARISON OF COST REPORTS

Thus there are four reports available containing costs expressed in such a way that they may be compared one with another. For the purpose of comparison the data are shown in two tables. Table 10.2 shows data from the Year A investigation alongside the production department quality cost forecasts for Year B and Year C. The most striking features of these data are, first, that many of the figures in the forecasted data appear to have been obtained by simply inflating the original Year A data by 2–3% per annum, and, second, that so many of the rates of expenditure are identical for each of the product sizes. On the first point, in only three of the 39 items listed is there a significant change in the rate of expenditure. The three items, which include product losses at the first roller grade and autotest stages and repair work, are a direct result of process improvement. On the second point, in view of the fact that there are significantly more problems with the smaller version of the product it is surprising that the rates of expenditure are the same for both products. It might have been expected that, for example, the prevention activities and some of the appraisal activities would reflect differences in process status of the two products. Equally, the reasons for some of the differences shown are not obvious either (e.g. epoxy coat operator inspection costs 20% more per unit for the larger product than for the smaller). Perhaps these apparent anomalies merely reflect the quality of the underlying estimated and technically based data.

Table 10.3 shows the combined (all-products) cost data from Table 10.2 alongside data from the Year B costing. It is immediately apparent that this latter report shows some substantial differences from the report for the same year compiled by the production department's technical service engineer.

Under the category of failure there is good agreement between the two on product losses. This is to be expected because most of the data are derived from a single intensive study carried out at the time of the original Year A investigation. Exceptions are the winding cell and autotest losses which are determined daily by counting and check-weighing. In general the losses are coroborated by the process materials efficiency records. There is also good

Table 10.2 Comparison of original and updated costing

Item	Data status	Original costing		Technical service engineer's costings			
		Year A	Year A	Year B	Year C	Year B	Year C
Annual production =		30 m	190 m	70 m	145 m	120 m	100 m
Product type =		7 mm	9 mm	7 mm	9 mm	7 mm	9 mm
1. Winding foil scrap	A	13.8	29.4	14.2	30.3	14.5	30.9
2. Winding cell loss	A	56.6	78.1	58.3	80.4	59.5	82.0
3. Detaping cell loss	A	71.6	57.6	73.7	5.9	7.5	6.0
4. 1st roller grade cell loss	A	130.5	152.3	33.6	39.2	34.3	40.0
5. 1st heal cell loss	A	49.9	58.2	51.4	49.9	52.4	61.0
6. 2nd roller grade cell loss	A	27.3	31.9	28.1	32.8	28.7	33.5
7. 2nd heal cell loss	A	22.6	26.4	23.3	27.2	23.7	27.7
8. Auto test cell loss	A	1250.6	645.2	776	428.8	601.0	437.4
9. Machine downtime	E	71.0	63.4	73.1	65.3	74.6	66.6
10. Mechanical engineering hours	E	29.8	61.6	29.8	63.4	30.4	64.7
11. Engineering orders	E	11.8	11.8	12.2	12.2	12.4	12.4
12. Stores items	E	32.3	32.3	33.3	33.3	34.0	34.0
13. Toolroom orders	E	19.1	19.1	19.7	19.7	20.1	20.1
14. Mechanical engineering hours	E	194.7	151.3	200.5	155.8	204.5	158.9
15. Toolroom orders	E	12.2	12.2	12.6	12.6	12.9	12.9
16. Electronic engineering hours	E	80.2	80.2	82.9	82.6	84.6	84.3
17. Repairs	TD	1132.1	51.9	291.5	53.5	96.2	54.6
18. Winding operator inspection	TD	53.0	50.0	54.6	51.5	55.7	52.5
19. Roller grade	TD	53.7	53.7	55.3	55.3	56.4	56.4
20. Heal and sort operator inspection	TD	148	183.6	152.4	111.2	155.4	113.4
21. Batch inspection	TD	86.5	86.5	89.1	90.9	90.9	90.9
22. Welding operator inspection	TD	46.0	46.1	47.4	47.5	48.3	48.3
23. Epoxy coat operator inspection	TD	36.0	45.0	37.1	46.4	37.8	47.3
24. Print operator inspection	TD	27.0	27.7	27.8	28.6	29.2	29.2
25. Sillner tape operator inspection	E	127	0	130.8	0	66.7	0
26. In-line quality	TD	170.4	170.4	175.5	175.5	179.0	179.0
27. 100% inspect	A	29.4	29.4	30.3	30.3	30.9	30.9
28. Raw material inspection	A	2.3	2.3	2.4	2.4	2.4	2.4
29. Quality laboratory	E	82.5	82.5	85.0	85.0	86.7	86.7
30. Works laboratory	A	9.4	9.4	9.7	9.7	9.9	9.9
31. Auto test man-hours	TD	159.9	195.9	164.7	164.7	167.9	167.9
32. Auto test machine hours	TD	707.5	707.5	728.7	728.7	743.0	743.0
33. Heal and sort machine hours	TD	274.5	274.5	282.7	282.8	288.3	288.3
34. Electronic engineering hours	E	20.9	20.9	21.5	21.5	21.9	21.9
35. Engineering orders	E	6.2	6.2	6.4	6.4	6.5	6.5
36. Quality engineering hours	E	23.4	23.4	24.1	24.1	24.6	24.6
37. Quality laboratory	E	54.6	54.6	58.1	58.1	59.3	59.3
38. Technical assistance	A	98.8	98.8	101.8	101.8	103.8	103.8
39. Works laboratory	A	2.6	2.6	2.7	2.7	2.8	2.8

Table 10.3 Comparison of costings of all-products data

Item		Data status	Original costing	Technical service engineers' costing		Quality engineer's costing
			Year A	Year B	Year C	Year B
Annual production =			220 m (m)	215 m	220 m	200 m
1.	Winding foil scrap	A	27.3	25	22	25
2.	Winding cell loss	A	75.1	73.2	69.7	73
3.	Detaping cell loss	A	5.95	6.4	6.8	6
4.	1st roller grade cell loss	A	149.3	37.4	36.9	69
5.	1st heal cell loss	A	57.1	57.1	56.3	83
6.	2nd roller grade cell loss	A	31.3	31.3	30.9	
7.	2nd heal cell loss	A	25.9	25.9	25.5	
8.	Auto-test cell loss	A	727.8	541.8	572	542
9.	Machine downtime	E	64.9	67.8	71	68
10.	Mechanical engineering hours	E	57.3	52.4	46	
11.	Engineering orders	E	11.8	12.2	12.4	
12.	Stores items	E	32.3	33.3	34.0	
13.	Toolroom orders	E	19.1	19.7	20.1	
14.	Mechanical engineering hours	E	157.2	170.4	183.4	212
15.	Toolroom orders	E	12.2	12.6	12.9	78
16.	Electronic engineering hours	E	80.2	82.6	84.5	82
17.	Repairs	TD	199.2	131	77.3	145
18.	Winding operator inspection	TD	28.9	52.5	54.2	68
19.	Roller grade	TD	53.7	55.3	56.4	112
20.	Heal and sort operator inspection	TD	113.6	124.6	135.3	12
21.	Batch inspection	TD	86.5	89.1	901	100
22.	Welding operator inspection	TD	46.1	47.5	48.3	41
23.	Epoxy coat operator inspection	TD	43.7	43.3	42.1	38
24.	Print operator inspection	TD	27.6	28.3	29.2	24
25.	Sillner tape operator inspect	E	(17.2)	(42.5)	(36.3)	40
26.	In-line quality	TD	170.4	175.5	179	162
27.	100% inspect	A	29.4	30.3	30.9	
28.	Raw materal inspection	A	2.3	2.4	2.4	3
29.	Quality laboratory	E	82.5	85	86.7	90
30.	Works laboratory	A	9.4	9.7	9.9	31
31.	Auto-test man-hour	TD	159.9	164.7	167.9	135
32.	Auto-test machine hours	TD	707.5	728.7	743	664
33.	Heal and sort machine hours	TD	274.5	282.7	288.3	271
34.	Electronic engineering hours	E	20.9	21.5	21.9	22
35.	Engineering orders	E	6.2	6.4	6.5	
36.	Quality engineer's hours	E	23.4	24.1	24.6	76
37.	Quality laboratory	E	56.4	58.1	59.3	28
38.	Technical assistance	A	98.8	101.8	103.8	102
39.	Works laboratory	A	2.6	2.7	2.8	

agreement on the costs of various engineering inputs, which suggests that the estimates of the proportion of this effort which is quality related has remained unchanged since the first investigation. Complaint returns and handling is a new element introduced by the quality engineer who has also combined repairs with other elements thus making exact comparison difficult.

In the appraisal category most of the data are from technical data prepared by the technical efficiency department of the company. Both Year B reports should therefore be the same. The fact that they are not, but that in many cases the differences are small, can be accounted for by use of an overall inflation figure in one set of figures (as mentioned earlier) and use of up-to-date technical data in the other. A difference which cannot be explained in this way is the factor of two of the cost of roller grade operator inspection. Attention to these machines is only a part-time activity for an operator but an increase in attention time to the machines may well have come about during investigations into high losses at this process stage. In the case of heal and sort operator inspection, where there is a difference of a factor of 10 between the reported figures, there has clearly been a change of definition. The definition used in the original investigation clearly included the whole of the machine operator's time. The latest view is that less than 10% of his time is spent on inspection. A surprising difference is a factor of three on works laboratory costs. These costs are charges-in to the department through the cost centre accounting system and hence should be identical.

Under the prevention category, the estimates of engineering and technical service input used in the original investigation still prevail but the quality engineer's estimates of the quality laboratory's and his own contributions to prevention are halved and trebled respectively.

10.5 DISCUSSION OF COSTS

For the purpose of calculating quality costs as fractions of annual sales turnover the latter is taken to be £3 million. Value of scrapped products is the standard price of the product at its process stage. Thus products scrapped before the welding stage are valued at about one-third of the value ascribed to products scrapped during and after the welding operation. Costs of all hourly paid staff include a proportion of the departmental overhead. Thus, for example, inspectors and fitters are costed at approximately twice as much as departmental engineers and supervisors.

Enquiries into costs always yield contradictory information. Company 4 is no exception. Enquiry into the cost of patrol inspection brought answers of 'two men full time' and 'one man 90% of the time' from two people very close to the manufacturing operation who would be expected to know the exact answer. Similarly three people's assessment of the proportion of machine downtime which is quality related are 'most', '85–90%' and '50–50'. Both of these quality topics fall into the 'estimated' category of cost status.

Much of the data used in calculating costs are fixed data (e.g. production level, machine and manning costs) so that the calculation of many costs could be reduced to measuring an operating variable and applying a factor to it. Some such simplification accompanied by judicious combining of elements will almost certainly be necessary if this type of reporting is to become routine in company 4. An analysis of the costing procedure shows the system to require inputs from 16 people working in 11 different departments or sections. It should be possible to reduce the number of contributors to four without sacrificing information or accuracy.

Referring to the quality engineer's Year B data, which are the most reliable after the original investigation, failure costs comprise £159 000 materials and added value losses, £37 800 additional labour costs directly associated with the losses, and a further £88 000 related costs. Many appraisal costs are unavoidable (e.g. operator inspection) and these amount to £214 000 leaving £177 000 as perhaps avoidable. Charges-in to the department under appraisal and prevention headings are challengeable and, possibly, reducible. In the period between this and the original costing there have clearly been improvements in quality performance and the effects on total quality costs are to reduce them by about 5% of annual sales turnover. Most of the reduction comes from significant reductions in roller grade cell losses, autotest cell losses and repairs. How real an apparent reduction in appraisal costs and an increase in prevention expenditure may be is difficult to gauge in view of the disparities discussed earlier.

One of the maxims of cost collecting seems to be that, in general, costs need to be large to hold attention. This creates something of a dilemma for the cost collector because large costs are often insensitive to changes. But the collector cannot omit large costs and concentrate only on smaller costs which may readily be seen to change. Hence cost groupings need to be chosen carefully so that cost reductions achieved are displayed in such a way that both the relative achievement and the absolute position are clearly shown. Another dilemma arises from the fact that one-off estimates do not change and that there is no point in collecting costs which do not change. The only way out of this is to measure directly, or through surrogates, those costs which are thought worth collecting.

10.6 QUALITY COST REPORTING

Apart from scrap sales in departmental accounts, quality-related costs are reported in only two contexts at company 4. One is the annual quality costs and the other is in quality improvement projects.

The original annual report which was prepared as a special project by an engineer from the company's quality engineering department was endorsed by the production manager and circulated widely in the department, to the quality fraternity on the site, and to the plant director. It comprises a 150-word covering note but otherwise leaves the figures to speak for themselves. The presentation of figures, though neat and clear, is essentially on working papers (i.e. typed format with handwritten figures and hand-drawn Pareto diagrams) and hence may not create the impact among senior management that such an excellent piece of work deserves. Another weakness is that all costs are expressed as costs per million of the product type so that to arrive at real costs the reader is constantly having to multiply by 140 and by 30 and sum the products. (Ironically the reports obtained by simply inflating the data in this original report are well presented but appear not to have made any impact.) However, the derived list of potential improvement projects does not suffer from either of these defects and clearly achieved its purpose when the top three projects were adopted and brought to successful conclusions.

The second annual report (for Year B), prepared by the quality engineer assigned to the department and incorporating the improvements noted earlier, also has a minimum of words and asks the figures to speak for themselves. Unfortunately, in this case, there has been no detailed analysis of the data leading to possible improvement projects. Nor is there a comparison with the original report to measure changes even though there were substantial improvements via the improvement projects in Year B. Combining the costs of the two main product types serves to obscure high-cost areas to some extent, because they have quite different quality cost rates per million. Clearly the report does not say as much as it could and may not make the impact that the work of compiling it deserves.

The reporting of quality costs in quality improvement project reports is sketchy and incomplete. It is also confusing. The confusion arises partly from poor form design of the quality improvement planning sheets (QUIPS) and partly because of some odd reporting practices. The poor form design contributes to the confusion because the three improvement projects have to share a sheet of A4 paper with customer problem reports such that the financial reporting of all three projects is squeezed into an area of 12 cm × 4 cm.

Reporting practices are odd in several respects. At the initiation of the project the annual expenditure and the expected annual savings (and hence the anticipated future annual expenditure) are clearly defined. Two months later, before the first review meeting, the assessment of the annual loss from 'mechanical losses due to poor levelling' had rocketed from £27 510 to £63 360 although it was then currently cruising along at a rate of £27 547 per annum. In the same period the annual expenditure rate of 'Sillner repairs' fell from £43 821 to £29 214 per annum – a considerable improvement until it is learned that the latter figure is based on an output level of two-thirds the original. The expenditure rate was later reduced to £14 600 per annum – but for one-third of the originally specified output level. The changes from expenditure to expenditure rates and the reasons for moving the goal posts are not indicated on the reporting format and must be gleaned from the minutes of quality improvement meetings which monitor the projects and consider these reports. These meetings were held at the intervals at which the QUIPS were produced (indeed the QUIPS predated the meetings by one day). They are attended by leaders of the project teams together with senior managers from the quality, production and site management functions. They are essentially reporting-upwards meetings in which situation and progress are reported, apparently without feedback (as judged by the minutes). It is probably fair to say that the minutes, apart from attendance, could be written before the meeting.

A point arising from the poor quality of reporting at company 4 is that the very fact of there being a multiplicity of reports with conflicting figures, all effectively from within the same department, undermines confidence in all of them, even the best.

A topic which is reported on at the meeting, and one which clearly is regarded by the company as being of the highest importance, is that of customer problems. Although the level of defects is very low (as indicated earlier, the individual capacitors are very cheap) the numbers returned (e.g. 40 000 in three months) plus the cost of personnel dealing with complaints may warrant costing. It is a surprising omission.

Another curious and disappointing feature of company 4 is that it has all the ingredients necessary for preparing excellent quality cost reports for improvement projects and total costs, but it does not do so. It employs high-calibre staff. The matrix organization ensures engineering, technical and quality assurance staff become fully integrated into the manufacturing function whilst maintaining strong links with their respective support functions. Technical engineering staff who provide a wealth of technical and cost data are similarly placed within the accounting function. Overall, the company is extremely well suited to tackle quality cost collection successfully. All the ingredients for effective quality cost reporting are there and all that is needed is some changes to attitudes and the will to do it.

The reasons why the state of quality cost reporting is not far better were not studied specifically. However, a number of matters noted during the study may have some bearing on the situation. Firstly, responsibility for quality seems to be divided. For example, the quality assurance department appeared to be preoccupied with customer-perceived quality, leaving the responsibility for in-house quality to the manufacturing department. The prime responsibility for product and service quality must of course lie with manufacturing departments, but quality assurance departments have a tacit responsibility in all matters relating to quality – especially failure. Secondly, the maverick behaviour of the manufacturing department's technical service engineer, in producing and pushing his own independent sets of data, is but an example of interdepartmental insularity at company 4. Management's acceptance or open reluctance to accept, or acknowledge, other figures, without attempting to determine the truth, is surely another. Thirdly, there was some evidence of a big-company syndrome of no one 'owning' problems, though there was much evidence of willingness to become involved with problems and contribute to solutions. Finally, there is a lack of expressed dissatisfaction on the part of senior management. (This may be related to the previous point about people not owning problems.) An example, quoted in the case study, is the apparent lack of response from members of the senior management team to quality improvement project reports. Quite apart from the poor standard of reporting, there surely must have been aspects of the work (technical, cost, rate of progress, changing priorities and changing targets) with which they were not entirely satisfied.

10.7 USES OF QUALITY COSTS

As mentioned earlier, company 4 is an adherent of the Juran [1] philosophy on TQM and quality costs. Very briefly, Juran advocates the use of costs to quantify threats or opportunities, to draw attention, and to initiate cost improvement projects using return on investment as the principal criterion for assessing projects. Hence it is not surprising that the investigator who carried out the original costing exercise did not end with the report described earlier in this chapter. Process, control and cost data were used to prepare cost-based Pareto diagrams of causes of scrap arising from each of the three principal process stages (i.e. widening, welding and coating) for each of the two major product sizes. Cost-based Pareto diagrams were also developed for scrap arising from the remaining process stages and untraceable faults. Examples are shown in Figure 10.1.

From this information a list of eight improvement projects was developed (Table 10.4). The basic problems and their associated failure costs are listed against the savings to be made. At this stage the whole of the particular failure cost was seen as a potential saving. The potential savings from eliminating the autotest scrap elements listed are about 35% of the total autotest scrap value and the total potential savings listed represent 30% and 13.7% of the failure costs and total quality costs respectively.

The top three problems were made the subject of quality cost improvement projects with teams, leaders, timescales, control criteria, and expected savings specified. Progress was formally reported after four, seven, ten and 12 months via a simple project reporting format and at quality improvement meetings with members of the senior management team.

Meanwhile, the manufacturing department's technical services engineer, anticipating the quality engineer's cost report, produced a quality improvement plan in which was listed an assortment of specific solutions to problems, proposals for trials of new techniques and materials, and a call for further

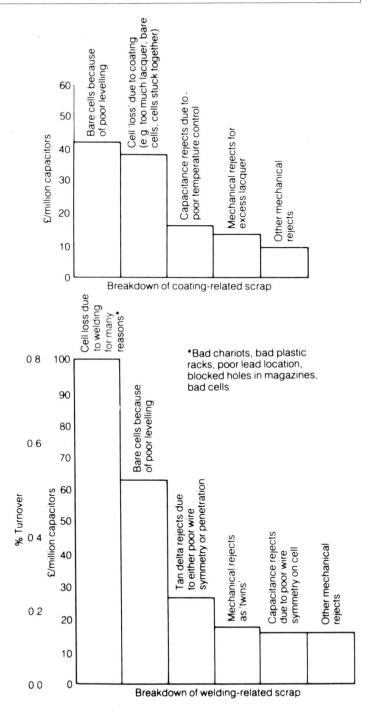

Figure 10.1 Pareto diagram examples.

Table 10.4 List of potential improvement projects

Number	Problem	Contribution	£/ annum	
1	Sillner	Machine Operator	20 364	
	Repairs	End Control	12 042	
				32 405
2	Winding faults	9 mm 1st rollergrade cell loss	28 880	
		7 mm 1st rollergrade cell loss	3 900	
				32 780
3	Levelling	9 Autotest scrap (due to weld)	11 970	
		9 mm Autotest scrap (due to epoxy coat)	7 980	
		7 mm Autotest scrap (due to weld)	1 470	
		7 mm Autotest scrap (due to epoxy coat)	960	
		9 mm Autotest level scrap	5 130	
				27 510
4	Unexplained capacitance	9 mm Autotest scrap	14 630	
		7 mm Autotest scrap	2 970	
	Rejects			17 600
5	Wire symmetry or penetration	9 mm Autotest scrap (tan delta)	5 130	
		9 mm Autotest scrap (capacitance)	3 040	
		7 mm Autotest scrap (tan delta)	5 310	
		7 mm Autotest scrap (capacitance)	630	
				14 110
6	Detaping	9 mm Stage loss	11 020	
		7 mm Stage loss	2 160	
				13 180
7	Winding faults:	Mechanical engineering hours 9 mm	5 135	
	Dropping foil,	Machine downtime hours 9 mm	1 182	
	No mylar pickup	Mechanical engineering hours 7 mm	268	
	Doubles	Machine downtime hours 7 mm	40	
				6 625
8	Welding faults:	Mechanical engineering hours	4 472	
	Weak weld	Machine downtime 9 mm	1 187	
	Missing weld	Machine downtime 7 mm	196	
				5 855

improvement to levelling of products prior to coating. The list was later condensed from 16 to five items with unexplained costs and appended to the cost report referred to earlier (which was obtained by inflating costs in the original report). The condensed plan or 'proposed strategy' must not have been adopted because the items appear again (albeit with different costs) appended to the next annual report by inflation.

REFERENCES

1. Juran, J.M. (ed.) (1988) *Quality Control Handbook*, McGraw-Hill, New York.
2. Juran, J.M. (1979) *Quality Management Work Book*, Juran Enterprises, New York.
3. BS6143 (1981) *The Determination and Use of Quality-Related Costs*, British Standards Institution, London.

Girobank PLC

11

11.1 INTRODUCTION

Girobank is a wholly owned subsidiary of the Alliance and Leicester Building Society. The bank was established in 1968 as a basic money transmission service (the banking arm of the Post Office) and in two decades has developed into major clearing bank with an account base of over 2 million personal and corporate customers and nearly 600 000 credit card holders. The bank offers a comprehensive range of financial services including: current, deposit and revolving credit accounts, overdrafts, personal loans, mortgages, VISA and ATM cards, international, insurance and collection services, pay schemes, cash cheques, business deposits and electronically formatted statement information. The bank employs over 6000 staff in 18 UK locations and each week handles some 8 million transactions and 250 000 customer accounts.

The introduction of TQM began in the Operations Directorate (the bank's 'paper factory') in 1987. In 1990, Girobank became the first financial institution to be awarded British registration to the BS5750 series of quality management system standards. The award covers Girobank's transaction processing operations at its main centre in Bootle, Merseyside. In 1991 they became the first bank and first service company to receive the British Quality Award. In the words of the judges they won the award for 'Four years of demonstrable and quantifiable business improvement achieved through a commitment to Total Quality'.

Total quality, innovation and caring are the foundations of the management approach adopted by Girobank. They have cultivated a management style which has moved from authoritative and directives to embrace the coaching, supportive and open style which encourages the creation of change agents and improvement champions from all levels and functions of the bank.

11.2 THE MOTIVATION FOR TOTAL QUALITY MANAGEMENT AND THE APPROACH ADOPTED

External customer service has always been of paramount importance to the bank. Until the mid 1980s internal improvement was largely driven by the traditional management services approach to methods and productivity. This was very successful and between 1980 and 1986 a 50% increase was achieved in customer transactions processed. Effective as this was, competitive pressures together with an increasingly discerning customer base made it apparent that a major new strategy was needed to enhance their competitive edge. The strategy adopted was TQM which was launched in the Operations Directorate in 1987. The TQM approach has been progressively extended to all areas of the bank – personnel, personal banking, corporate banking, finance division and management services.

Girobank's approach to TQM, which, at the outset, drew on the philosophy of Crosby [1], has a threefold focus, placing equal emphasis on: quality improvement, customer care and quality assurance (Fig. 11.1). The approach encompasses 10 'quality values'.

Figure 11.1 Girobank's TQM focus.

1. Make the *satisfaction* of our customers' needs our *primary goal* by working with them to identify and *satisfy* their requirements now and in the future.
2. Develop a working environment which *recognizes* and *rewards* our employees contribution to the business and *encourages* their personal involvement and development.
3. To ensure profitable growth of the business which provides an acceptable return on investments to our shareholders by delivering *value for money* products to our customers.
4. Adopt a consistently open, participative leadership style to *harness* the *skills* and enthusiasm of the whole workforce.
5. Provide the *educational* and *training* opportunities and resources to support the achievement of business objectives.

6. It is management's responsibility to lead the quality programme and involve all our people through *effective team working*.
7. Continuous quality improvement will be tackled through a *planned* and *structured* programme throughout.
8. To aim to provide better products, *delivery* and *service* than our competitors in those markets in which we choose to compete.
9. To *maintain* beneficial relationships with all our suppliers.
10. To recognize our *responsibility* to the wider commercial and social communities in which we operate.

The basic steps in Girobank's approach to TQM are illustrated in Fig. 11.2 and are now described, in brief:

Figure 11.2 Girobank's Approach to TQM.

(a) *Preparation.* A supportive management and facilitating structure was put into place. For example, a top level quality council was formed consisting of six senior managers and a quality co-ordinator from each department in the Operations Directorate.
(b) *Awareness and motivational training.* To get the TQM message across and emphasize the need for continuous improvement a series of workshops were devised and run. An integral part of Girobank's TQM strategy is to introduce each year a different initiative which is both innovative and exciting. The aim is to renew and reinforce the commitment of every individual. These initiatives have included: Journey to Excellence seminars, Quality Challenge seminars, Quest for Quality, Quality Fair, Customer Care workshops, Investment in Excellence and Customer Watch.
(c) *Audits.* To identify and prioritize improvement action a series of systematic audits followed the quality awareness training. The audits had an external and internal focus and included: market research study, staff attitude survey, customer-supplier quality review, letter and telephone analysis, and supplier audit. The outcome of these audits identified a list of improvement projects and initiatives.

(d) *Projects*. A project by project approach has been adopted. The aim is to involve people from all levels and functions of the bank in project activity.

(e) *Suggestion schemes*. To generate participation in the process of continuous improvement, a formal staff suggestion scheme is operated.

(f) *Communications*. The size and regional spread of the bank means that communication needs to be efficient, practical, thorough and simple. The bank has gone to considerable lengths to ensure that the lines of communication are interesting, informative and memorable. The bank's Team Brief initiative has proved to be extremely successful and the model has recently been adopted by the Alliance and Leicester Bulding Society for group-wide communication.

(g) *Competitions*. The experience is that the use of competitions achieves excellent levels of involvement while providing the opportunity for people to use their imagination and innovative powers to gain satisfaction and recognition.

(h) *Quality management system (QMS)*. A quality assurance programme was set up to establish standards for performance and develop a system which meets the requirements of the quality management system series BS5750 [2].

The details of these initiatives are given by Rowe *et al*. [3].

11.3 WHY DID GIROBANK UNDERTAKE A QUALITY COSTING EXERCISE?

As is the case with many organizations Girobank, prior to its launch of TQM, commissioned a firm of major management consultants to undertake a quality cost analysis. This first quality cost audit was badly designed and involved a lot of management and staff time and the quality cost were presented in such a way that they could not be compared against a suitable internal benchmark; it was a typical 'one-shot' exercise.

More recently a cost of quality analysis (termed cost of failure) has been carried out in various departments of the bank. The purpose of this tailored measurement system were as follows.

- The success of Girobank's bank-wide process of continuous quality improvement was to be monitored and measured. For example, (i) over 2500 quality-related projects undertaken by Project Action Teams (PAT) had been registered and 900 or so projects had been completed, leading to a net financial benefit of over £6M and (ii) over 7000 suggestions had been adopted with net financial savings of around £5.5M.

- Areas of failure costs (i.e. waste, rework, errors and complaints) were to be identified and the improvement opportunities for project work prioritized.

- A better understanding of the quality-related activities to which time and effort is being devoted was to be developed. In this way an understanding of true 'failure' costs at all levels in the bank could be obtained.

It is a bank-wide activity covering both processing and non-processing areas.

11.4 APPROACH ADOPTED TO QUALITY COST COLLECTION

A prevention, appraisal and failure model along the lines of BS6143: Part 2 [4] has been adopted by the Bank for the exercise. The data for this model are collected by the line managers, using various data sources as a self-recording exercise but relating only to operational activities. Prior to line managers going about data collection they were briefed on the philosophy and concepts underpinning the cost of failure model. A manager will usually have more than one section under his/her control (e.g. data capture and technical support).

The key activities undertaken within the department are first listed and, together with an advisor from the Quality Department, categorized into the four categories of Task, Failure, Appraisal and Prevention. Following this each line manager completes a simple sheet in relation to the process and the Task, Failure, Appraisal and Prevention activities and cause (Fig. 11.3). These major headings are explained as follows:

1. *Failure, appraisal and prevention*. These activities are along the lines of the definitions as typically outlined in BS6143 Part 2 [4], which have been outlined a number of times already in the book. The following description of failure, appraisal and prevention were given as notes to the line managers to assist them in the cost of failure exercise.
   (a) Failure costs are the costs of not doing it right the first time. Correction may or may not be done in the area where the fault was committed (e.g. a document not associated with the relevant cheque envelope and a document keyed in twice).
   (b) Appraisal costs are the costs of checking for faults (e.g. checking that the details on a journal voucher are correct). Appraisal takes place irrespective of whether or not faults are actually present. It is usually part of the formal organisation and procedures of a business.
   (c) Prevention costs are the costs of setting up things beforehand so that faults are not made in the first place (e.g. planning work and cleaning machines before use).
2. *Task*. This is considered as basic work activity and practice and is related to the essential elements undertaken by a function.
3. *Process*. A breakdown of the main activities is carried out by the section/ function under study. As appropriate, a flowchart is prepared and used to confirm the main aspects of the process.

MGD NAME _____ BRANCH _____ DATE _____

SECTION _____

PROCESS	TASK	FAILURE	APPRAISAL	PREVENTION	CAUSE
TOTALS					

Figure 11.3 Cost of failure collection sheet.

For example: pouch opening, the opening of the pouches containing cheques and documents from the Post Masters', includes the following process activities:

(a) open pouch and outsort (task);
(b) check cash value (appraisal);
(c) check the number of cheques (appraisal);
(d) enter number of cheques on document (task);
(e) remove staples (failure);
(f) amend batch header (failure);
(g) correct pouch presentation errors (failure);
(h) check empty envelopes (appraisal).

Data capture typically includes:

(a) receive raw credits, strip and split, batch and bin (task);
(b) microfilm (task);
(c) key in credits (task);
(d) re-keying because of errors and balance errors (failure);
(e) reconciliation keying (failure).

4. *Cause*. Notes are made under this section of the form of any known underlying reasons for failures (e.g. correcting postmasters' errors and dealing with document jams in microfilm camera).

The sheet is filled-in using as much data, which is already generated currently within each manager's section or by carrying out short activity sampling activities, as appropriate. The data collected relates to the volume of work flowing through each stage of the process, duration of activity and the grade of person undertaking the identified activities, categorized as task, failure, appraisal or prevention respectively. The yearly budget statistics are also taken into account in making the assessment.

The completed sheets are sent to the Improvement Services section of Operations Support Services. The data is put on to a spreadsheet on a central personal computer and converted into the staff time (full-time equivalents), percentages and monetary values and the results are then summarized for the whole of the operations Directorate. Departmental results are then fed back to the appropriate manager for final verification and signed off before they are published.

11.5 REPORTING AND USE OF THE DATA

The failure cost data is reported to each department, the Director of Operations and the Improvement Council. The format used is shown in Table 11.1. The Improvement Council reviews the results and monitors progress in relation to the cost of failure reduction.

Based on the findings of the exercise each line manager is given objectives to reduce the failure costs. This results in the setting-up of projects to

Table 11.1 Cost of failure analysis

Department	Total staff cost of areas audited	Failure cost	Failure cost as a % of the total staff cost of areas audited	Appraisal cost	Appraisal cost as a % of the total staff cost of areas audited	Prevention cost	Prevention cost as a % of the total staff cost of areas audited	Total non-quality cost (failure, appraisal and prevention)	Total non-quality cost as a % of the total staff cost of areas audited

achieve localized improvement and the development of the internal customer-supplier relationship between functions.

The potential for cost of failure reduction is greater in some departments than others. Some departments, as a result of the direct nature of their work, have high levels of correction costs as a result of mistakes by other banks (i.e. inter-bank difference).

The cost of failure exercise is undertaken on an annual basis. The main emphasis of being used as a management tool to assist in the prioritization of improvement work will lead to the driving down of costs. The line managers are always keen to compare their results from year to year. This is not, however, encouraged because as part of the bank's continuous improvement activity a number of work processes will have been re-engineered and some aspects of work will come under the responsibility of other departments and managers.

11.6 SUMMARY

There is a shortage of published material on how quality costing can be applied to non-manufacturing situations. The case study of Girobank has shown how the basic methodology can be tailored to suit this type of situation.

The cost of failure data has given an added impetus to Girobank's error reduction programme. Agreeing cost of failure reduction targets built into improvement objectives has been of particular benefit to the bank-wide improvement process.

REFERENCES

1. Crosby, P.B. *Quality is Free*, McGraw-Hill, New York.
2. BS5750, (1987) *Quality Systems*, British Standards Institution, London.
3. Rowe, S., Gosling, C. and Dale, B.G. (1994) Girobank, Chapter 24 of *Managing Quality* 2nd edn (ed. by B.G. Dale) Prentice Hall, Herts.
4. BS6143: Part 2, (1990) *Guide to the Economics of Quality – Prevention, Appraisal and Failure Model*, British Standards Institution, London.

ACKNOWLEDGEMENTS

The author wishes to thank Steve Rowe, Lyn Grugel and Catie Gosling for providing the material on which this chapter is based and for their suggestions on the text.

Total cost of ownership at ICL | 12

12.1 INTRODUCTION

This chapter outlines the development and use of a total cost of ownership (TCO) model which has been developed for use at the ICL manufacturing operations plant at Ashton-under-Lyne. Central to the model are three key categories of cost – acquiring, possessing and sustaining. The background to these three types of cost and their definitions are examined in the chapter.

Total cost of ownership is a new management concept for dealing with supplier selection, partnership sourcing and other issues. It is based on a computer-aided model to track the performance of a supplier in terms of a series of defined cost elements, rather than subjective measures such as a points system typically used in vendor accreditation. The model seeks to provide a change in culture away from lowest cost per piece towards the lowest total cost of owning parts during their life cycle. It was developed as a tool to analyse the total costs associated with procuring parts from outside vendors and assist the partnership effort to optimize cost and improve quality. The application of the TCO model lies within the procurement and vendor quality (this department deals with supplier problems and acts as an interface to deal with problems that have occurred within the Ashton factory operations). These areas have responsibility for product cost and quality standards of externally sourced parts. Potential uses of the model are outlined in the chapter, including supplier selection and negotiation, supplier education and partnership, strategic purchasing decisions, and internal manufacturing issues.

12.2 COMPANY BACKGROUND INFORMATION

The ICL plant at Ashton-under-Lyne is responsible for the manufacture of mid-range systems, mainframe systems, storage units and other contract manufacture. The site employs over 400 people and uses parts procured from external vendors and printed circuit boards (PCBs) sourced from a sister ICL company. The site operates to exacting quality standards and uses systems and tools such as material requirements planning (MRP), just in time (JIT), flexible manufacturing systems (FMSs), electronic kanban, electronic data interchange (EDI) and a variety of teamwork initiatives. It has developed an overall quality culture for which it has received external recognition (i.e. the British Quality Award).

A manufacturing plant such as this, which buys in most of its parts from external suppliers, is liable to purchase many of its quality costs from its suppliers. According to Smock [1], Crosby estimates that 50% of a company's quality problems are caused by defective purchased materials. The company is currently forecast to spend £134m on externally procured items, excluding purchases from its sister plant. It was against this background that a TCO model was developed as a tool to analyse the cost interface between ICL and its suppliers. The development of the model was undertaken by Andrew Nix during a Teaching Company Programme between ICL and the UMIST Quality Management Centre, for details see Dale and Hollier [2].

12.3 THE TOTAL COST OF OWNERSHIP MODEL CONCEPT

The model provides a measurement system to track the performance of procured parts and show the effect of actions to improve quality and reduce cost. It is designed to improve the interface between the purchasing and quality functions. The TCO model is a method to show in financial terms the effects of the relationship of ICL with its suppliers, to highlight, prioritize and measure the effectiveness of actions taken by both parties to reduce total costs. It is based on a set of definitions from which different cost elements are used according to the specific business use. In this way the model provides a rigorously defined measurement system for examining the relationship with suppliers along with other key internal issues.

The model seeks to analyse the costs of owning a part that is procured from an external supplier. This enables improvement targets with suppliers to be agreed, priorities set and actions planned and taken to reduce costs. The model tracks the success of these actions and initiatives. It also aims to harmonize the approaches of purchasing and quality functions by emphasizing that changes away from lowest unit cost to lowest TCO plus unit cost are necessary if ICL is to operate in the most efficient manner.

The definitions of TCO is divided into three specific areas: acquiring, possessing and sustaining. The definitions are:

- *Total cost of ownership*. These are the costs associated with acquiring, possessing and sustaining a conforming product as it exists throughout its life cycle.
- *Costs of acquiring a product*. These are the costs which are concerned with ensuring that a conforming product is available for manufacture.
- *Costs of possessing*. These are the reactive costs which ensure the conformance of a product.
- *Costs of sustaining*. These are the proactive costs that ensure conformance will be maintained in the future.

Any cost element can be placed within one of the areas. The definitions are set up in such a way as to show the effect of changes in one cost area on another (i.e. what a change made in sustaining costs has on possessing costs and to establish the elasticity of the influence of sustaining on possessing costs). ICL has sufficient purchasing power with its vendors to request cost reductions. However, many of the proposals require extra resources (e.g. procurement investigation, design input, evaluation exercises) from within ICL. The model allows ICL to track the effect of initiatives taken in one area against changes in other area. For example, if a cost were placed within the sustaining category, measures would be put in place to ensure that possessing costs would be reduced in the future. This split into three areas also seeks to avoid discriminating against a supplier willing to work proactively with ICL to improve conformance (i.e. cost of sustaining versus costs of possessing). By showing the different biasing of costs to ICL and the influence this has on other areas of cost ownership the longer term trends in a suppliers' performance are highlighted.

The categories have been developed in such a way that only certain cost elements need be extracted as appropriate to the particular business environment in which the model is designed to operate. Appendix 12.1 details the cost elements within each of the three categories that an ideal TCO model should have. In applying the model the three cost categories and associated elements are analysed by a team. It is suggested that the team members should comprise representatives of purchasing, quality, vendor quality, manufacturing and finance functions. The team in deciding the elements to be used in the model should take into account how management are to use the model, the company environment and the relationship which currently exists with suppliers.

As already stated in this book quality cost experience indicates that it is best to start with a number of major costs and once confidence has been gained in the collection, measurement and use of costs the system can be expanded. This also applies to the TCO model and it is suggested than an initial model be developed to show the benefits. As the model is developed, it can be used to look at smaller cost elements and those costs elements that are difficult to measure.

12.4 USES OF THE TOTAL COST OF OWNERSHIP MODEL

The primary use of the TCO model is to establish a forum to bring suppliers and ICL together in a business partnership, with a focus on reducing the total cost of ownership.

There are specific management/business uses of the TCO model, aside from those addressing changes in practice for the purchasing function. It is of major importance to the development of the model that specific management uses are defined at an early stage so that the relevant cost elements are included. The management uses that were initially developed for the model at ICL include: supplier selection and negotiation, supplier education and partnership, warranty issues, strategic purchasing decisions, and internal manufacturing issues. These uses are now reviewed.

12.4.1 Supplier selection and negotiation

A potential use of the TCO model is to provide cost of owning parts data from similar suppliers so that sourcing decisions can be made and assessed. This should be undertaken in conjunction with other data, for example that provided from vendor accreditation/rating schemes. The costings developed by the TCO model should show all the relevant costs, not just the unit costs involved. The model is designed to take away emotions and introduce a rigidly defined set of costs and data for sound business decision making.

Once confidence has been developed in the model by both the company and supplier, it can be used as a negotiating tool for cost reduction exercises with suppliers. The supplier must have confidence in the way that the model has been constructed and how it works, clearly it would be counterproductive to argue over the concept of the model and its associated elements.

12.4.2 Supplier education and partnership

For high value procured parts such as disk drives, power supplies and PCBs, zero defect meetings are held between ICL and its suppliers on a monthly basis to discuss supplier performance (internal and external) and any product issues. A major use of the TCO model is to translate a performance percentage into an actual cost on the non-conformances. This cost then becomes the focal point of the zero defect meetings.

By making suppliers aware of the costs to ICL of their product compared to suppliers of similar products a new concept of supplier partnership development is opened up. ICL and its suppliers can work together to reduce the total cost of ownership. If the data is used consistently over a period of time it can lead to possible negotiations with suppliers in relation to the performance of their products, price structure and changes in warranty conditions.

Using the concept of costs to track a supplier's performance enables the TCO model to be used as a tool to prioritize actions, set non-conformance reduction targets for suppliers and it will enable the supplier to be tracked against these targets. The model will also act as an indicator of the success of any corrective actions taken to reduce the non-conformances of a part.

12.4.3 Warranty issues

The model can be used to provide strict guidelines for negotiations of warranty details. By analysing some of the parameters of the warranty terms (e.g. transportation cost and liability definitions) the model would help to minimize cost, based on past data for the supplier/product area.

12.4.4 Strategic purchasing decisions

At an advanced level the model could be used for strategic decision making in relation to single or dual sourcing, make or buy and defining optimum purchase patterns, for example. For the make or buy decision the sum of all the TCO outputs for a sub-assembly can be compared to a TCO output from a supplier who can source the finished product.

12.4.5 Internal manufacturing issues

There is also scope for different types of TCO models to deal with internal issues such as: analysis of internal processes to identify those of high cost, deciding the most efficient level of testing, analysis of cost savings arising from initiatives such as ship to stock, inventory handling, and tracking a new product's introduction into the factory.

To use the model in this way requires that sufficient data are built up over a period of time, along with suitable confidence in the robustness of the model.

12.5 DEVELOPMENT AND IMPLEMENTATION OF THE TOTAL COST OF OWNERSHIP MODEL

Important questions which need to be kept in mind when developing the list of cost elements for an initial TCO model are the following.

- What are the major cost elements that concern TCO?
- Is the cost element relevant to the definition?
- Is the cost element of a significant relative size?
- Is the cost element currently measured?
- Is the cost element easy to measure?
- Is there a degree of confidence in the quality of data?

- What are the current supplier/company interfaces, and what role could TCO have within these interfaces?
- What are the current strategic initiatives that may effect the TCO model?
- Are other issues involved (i.e. product liability)?

The model should be built starting with the larget perceived cost elements and those that are easily measurable. In developing a model, the priorities should be to produce a simple and easily understood model that will be accepted by all users; this must include the suppliers who will be ultimately measured by the model. It is therefore important only to include costs that are relevant to the definition of TCO. For example, it may not be appropriate to measure the costs of testing done on finished products, as these costs may be an internal requirement rather than a supplier related cost. Within ICL an initial concern was raised with this approach of cost analysis. It was felt that when the detail of the costing mechanism was being discussed with suppliers they might query the cost of some of the processes that ICL operate.

Initial work was carried out to develop a system to extract data from the various mainframe and database applications that exist throughout the factory. Examples of output were developed and analysed and these showed that significant items of cost are field failures, returning parts to suppliers and interaction with suppliers concerning product issues failure. These types of cost are perhaps specific to the computer industry due to high costs of call out for field failures and expensive returns, often to overseas locations. The basic concept behind the model is to establish specific occurrences of process. This requires an electronic database where this information is stored, an ability to read the information and a process cost. The model then extracts the data and attaches a total cost of the process occurring. Its operation is based upon the electronic extraction of flags that indicate that a certain process has occurred. Information on the number and type of flags is passed to a central processor, where process costs are attached and a final cost is extracted with the correct division of costs. The model has been written using a Windows based spreadsheet. This acts as a central controller for all the data, bringing together the process costs and data concerning occurrences.

The data is extracted from a number of databases.

1. Local quality system (LQS) mainframe:
    (a) supplier details,
    (b) inspection details,
    (c) inspection history,
    (d) fault details,
    (e) repair details,
    (f) goods inward received quantity,
    (g) goods inward batch sampling,
    (h) details on passed tests,

(i)   details on failed tests,
(j)   installation and commissioning field returns to the Ashton manufacturing site.

2.   Networked computer:
     (a) supplier visits
     (b) supplier meetings
     (c) permits raised,
     (d) first-off appraisal details,
     (e) first-off corrective actions,
     (f) DAN database.

3.   Other databases available for the model include OMAC, PAM database and other purchasing and engineering databases on different networks.

Once the concept of the model was accepted by ICL's management initial work was carried out to transfer data held electronically on the various systems within the plant. This was mainly based on finding a flag that indicated that a cost had been incurred. An example of this is the raising of a defect advice note (DAN) which shows the quantity of parts rejected in relation to a particular supplier. Work was carried out to attach a cost to the occurrence of a DAN. An example of the format of the data is contained in Appendix 12.2. Many of the processes within ICL that are relevant to the TCO are cross-departmental and it was decided to look at the process cost as a time and unit cost per hour function. The processes were analysed in terms of time elapsed for actions and the unit cost per hour with built-in over-heads.

An important issue is the interface of the model with current supplier development initiatives which are already going on within ICL. For example, ICL operates a vendor accreditation scheme, zero defect meetings (a forum for analysing and improving the performance of parts) and quality review meetings with its major suppliers in relation to product issues. Due to the advanced nature of these vendor interfaces through these types of initiatives, which are often product and vendor specific, they had to be considered and catered for in development of the model. It was also felt that three significant costs – field failures, returning parts to suppliers and interaction with suppliers on product issues – were already managed to produce corrective action plans to reduce non-conformance and hence costs. This presented a problem in that the model appeared to measure issues that were already being tracked.

Various developments were required to implement and demonstrate the use of the model. The issues that were faced at ICL are now discussed.

12.5.1 Vendor quality corrective action database

Product issues that arise are not currently recorded electronically. This information would be used by the Vendor Quality Department and is a major cost item for TCO. It was necessary to set up an electronic database to record and track the following:

- a detailed analysis of the product issue;
- a description of actions and corrective actions taken;
- an analysis of resources utilized;
- a closed field for the product issue; and
- forecasting device closure dates.

This database, as well as being a major cost element to a TCO model, has many strategic features for vendor quality. It allows the tracking of a part's history and can provide the basis of a system to use as a resource to solve future problems. It also sets up a control, scheduling, communication and feedback facility for vendor quality to tackle supplier quality-related issues.

This database is crucial to the TCO model since without it a major cost element is missing in terms of product issues that cannot currently be captured from any system with the Ashton manufacturing facility.

12.5.2 LQS development

Changes were required to the LQS to track and cost suitable items. These included:

- tracking liability on failed tests;
- tracking time taken to test parts at goods inward inspection and on the line; and
- other measures that are included in vendor accreditation, for example, tracking:
  - packaging issues,
  - meeting documentation requirements,
  - failure to supply certificate of conformance,
  - quality notices issued due to defects,
  - vendor self measurement,
  - vendor appraisal.

12.5.3 Costing for other systems

Systems need to be developed to provide for time spent on certain process on the other systems that exist in ICL, for example on engineering database costing of engineering changes.

12.5.4 Establish a TCO input to zero defect meetings

It was necessary to establish a TCO input to the zero defect meetings, showing the cost of internal and external failures (DAN and ICOR returns). The TCO model needed to be designed to automatically produce the statistics concerning a supplier's performance and the process costs. In this way the model would then provide a tracking and measuring facility to set realistic targets for suppliers. However, there are implications to negotiations with vendors that require consideration before this is accepted.

12.5.5 A TCO element for vendor accreditation

It is necessary to develop a TCO element for suppliers failing to score maximum points on the vendor accreditation measures. The purpose of this is to focus on the exact costs of a supplier failing to perform rather than a simple points score. These measures of points and costs can co-exist with each other.

12.5.6 Establish database for supplier/ICL interfaces

This database would show accurately direct interfaces with suppliers in the form of meetings/visits, the purpose of the visits and the resources utilized. It would enable this area of activity to be fully costed and measured.

12.6 POTENTIAL BENEFITS

There are benefits of using a TCO model. However, in any organization significant initial work is required to develop the underlying model. The benefits that can be realized are numerous, including a common tracking tool for analysis of costs, a mechanism for focusing on key issues, an indicator of success and a significant negotiating tool. These are now examined under the broad headings of costs reductions and resource allocation.

12.6.1 Cost reductions

ICL enters into negotiations with its suppliers in order to reduce the unit costs. However, TCO principles can be applied to look at costs other than from simple unit costs to those such as basic material cost, transportation, packaging costs, unpacking costs, inspection costs, testing costs and assembly costs.

A project arising from the TCO model concept has started at ICL. This is to develop negotiations away from the unit costs to allow suppliers to examine the way they make parts, for example asking them to suggest a change of material and/or improve packaging in order to save unnecessary costs. By allowing the supplier to examine and redesign the parts and increased flexibility for the supplier to independently examine cost reduction opportunities, a stronger partnership has developed between ICL and its suppliers. The development of a process to look at other cost reduction proposals releases costs to ICL and its suppliers. Recognition is given to suppliers for their ability to develop cost reductions.

12.6.2 Resource allocation

For a supplier to redesign a part (e.g. a cable, a metalwork fabrication or something more complicated), it is necessary that ICL spend resources before the new design can be accepted. For example a cable will require evaluation for checks on radio frequency interference (RFI) controls, functionability and fit. Further resources will be required to update drawings and other systems that exist.

There is a requirement to improve the framework within which cost reduction proposals are developed in order to arrive at a more accurate estimate of the cost savings of a proposal. The standardization of this process through the TCO model will eliminate some of the emotion associated with cost reductions to arrive at a sound business decision.

It is important to ensure that the resources are used in the most cost effective way to provide the greatest benefit. The model is designed to be used as a central forum with all current cost reductions and resources being available. This will assist in maximizing the total cost benefits that can be released within the constraints of available resources. A central forum is planned to allow all proposals raised in a given period and the current resources available for cost reductions to be matched for greatest release of benefit. This process is expected to be via a computer spreadsheet and is designed to take out any emotions surrounding cost reductions and deal with specific figures.

12.7 SUMMARY

The TCO model has got two main purposes. The first is to act as a catalyst to bring a company and its suppliers together with the common purpose of reducing the TCO. The second is to attach a cost that a company actually incurs from procuring a part from a supplier. Within this there are many worthwhile projects that come under the TCO umbrella, as outlined in this chapter.

Total cost of ownership is a strategic management technique which establishes a new way of dealing with supplier issues and specific cost items. Careful thought is required to ensure that well defined and correct cost elements are extracted from existing databases to be used in the TCO model.

If TCO is to be used successfully it is important to ensure the integrity of the data, its capture and analysis. To introduce TCO with suppliers before this is complete would be unprofessional and dangerous.

The TCO model is still under development at ICL and final models are being prepared for use. As part of this development it is planned to use the initial model to act as the catalyst with both internal users and suppliers to develop and produce the ideas for cost reduction. It is also planned to educate the suppliers by a visit to ICL to show the complete process for the supplier's parts and to initiate ideas for cost reductions. It can be said that the ideas of TCO are now well integrated into the strategy of the company's purchasing, materials and supply function.

REFERENCES

1. Smock, D. (1982) How to stem the tide of shoddy materials. *Purchasing*, **92** (9), 51–7.
2. Dale, B.G. and Hollier, R.H. (1992) Technology transfer: some total quality management examples. *Proceedings of the 1992 Technology Transfer and Implementation Conference*, Teaching Company Scheme in association with the IT and ACME Directorates, London, July, 149–54.

ACKNOWLEDGEMENTS

Barrie Dale is grateful to Andrew Nix for allowing his material to be used in this chapter and to ICL for permission to publish.

APPENDIX 12.1 Cost elements of the TCO model

A Acquiring

A1 Non-attaining

These are any costs that are incurred without securing a conforming product, i.e. price of non-conformance (PONC) items.

A2 Design

These are any costs in designing a conforming product, including any specification or verification costs.

A3 Sourcing

These are costs of sourcing for a given product.

A4 Selecting

These are the costs of any assessment or negotiation with suppliers.

A5 Appraisal

These are the costs of checking the conformance of a product. This includes the cost of any quality measuring equipment (and consumables used), any costs of inspection, sampling or resting (receiving, in-house, final or on-site), the running of any statistical controls and any costs of external approval that is required.

B Possessing

B1 Inventory

There are all the costs associated with the maintaining and tracking of inventory, including any costs of storage or extra handling equipment (external or internal), costs of safeguarding the product, costs of holding extra buffer stock above a normal level, evaluation of the stock, special storage costs of stock lost or obsolescence.

B2 External failure

These are the costs of all external failures (i.e. errors found after the product is dispatched to customer). These costs include any processing of customer complaints or warranty claims, costs of product recalls and returns and any costs as a result of lawsuits. All these have associated losses of goodwill that should be taken into account.

B3 Internal failure

These are the costs of all internal failures (i.e. errors found before the product is dispatched to the customer). These costs include any scrapped products (including any added value incorporated into the item that cannot be salvaged), repairs needed (including any labour costs), returning, replacement, re-order costs and any downtime costs as a result of a line shutdown.

B4 Process control

These are the costs of maintaining any records and systems that indicate that a product does not conform to requirements. This includes the costs of processes and costs due to delay, 'first-offs', permits/concessions and DANs.

B5 Process state

These are any costs associated with transferring the ownership of items between processes, internally or externally including any handling, storage, packaging and delivery costs.

C Sustaining

C1 Quality improvement

This section covers all costs that are associated with a process of continuous improvement that ensure and sustain product and service quality. It covers all general improvement and awareness initiatives, internal audits of the company, and other product-specific improvement costs.

C2 Prevention

These comprise any costs that can be attributed to actually preventing non-conformances in the future. This element is concerned with liaising with relevant parties, corrective actions, troubleshooting, any system updating and follow-up.

C3 Training/Education

This includes any product-specific costs which are related to either training or educating for the sustaining of conforming products.

C4 Initiatives

These are the cost of initiatives to reduce costs, especially those concerned with the total cost of ownership. These may include initiatives concerned with suppliers, manufacturing and process.

C5 Supplier linking

These are costs attributable to suppliers that will ensure and sustain a conforming product. Such costs are performance monitoring of a company or product, joint ventures linking ICL and the supplier, any recognition given to the company (e.g. exclusive contracts, top vendor awards, letters to management), or any poor performance recognition (e.g. return of goods, cancellation of contracts, rework scrap charges, legal action), any costs of suppliers surveys or audits and any costs of re-selecting a product due to product failure.

APPENDIX 12.2 EXAMPLE OF PROCESS COST DOCUMENT

Table 12.1 shows how the DAN process loop is costed. The letter shown after the time relates to a rate of pay table that is stored within the spreadsheet.

The colons act as delimiters for the spreadsheet program to read in the time and rate to give an overall process time. This document is designed so any process can be costed in a simple time/pay rate – whilst still giving information on the actual process.

Table 12.1 Example of a process cost document

	: Time (min)	: Rate
Operator realizes that part(s) has (have) been assembled incorrectly	: 01.00	: A
Operator takes the workpiece to supervisor/manager	: 01.00	: B
Supervisor/manager decides whether work piece can still be used, has to be reworked or has to be scrapped	: 01.00	: B
Rejection label attached to workpiece	: 05.00	: A
Quality control to be called to decide whether workpiece can be used, reworked or scrapped	: 05.00	: C
Quality control stamp reject label	: 05.00	: C
Workpiece is transferred to cell control	: 05.00	: A
Cell control originate an 078 form on OMAC	: 01.00	: B
Workpiece sent off to defect control centre	: 05.00	: A
Defect control centre check 074 OMAC form	: 01.00	: B
Defect control centre update QPOM	: 03.00	: B
Defect control centre log DAN on database	: 01.00	: B
Defect control centre prepare and raise DAN	: 05.00	: B
Defect control centre paperwork/copies of DANs	: 01.00	: B
DAN circulated	: 02.00	: A
Vendor quality to be signed off	: 01.00	: C
Purchasing to be signed off	: 01.00	: D
Consignment notes/labels	: 03.00	: A
DAN is taken to pigeon hole	: 02.00	: F
074 OMAC form is raised	: 01.00	: B
Defect control centre update database	: 02.00	: B
	: 33.00	: Total

<table>
<tr><td>

Setting up a quality costing system

</td><td>

13

</td></tr>
</table>

13.1 INTRODUCTION

This short concluding chapter of quality costing, by drawing on the previous 12 chapters, offers a number of pointers to organizations on how they might approach the collection, analysis and reporting of quality costs. A checklist of dos and don'ts are also presented which may help organizations avoid some typical difficulties encountered in quality costing.

13.2 QUALITY COSTING POINTERS

It is unlikely that an organization's management accounts will contain the necessary information in the right form. Hence it is essential right from the outset to involve accountants, as part of the team, in the cost collection exercise. This team, once formed, should set about educating itself about the concept of quality costing. Quality costing is a management technique which needs to be reported accordingly in terms of management accounting. However, it should be viewed in improvement terms and not just as another financial performance measure.

There is no point in collecting quality-related costs just to see what they may reveal – the criterion should be 'need to know' rather than 'nice to know'. Many executives have successfully resisted pressure to co-operate in the collection of quality costs on the grounds that they would not reveal any problems of which they were not already aware from the quality management information system. The purpose of quality costing should be clarified at the start of the project as this may influence the strategy of the exercise and will help to avoid difficulties later. If, for example, the main objective of the exercise is to identify high-cost problem areas, approximate costs will suffice. If, on the other hand, the purpose is to set a percentage cost-reduction target for the organization's total quality costs, it will be necessary to identify and measure all the contributing cost elements in order to be sure that costs are reduced and not simply transferred elsewhere.

It will also be necessary to decide how to deal with overheads, since many quality costs are normally included as part of the overhead, whilst others are treated as direct costs and attract a proportion of overheads. Failure to clarify this can lead to a gross distortion of the picture derived from the analysis. It is also easy to fall into the trap of double counting. For these and other reasons quality costs should be made the subject of a memorandum account. However, the costs should not include recovery of overheads in calculating costs of personnel. Another issue to be decided is how costs are allocated to components, material and so forth which are scrapped. A common practice is to value scrap at 100% material cost plus 50% of the finished part total labour/burden costs, irrespective of the actual state of manufacture of the rejected part.

Another area of difficulty is deciding whether some activities, usually of a setting-up, testing or running-in type, are quality activities or an integral and essential part of the production/operations activity. These costs often can be substantial and can alter quite markedly the relative proportions of quality-related costs categories. There are also factors which serve to ensure the basic utility of the product and/or service, guard against errors, and protect and preserve quality. Examples are the use of design codes, preparation of engineering, technical and administrative systems and procedures, capital premiums on machinery, and equipment, document and drawing controls, and handling and storage practices. Whether such factors give rise to costs which may be regarded as being quality related is a matter for judgement in individual cases. These problems need to be discussed with purchasing, engineering, production/operations, and accountancy personnel, as appropriate, in order to resolve them. There is little doubt that deciding which activities should be included under the quality-related cost umbrella is by no means straightforward and there are many grey areas. Some quality assurance managers have a tendency to include costs that are difficult to justify as being quality related and over which they have no control or influence. This overzealousness should be guarded against.

One of the maxims of quality cost collection seems to be that, in general, costs need to be large to hold the attention of people – in particular, that of senior management. Magnitude is often regarded as being synonymous with importance, though it is magnitude coupled with relevance and potential for reduction which determines the real importance of costs. Clearly it may be much more advantageous to pursue a small percentage reduction in a large cost than a large reduction in a small cost, depending on the ease of achievement. This creates something of a dilemma for the cost collector because large costs are often insensitive to changes. But the collector cannot omit large costs and concentrate only on smaller costs which may be readily seen to change. Hence cost groupings need to be chosen carefully so that the cost reductions which are achieved are displayed in such a way that both the relative achievement and absolute position are clearly shown. Another dilemma facing the cost collector arises from the fact that one-off estimates of quality costs tend not to change and some people take the view that there is no point in collecting costs which do not change. The only way out of this dilemma is to measure directly, or through surrogates, those costs which it is thought worth collecting.

Prior to the collection of costs an assessment should be made of the type of data which is available from the quality management information system. This assessment should also encompass accuracy and reliability.

A checklist of quality cost elements can provide a useful starting point for the cost collection exercise. However, there is no substitute for a thorough analysis of all an organization's activities and some key elements may be missed if only this method is used. BS6143: Part 2 [1] and Campanella [2] provide such a list of elements under the cost categories of prevention, appraisal, internal failure, and external failure. In some organizations cost elements have been identified by scanning the quality costing literature, and other organizations from analysis of their processes using, for example, a process cost model as typically outlined in BS6143: Part 1 [3], have identified the costs incurred from not getting operations right the first time.

A point to be borne in mind is that the staff from manufacturing departments are used to being measured. This is not the case with non-manufacturing departments, where there is likely to be more of a challenge to the concepts involved in a quality costing exercise. It is also likely that some departmental managers will express strong emotions about the costs identified in their area of responsibility. Departmental managers may also not give a high priority to the identification and measurement of costs, particularly if the importance of quality costing has not been made clear by senior management.

In the absence of an established quality-related cost reporting system, start by looking into failure costs, i.e.:

- failure costs attributable to suppliers or sub-contractors,
- in-house mistakes, scrap, rework, and rectification costs,
- downgraded products or 'seconds',
- free repairs or replacements for products which are defective as delivered and/or fitted,
- compensations for service failure,
- warranty and guarantee costs and field failures,
- litigation costs.

This should be followed by inquiring into the costs of inspection, checks, false starts, disruption to routine production and operations activities, and quality-related inefficiencies built into standard costs. The way in which quality-related costs are computed should be recorded so that the validity of comparisons made across departments, products, processes or time may be checked.

When cost information is available analyse it and costs attributed to department, defect type, product, project, cause and supplier. The responsibility for costs should be identified with functions and people. Problems and cost reduction projects need to be ranked by size and importance. The collection, analysis, and reporting of quality-related costs should be integrated into the company accounting system – with the aim of keeping paperwork to a minimum.

The reporting of quality costs should be carried out in a disciplined manner and in such a way that the costs make an impact and the data used to its full potential. It is important to ensure that the data collected is comparable with previous cost reporting exercises. In most organizations the standard of quality costs reporting is poor. Consideration needs to be given to issues such as: a standardized reporting format, clarity and simplicity of reporting with minimum use of words, the quality costs data are well presented, the data is complete, and the decisions to be taken by management from the reported data are clear. The summarized data should be supported by detailed information – especially the failure costs. Attention should be given to the use of bar charts and pie charts with standard range and scales. This ensures that the relative magnitude of cost elements plotted on separate charts is kept in perspective, thus making comparisons and judgements easier. The quality costs should always be separated from other aspects of quality and presented in the context of other costs.

Successful quality costing systems, as an everyday feature of an organization's management activities, takes a long time to establish. It can take up to five years to reach the status of credibility and usefulness that should be expected of data featured in a management information system. A measure of the organizational status of quality costing is if it features in the quality manual.

13.3 QUALITY COSTING DOS AND DON'TS

A few dos and don'ts which may help organizations to avoid some of the difficulties and traps typically encountered in a quality cost collection exercise are:

13.3.1 Dos

- Get the purpose and the strategy clear at the start.
- Report only costs produced or endorsed by the accounts departments.
- Make a friend of the accountant.

- Make it clear to the accountant that precise information is not always essential in a quality costing exercise.
- Get data and costs from standard data wherever possible.
- Assess the accuracy and reliability of the data produced by quality management information system.
- Seek independent corroboration of any data which is doubtful.
- Avoid getting bogged down with trying to understand all the underlying details.
- Start with failure costs.
- Consider appraisal costs as a target for cost reduction.
- Consider ease of collection and start with the easiest cost elements.
- Ensure that any first-off quality costing is soundly based.
- Exercise caution in extrapolation of quality costs.
- Refine large costs rather than attempt to quantify small unknown costs.
- Concentrate on costs that do or can change with quality improvement activities.
- Remember that rigid systems make for easier quality cost collection.
- Expect to modify the quality costing system in the light of operational experience.
- Indicate all existing cost sources in reports, including those which may not be currently quantifiable.
- Prepare a procedure for the collection and reporting of quality costs; this will help to ensure consistency.
- Analyse and report costs clearly in a business context and ensure that the format is of immediate value to senior management.
- Relate quality costs to the profit of the organization.
- Ensure that the data is used and the quality costing system meets its objectives, also encourage feedback on this.
- Avoid a multiplicity of quality costing reports.
- Consider displaying, as part of an organization's visual management system, the main elements of failure.
- Consider reporting warranty and guarantee payments as a separate quality cost category.
- Exercise caution in the choice of use of ratios used to assess changes in quality costs.
- Treat 'economic cost of quality' models with suspicion: their validity is disputed.

Don'ts

- Forget that there are many complexities and difficulties in the measurement and collection of quality-related costs.
- Go it alone – seek accounting, engineering, and technical help as appropriate.

- Expect accountants to take the initiative.
- Expect accountants to arbitrate on what is, or is not, quality-related; accountants dread dealing with 'grey areas'.
- Believe that standard accounting systems will yield the information needed, there is a certain inaptness of some conventional accounting systems for dealing with quality-related costing.
- Forget that the cost collector has often to adopt a 'Sherlock Holmes' type approach in sifting through the data in order to identify costs which are quality-related.
- Forget that the definition of quality-related costs, or the relevance of cost elements to quality is not always obvious.
- Underestimate the difficulties with definitions of quality costs.
- Be too ambitious – start small.
- Expect too much from the first attempt, any such attempt is likely to underestimate the costs.
- Lose sight of the fact that it is primarily a cost collection exercise.
- Agonize over relatively trifling costs, keep the cost elements and/or categories in perspective.
- Use guessed costs or costs based on guessed data – not even informed guesses.
- Make comparisons unless you can guarantee comparability.
- Assume straightforward operations will necessarily be easy to cost.
- Overlook the fact that transactions between companies and their customers and suppliers are often as difficult to cost as in-house transactions.
- Forget that prevention is the most difficult category to cost.
- Deduct from quality costs income from scrap.
- Forget that costs derived from estimates of time or from special intensive studies often do not get revised.
- Concentrate exclusively on what is already known.
- Overlook the fact that concessions, design, document, and engineering changes are a major source of quality-related costs which often do not receive the attention they merit.
- Be constrained by the traditional prevention-appraisal-failure categorization of quality costs, there are other categorizations which are closer to standard business practices.

13.4 CONCLUDING SUMMARY

In conclusion, total quality management as a key organizational business parameter is here to stay, and needs to be seen and treated by organizations as such. One of the factors in promoting a process of continuous quality improvement is the collection, reporting and use of quality-related cost information. Quality costs need to be formally stated as part of an organization's operational planning and budgetary system and operated as such by executives.

The task of quality costing is not easy. There may be internal opposition to the concept and obscuration of the data, but those individuals and organizations who have persevered and succeeded have found the exercise very rewarding – indeed some see it as vital if they are to remain profitable in an increasingly tough, competitive market. The difficulties associated with quality costing touched upon in this book should not be regarded as a deterrent by organizations considering quality cost collection. Those who have undertaken quality costing have benefited from the experience and from the findings. A number of organizations claim that quality costing has assisted them in achieving world class status. Many organizations are surprised when they learn of the potential savings and soon want to develop their quality-related costing systems to gain greater benefits and cost control. However, they should not overlook the fact that improvements in quality performance do not necessarily produce *pro rata* changes in quality-related costs.

Organizations should seek help if they need it. Collection and use of quality-related costs can and does pay off. However, it should not be forgotten that it is not enough to have the necessary mechanisms for collecting quality-related costs in place, it is also necessary for the organization's senior management team to have the will to carry it out and to use the data.

REFERENCES

1. BS6143: Part 2 (1990) *Guide to the Economics of Quality: Prevention, Appraisal and Failure Model*, British Standards Institution. London.
2. Campanella, J. (1990) *Principles of Quality Costs: Principles, Implementaion and Use*, ASEC Quality Press, Milwaukee.
3. BS6143: Part 1 (1992) *Guide to the Economics of Quality: Process Cost Model*, British Standards Institution, London.

Index

Page numbers appearing in **bold** refer to figures.